STONYHURST   PHILOSOPHICAL   SERIES.

ROEHAMPTON :

PRINTED BY JOHN GRIFFIN.

STONYHURST PHILOSOPHICAL SERIES

MORAL PHILOSOPHY

OR

ETHICS AND NATURAL LAW

BY

JOSEPH RICKABY, S.J.

NEW IMPRESSION

LONGMANS, GREEN, AND CO.
39 PATERNOSTER ROW, LONDON
NEW YORK, BOMBAY, AND CALCUTTA
1908

17114
R421.2

49422

PREFACE TO THE LAST EDITION (1905).

FOR fifteen years this Manual has enjoyed all the popularity that its author could desire. With that popularity the author is the last person to wish to interfere. Therefore, not to throw previous copies out of use, this edition makes no alteration either in the pagination or the text already printed. At the same time the author might well be argued to have lapsed into strange supineness and indifference to moral science, if in fifteen years he had learnt nothing new, and found nothing in his work which he wished to improve. Whoever will be at the expense of purchasing my *Political and Moral Essays* (Benziger, 1902, 6s.) will find in the first essay on the *Origin and Extent of Civil Authority* an advantageous substitute for the chapter on the State in this work. The essay is a dissertation written for the degree of B. Sc. in the University of Oxford; and represents, I hope, tolerably well the best contemporary teaching on the subject.

If the present work had to be rewritten, I should make a triple division of Moral Philosophy, into Ethics, Deontology (the science of τὸ δέον, i.e., of what *ought* to be done), and Natural Law. For if "the principal business of Ethics is to determine what moral obligation is" (p. 2), then the classical work on the subject, the *Nicomachean Ethics* of Aristotle, is as the play of Hamlet with the character of Hamlet left out: for in that work there is no analysis of moral obligation, no attempt to "fix the comprehension of the idea I *ought*" (ib.). The system there exposed is a system of Eudaemonism, not of Deontology. It is not a treatise on Duty, but on Happiness: it tells us what Happiness, or rational well-being, is, and what conduct is conducive to rational well-being. It may be found convenient to follow Aristotle, and avow that the business of Ethics is not Duty, not Obligation, not Law, not Sanction, but Happiness. That fiery little word *ought* goes unexplained in Ethics, except in an hypothetical sense, that a man *ought* to do this, and avoid that, *if* he means to be a happy man: cf. p. 115. Any man who declares that he does not care about ethical or rational happiness, stands to Ethics as that man stands to Music who "hath no ear for concord of sweet sounds."

All that Ethics or Music can do for such a Philistine is to "send him away to another city, pouring ointment on his head, and crowning him with wool," as Plato would dismiss the tragedian

(*Republic* III. 398). The author of the *Magna Moralia* well says (I. i. 13) : "No science or faculty ever argues the goodness of the end which it proposes to itself: it belongs to some other faculty to consider that. Neither the physician says that health is a good thing, nor the builder that a house is a good thing : but the one announces that he produces health and how he produces it, and the builder in like manner a house." The professor of Ethics indeed, from the very nature of his subject-matter, says in pointing out happiness that it is the rational sovereign good of man : but to any one unmoved by that demonstration Ethics can have no more to say. Ethics will not threaten, nor talk of duty, law, or punishment.

Ethics, thus strictly considered on an Aristotelian basis, are antecedent to Natural Theology. They belong rather to Natural Anthropology : they are a study of human nature. But as human nature points to God, so Ethics are not wholly irrespective of God, considering Him as the object of human happiness and worship,—the Supreme Being without whom all the aspirations of humanity are at fault (pp. 13—26, 191—197). Ethics do not refer to the commandments of God, for this simple reason, that they have nothing to say to commandments, or laws, or obligation, or authority. They are simply a system of moral hygiene, which a man may adopt or not : only, like any other physician, the professor of Ethics utters a friendly warning that misery must ensue upon the neglect of what makes for health.

Deontology, not Ethics, expounds and vindicates the idea, *I ought*. It is the science of Duty. It carries the mild suasions of Ethics into laws, and out of moral prudence it creates conscience. And whereas Ethics do not deal with sin, except under the aspect of what is called 'philosophical sin' (p. 119, § 6), Deontology defines sin in its proper theological sense, as "an offence against God, or any thought, word, or deed against the law of God." Deontology therefore presupposes and is consequent upon Natural Theology At the same time, while Ethics indicate a valuable proof of the existence of God as the requisite Object of Happiness, Deontology affords a proof of Him as the requisite Lawgiver. Without God, man's rational desire is frustrate, and man's conscience a misrepresentation of fact.[1]

---

[1] This is Cardinal Newman's proof of the existence of God from Conscience: see pp. 124, 125, and *Grammar of Assent*, pp. 104 —111, ed. 1895. With Newman's, "Conscience has both a critical and a judicial office," compare Plato, *Politicus*, 260 B, συμπάσης τῆς γνωστικῆς τὸ μὲν ἐπιτακτικὸν μέρος, τὸ δὲ κριτικόν. The 'critical' office belongs to Ethics: the 'judicial,' or 'preceptive' office τὸ ἐπιτακτικόν) to Deontology; and this latter points to a Person who commands and judges, that is, to God.

In this volume, pp. 1—108 make up the treatise on Ethics: pp. 109—176 that on Deontology.

Aristotle writes: " He that acts by intelligence and cultivates understanding, is likely to be best disposed and dearest to God. For if, as is thought, there is any care of human things on the part of the heavenly powers, we may reasonably expect them to delight in that which is best and most akin to themselves, that is, in intelligence, and to make a return of good to such as supremely love and honour intelligence, as cultivating the thing dearest to Heaven, and so behaving rightly and well. Such, plainly, is the behaviour of the wise. The wise man therefore is the dearest to God " (Nic. Eth. X. ix. 13). But Aristotle does not work out the connexion between God and His law on the one hand and human conscience and duty on the other. In that direction the Stoics, and after them the Roman Jurists, went further than Aristotle. By reason of this deficiency, Aristotle, peerless as he is in Ethics, remains an imperfect Moral Philosopher.

CONTENTS.

PART I.—ETHICS.

CONTENTS. xiii

CORRIGENDA.

p. 43, lines 20, 26 from top, for *daring* read *impetuosity*.

p. 49, § 1, line 2, for *physical* read *psychical*.

p. 74, line 8 from top, read *facilitate*.

p. 79, line 3 from top, for *spoiled* read *spoilt*.

p. 84, foot, for *ways* read *way*.

p. 95, § 2, line 4, for *Daring* read *Impetuosity*.

p. 106, § 6, add note: *On the Aristotelian division of justice see Political and Moral Essays (P.M.E.), pp.* 285–6.

p. 125, foot. Add to the *Readings, Oxford and Cambridge Conferences,* 1900, 1901, *pp.* 184—222.

pp. 150, 151, cancel §§ 4, 5, and for the note to § 4, read: *See the Appendix to the Third Edition, and still further, P.M.E. pp.* 185—191.

p. 218, lines 13—16 from top, cancel the sentence, *To this query* &c., and substitute: *The reply is, that God is never willing that man should do an inordinate act : but suicide is an inordinate act, as has been shown (nn.* 3, 4) : *capital punishment is not (c. viii. s. viii. n.* 7, *p.* 349).

p. 237, in the *Readings*, for *The Month for March* 1883, read *P.M.E. pp.* 215—233.

p. 251, to the *Reading* add *P.M.E. pp.* 267—283.

pp. 322-3. Cancel § 7 for reasons alleged in P.M.E. pp 50—72 Substitute : *States are living organisms and grow, and their powers* **vary** *with the stage of their development.*

p. 323, § 8. For *This seems at variance with,* read *This brings us to consider.*

ETHICS AND NATURAL LAW.

PART I. ETHICS.

CHAPTER I.

OF THE OBJECT-MATTER AND PARTITION OF MORAL PHILOSOPHY.

1. MORAL PHILOSOPHY is the science that considers human acts inasmuch as they befit man's rational nature and make towards man's last end.

2. Those acts alone are properly called *human*, which a man is master of to do or not to do. A *human act*, then, is an act voluntary and free. A man is what his human acts make him.

3. A *voluntary* act is an act that proceeds from the will with a knowledge of the end to which the act tends.

4. A *free* act is an act which so proceeds from the will that under the same antecedent conditions it might not have proceeded.

5. *Human acts*, as defined above, are the subject-matter of moral philosophy. The special light in which it considers them is their agreement with, or opposition to, man's rational nature. That agree-

B

ment or opposition is their moral good or evil, and
is called *morality*.

6. Moral Philosophy is divided into Ethics and
Natural Law. The principal business of Ethics is
to determine what moral obligation is, or to fix what
logicians call the *comprehension* of the idea *I ought*.
It belongs to Natural Law to consider what things
are morally obligatory, or to determine the *extension*
of the idea *I ought*.

7. Ethics stand to Natural Law as Pure Mathematics to Mixed.

Readings.—St. Thos., *in Eth.*, I., lect. 1, init.;
ib., 1a 2æ, q. 1, art. 1, in corp.; *ib.*, q. 58, art. 1,
in corp.

CHAPTER II.

OF HAPPINESS.

SECTION I.—*Of Ends.*

1. EVERY human act is done for some end or purpose. The end is always regarded by the agent in the light of something good. If evil be done, it is done as leading to good, or as bound up with good, or as itself being good for the doer under the circumstances; no man ever does evil for sheer evil's sake. Yet evil may be the object of the will, not by itself, nor primarily, but in a secondary way, as bound up with the good that is willed in the first place.

2. Many things willed are neither good nor evil in themselves. There is no motive for doing them except in so far as they lead to some good beyond themselves, or to deliverance from some evil, which deliverance counts as a good. A thing is willed, then, either as being good in itself and an end by itself, or as leading to some good end. Once a thing not good and desirable by itself has been taken up by the will as leading to good, it may be taken up again and again without reference to its tendency. But such a thing was not originally taken up except in view of good to come of it. We

may will one thing as leading to another, and that to a third, and so on; thus one wills study for learning, learning for examination purposes, examination for a commission in the army, and the commission for glory. That end in which the will rests, willing it for itself without reference to anything beyond, is called the *last end*.

3. An end is either *objective* or *subjective*. The *objective end* is the thing wished for, as it exists distinct from the person who wishes it. The *subjective end* is the possession of the objective end. That possession is a fact of the wisher's own being. Thus *money* may be an objective end: the corresponding subjective end is *being wealthy*.

4. Is there one subjective last end to all the human acts of a given individual? Is there one supreme motive for all that this or that man deliberately does? At first sight it seems that there is not. The same individual will act now for glory, now for lucre, now for love. But all these different ends are reducible to one, *that it may be well with him and his*. And what is true of one man here, is true of all. All the human acts of all men are done for the one (subjective) last end just indicated. This end is called *happiness*.

5. Men place their happiness in most different things; some in eating and drinking, some in the heaping up of money, some in gambling, some in political power, some in the gratification of affection, some in reputation of one sort or another. But each one seeks his own speciality because he thinks that he shall be happy, that it will be well with him,

when he has attained that. All men, then, do all things for happiness, though not all place their happiness in the same thing.

6. Just as when one goes on a journey, he need not think of his destination at every step of his way, and yet all his steps are directed towards his destination: so men do not think of happiness in all they do, and yet all they do is referred to happiness. Tell a traveller that this is the wrong way to his destination, he will avoid it; convince a man that this act will not be well for him, will not further his happiness, and, while he keeps that conviction principally before his eyes, he will not do the act. But as a man who began to travel on business, may come to make travelling itself a business, and travel for the sake of going about; so in all cases there is a tendency to elevate into an end that which was, to start with, only valued as a means to an end. So the means of happiness, by being habitually pursued, come to be a part of happiness. Habit is a second nature, and we indulge a habit as we gratify nature. This tendency works itself to an evil extreme in cases where men are become the slaves of habit, and do a thing because they are got into the way of doing it, though they allow that it is a sad and sorry way, and leads them wide of true happiness. These instances show perversion of the normal operation of the will.

Readings.—St. Thos., Ia 2æ, q. 1, art. 4, in corp.; *ib.*, q. 1, art. 6, 7; *ib.*, q. 5, art. 8; Ar., *Eth.*, I., vii., 4, 5.

Section II.—*Definition of Happiness.*

1. Though all men do all things, in the last
resort, that it may be well with them and theirs,
that is, for happiness vaguely apprehended, yet when
they come to specify what happiness is, answers so
various are given and acted upon, that we might be
tempted to conclude that each man is the measure
of his own happiness, and that no standard of happiness for all can be defined. But it is not so. Man
is not the measure of his own happiness, any more
than of his own health. The diet that he takes to
be healthy, may prove his poison ; and where he
looks for happiness, he may find the extreme of
wretchedness and woe. For man must live up to
his nature, to his bodily constitution, to be a healthy
man ; and to his whole nature, but especially to his
mental and moral constitution, if he is to be a happy
man. And nature, though it admits of individual
peculiarities, is specifically the same for all. There
will, then, be one definition of happiness for all men,
specifically as such.

2. *Happiness is an act, not a state.* That is to say,
the happiness of man does not lie in his having
something done to him, nor in his being habitually
able to do something, but in his actually doing
something. "To be up and doing," that is happiness,—ἐν τῷ ζῆν καὶ ἐνεργεῖν. (Ar., *Eth.*, IX., ix., 5.)
This is proved from the consideration that happiness is the crown and perfection of human nature ;
but the perfection of a thing lies in its ultimate act,
or "second act," that is, in its not merely being able

to act, but acting. But action is of two sorts. One proceeds from the agent to some outward matter, as cutting and burning. This action cannot be happiness, for it does not perfect the agent, but rather the patient. There is another sort of act immanent in the agent himself, as feeling, understanding, and willing: these perfect the agent. Happiness will be found to be one of these immanent acts. Furthermore, there is action full of movement and change, and there is an act done in stillness and rest. The latter, as will presently appear, is happiness; and partly for this reason, and partly to denote the exclusion of care and trouble, happiness is often spoken of as *a rest*. It is also called *a state*, because one of the elements of happiness is permanence. How the act of happiness can be permanent, will appear hereafter.

3. *Happiness is an act in discharge of the function proper to man, as man.* There is a function proper to the eye, to the ear, to the various organs of the human body: there must be a function proper to man as such. That can be none of the functions of the vegetative life, nor of the mere animal life within him. Man is not happy by doing what a rose-bush can do, digest and assimilate its food: nor by doing what a horse does, having sensations pleasurable and painful, and muscular feelings. Man is happy by doing what man alone can do in this world, that is, acting by reason and understanding. Now the human will acting by reason may do three things. It may regulate the passions, notably desire and fear: the outcome will be the moral virtues of

temperance and fortitude.   It may direct the understanding, and ultimately the members of the body,
in order to the production of some practical result
in the external world, as a bridge.   Lastly, it may
direct the understanding to speculate and think,
contemplate and consider, for mere contemplation's
sake.   Happiness must take one or other of these
three lanes.

4. First, then, *happiness is not the practice of the
moral virtues of temperance and fortitude.*   Temperance
makes a man strong against the temptations to irrationality and swinishness that come of the bodily
appetites.   But happiness lies, not in deliverance
from what would degrade man to the level of the
brutes, but in something which shall raise man to
the highest level of human nature. Fortitude, again,
is not exercised except in the hour of danger ; but
happiness lies in an environment of security, not of
danger.   And in general, the moral virtues can be
exercised only upon occasions, as they come and
go ; but happiness is the light of the soul, that must
burn with steady flame and uninterrupted act, and
not be dependent on chance occurrences.

5. Secondly, *happiness is not the use of the practical
understanding with a view to production.*   Happiness
is an end in itself, a terminus beyond which the act
of the will can go no further ; but this use of the
understanding is in view of an ulterior end, the thing
to be produced.   That product is either useful or
artistic ; if useful, it ministers to some further end
still ; if artistic, it ministers to contemplation.
Happiness, indeed, is no exercise of the practical

understanding whatever. The noblest exercises of practical understanding are for military purposes and for statesmanship. But war surely is not an end in itself to any right-minded man. Statecraft, too, has an end before it, the happiness of the people. It is a labour in view of happiness. We must follow down the third lane, and say :

6. *Happiness is the act of the speculative understanding contemplating for contemplation's sake.* This act has all the marks of happiness. It is the highest act of man's highest power. It is the most capable of continuance. It is fraught with pleasure, purest and highest in quality. It is of all acts the most self-sufficient and independent of environment, provided the object be to the mind's eye visible. It is welcome for its own sake, not as leading to any further good. It is a life of ease and leisure : man is busy that he may come to ease.

7. Aristotle says of this life of continued active contemplation :

"Such a life will be too good for man; for not as he is man will he so live, but inasmuch as there is a divine element in his composition. As much as this element excels the compound into which it enters, so much does the act of the said element excel any act in any other line of virtue. If, then, the understanding is divine in comparison with man, the life of the understanding is divine in comparison with human life. We must not take the advice of those who tell us, that being man, one should cherish the thoughts of a man, or being mortal, the thoughts of a mortal, but so far as in us lies, we must play the

immortal (ἀθανατίζειν), and do all in our power to
live by the best element in our nature : for though
that element be slight in quantity, in power and in
value it far outweighs all the rest of our being. A
man may well be reckoned to be that which is the
ruling power and the better part in him. . . . What
is proper to each creature by nature, is best and
sweetest for each : such, then, is for man the life
of the understanding, if the understanding pre-
eminently is man." (Ar., *Eth.*, X., vii., 8, 9.)

8. But if happiness is an act in discharge of the
function proper to man as man (n. 3), how can it be
happiness to lead a life which Aristotle says is too
good for man ? The solution of this paradox is
partly contained in the concluding words of Aristotle
above quoted, and will still further appear presently
(s. iv., n. 1, p. 21), where we shall argue that human
life is a state of transition in preparation for a
higher life of the soul, to be lived, according to the
natural order, when the compound of soul and body
would no longer exist.

9. *The act of contemplation, in which happiness consists, must rest upon a habit of contemplation, which is
intellectual virtue.* An act, to be perfection and happiness, must be done easily, sweetly, and constantly.
But no act of the intellect can be so done, unless it
rests upon a corresponding habit. If the habit has
not been acquired, the act will be done fitfully, at
random, and against the grain, like the music of an
untrained singer, or the composition of a schoolboy.
Painful study is not happiness, nor is any studied
act. Happiness is the play of a mind that is, if not

master of, yet at home with its subject. As the intellect is man's best and noblest power, so is intellectual virtue, absolutely speaking, the best virtue of man.

10. The use of the speculative understanding is descernible in many things to which even the common crowd turn for happiness, as news of that which is of little or no practical concern to self, sight-seeing, theatre-going, novels, poetry, art, scenery, as well as speculative science and high literature. A certain speculative interest is mixed up with all practical work: the mind lingers on the speculation apart from the end in view.

11. *The act of contemplation cannot be steadily carried on, as is necessary to happiness, except in the midst of easy surroundings.* Human nature is not self-sufficient for the work of contemplation. There is need of health and vigour, and the means of maintaining it, food, warmth, interesting objects around you, leisure, absence of distracting care or pain. None would call a man happy upon the rack, except by way of maintaining a thesis. The happiness of a disembodied spirit is of course independent of bodily conditions, but it would appear that there are conditions of environment requisite for even a spirit's contemplation.

12. *Happiness must endure to length of days.* Happiness is the perfect good of man. But no good is perfect that will not last. One swallow does not make a summer, nor does one fine day: neither is man made blessed and happy by one day, nor by a brief time. The human mind lighting upon

good soon asks the question, Will this last ? If the
answer is negative, the good is not a complete good
and there is no complete happiness coming of it
If the answer is affirmative and false, once more
that is not a perfect happiness that rests on a
delusion. The supreme good of a rational being is
not found in a fool's paradise. We want an answer
affirmative and true : *This happiness shall last.*

13. We now sum up and formulate the definition
of happiness as follows : *Happiness is a bringing of
the soul to act according to the habit of the best and most
perfect virtue, that is, the virtue of the speculative intellect, borne out by easy surroundings, and enduring to
length of days*—ἐνέργεια ψυχῆς κατ' ἀρετὴν τὴν
ἀρίστην καὶ τελειοτάτην ἐν βίῳ τελείῳ. (Ar., *Eth.*,
I., vii., 15, 16.)

14. Man is made for society. His happiness
must be in society, a social happiness, no lonely
contemplation. He must be happy in the consciousness of his own intellectual act, and happy in
the discernment of the good that is in those around
him, whom he loves. Friends and dear ones are
no small part of those *easy surroundings* that are the
condition of happiness.

15. Happiness—final, perfect happiness—is not
in fighting and struggling, in so far as a struggle
supposes evil present and imminent ; nor in benevolence, so far as that is founded upon misery
needing relief. We fight for the conquest and
suppression of evil ; we are benevolent for the healing of misery. But it will be happiness, *in the
limit,* as mathematicians speak, to wish well to all

in a society where it is well with all, and to struggle with truth for its own sake, ever grasping, never mastering, as Jacob wrestled with God.

Readings.—Ar., *Eth.*, I., vii. viii., 5 to end; I., x., 8 to end; I., v., 6; VII., xiii., 3; IX., ix.; X., vii.; X., viii., 1—10; Ar., *Pol.*, IV. (al. VII.), i., 3—10; IV., iii., 7, 8; St. Thos., 1a 2æ, q. 3, art. 2; *ib.*, q. 3, art. 5. in corp., ad 3; *ib.*, q. 2, art. 6.

Section III.—*Happiness open to man.*

" And now as he looked and saw the whole Hellespont covered with the vessels of his fleet, and all the shore and every plain about Abydos as full as possible of men, Xerxes congratulated himself on his good fortune; but after a little while, he wept. Then Artabanus, the King's uncle, when he heard that Xerxes was in tears, went to him, and said: 'How different, sire, is what thou art now doing from what thou didst a little while ago! Then thou didst congratulate thyself; and now, behold! thou weepest.' 'There came upon me,' replied he, 'a sudden pity, when I thought of the shortness of man's life, and considered that of all this host, so numerous as it is, not one will be alive when a hundred years are gone by.' 'And yet there are sadder things in life than that,' returned the other. 'Short as our time is, there is no man, whether it be among this multitude or elsewhere, who is so happy, as not to have felt the wish—I will not say once, but full many a time—that he were dead rather than alive. Calamities fall upon us, sicknesses vex and harass us, and make life, short though it be, to appear long. So death, through the wretchedness of our life, is a most sweet refuge to our race; and God, who gives us the tastes that we enjoy of pleasant times, is seen, in his very gift, to be envious." (Herodotus, vii., 45, 46.)

1. It needs no argument to show that happiness, as defined in the last section, can never be perfectly realized in this life. Aristotle took his definition to represent an ideal to be approximated to, not attained. He calls his sages "happy as men" (*Eth.*, I., x., 16), that is, imperfectly, as all things human are imperfect. Has Aristotle, then, said the last word on happiness? Is perfect happiness out of the reach of the person whom in this mortal life we call man? However that may be, it is plain that *man desires perfect happiness.* Every man desires that it may be perfectly well with him and his, although many have mistaken notions of what their own well-being consists in, and few can define it philosophically. Still they all desire it. The higher a man stands in intellect, the loftier and vaster his conception of happiness, and the stronger his yearning after it. This argues that *the desire of happiness is natural to man*: not in the sense in which eating and drinking are natural, as being requirements of his animal nature, but in the same way that it is natural to him to think and converse, his rational nature so requiring. It is a natural desire, as springing from that which is the specific characteristic of human nature, distinguishing it from mere animal nature, namely reason. It is a natural desire in the best and highest sense of the word.

2. Contentment is not happiness. A man is content with little, but it takes an immensity of good to satisfy all his desire, and render him perfectly happy. When we say we are content, we signify that we should naturally desire more, but acquiesce in our present portion, seeing that more is not to be had. "Content," says Dr. Bain, "is not the natural frame of any mind, but is the result of compromise."

3. But is not this desire of unmixed happiness unreasonable? Are we not taught to set bounds to our desire? Is not moderation a virtue, and contentment wisdom? Yes, moderation is a virtue, but it concerns only the use of means, not the apprehension of ends. The patient, not to say the physician, desires medicines in moderation, so much as will do him good and no more; but, so far as his end is health, he desires all possible health, perfect health. The last end, then, is to be desired as a thing to possess without end or measure, fully and without defect.

4. We have then these facts to philosophise on: that all men desire perfect happiness: that this desire is natural, springing from the rational soul which sets man above the brute: that on earth man may attain to contentment, and to some happiness, but not to perfect happiness: that consequently nature has planted in man a desire for which on earth she has provided no adequate satisfaction.

5. If the course of events were fitful and wayward, so that effects started up without causes, and like causes under like conditions produced unlike

effects, and anything might come of anything, there would be no such thing as that which we call *nature*. When we speak of nature, we imply a regular and definite flow of tendencies, this thing springing from that and leading to that other; nothing from nothing, and nothing leading nowhere; no random, aimless proceedings; but definite results led up to by a regular succession of steps, and surely ensuing unless something occurs on the way to thwart the process. How this is reconciled with Creation and Freewill, it is not our province to enquire: suffice it to say that a *natural* agent is opposed to a *free* one, and creation is the starting-point of nature. But to return. Everywhere we say, "this is for that," wherever there appears an end and consummation to which the process leads, provided it go on unimpeded. Now every event that happens is a part of some process or other. Every act is part of a tendency. There are no loose facts in nature, no things that happen, or are, otherwise than in consequence of something that has happened, or been, before, and in view of something else that is to happen, or be, hereafter. The tendencies of nature often run counter to one another, so that the result to which this or that was tending is frustrated. But a tendency is a tendency, although defeated; *this* was for *that*, although that for which it was has got perverted to something else. There is no tendency which of itself fails and comes to naught, apart from interference. Such a universal and absolute break-down is unknown to nature.

6. All this appears most clearly in organic beings,

plants and animals. Organisms, except the very lowest, are compounds of a number of different parts, each fulfilling a special function for the good of the whole. There is no idle constituent in an organic body, none without its function. What are called *rudimentary organs*, even if they serve no purpose in the individual, have their use in the species, or in some higher genus. In the animal there is no idle natural craving, or appetite. True, in the individual, whether plant or animal, there are many potentialities frustrate and made void. That is neither here nor there in philosophy. Philosophy deals not with individuals but with species, not with Bucephalus or Alexander, but with *horse, man*. It is nothing to philosophy that of a thousand seeds there germinate perhaps not ten. Enough that one seed ever germinates, and that all normal specimens are apt to do the like, meeting with proper environment. That alone shows that seed is not an idle product in this or that class of living beings.

7. But, it will be said, not everything contained in an organism ministers to its good. There is refuse material, only good to get rid of: there are morbid growths; there is that tendency to decay, by which sooner or later the organism will perish. First, then, a word on diseases. Diseases are the diseases of the individual; not of the race. The race, as such, and that is what the philosopher studies, is healthy: all that can be imputed to the race is liability to disease. That liability, and the tendency to decay and die, are found in living things, because their essence is of finite perfection;

c

there cannot be a plant or animal, that has not these drawbacks in itself, as such. They represent, not the work of nature, but the failure of nature, and the point beyond which nature can no further go.

8. On the preceding observations Aristotle formulated the great maxim—called by Dr. Thomas Browne, *Religio Medici*, p. i., sect. 15, "the only indisputable axiom in philosophy,"—*Nature does nothing in vain*. (Ar., *Pol.*, I., viii., 12; *De Anima*, III., ix., 6; *De part. animal.*, l. i., p. 641, ed. Bekker.)

9. *The desire of happiness, ample and complete, beyond what this world can afford, is not planted in man by defect of his nature, but by the perfection of his nature, and in view of his further perfection.* This desire has not the character of a drawback, a thing that cannot be helped, a weakness and decay of nature, and loss of power, like that which sets in with advancing years. A locomotive drawing a train warms the air about it : it is a pity that it should do so, for that radiation of heat is a loss of power : but it cannot be helped, as locomotives are and must be constructed. Not such is the desire of perfect happiness in the human breast. It is not a disease, for it is no peculiarity of individuals, but a property of the race. It is not a decay, for it grows with the growing mind, being feeblest in childhood, when desires are simplest and most easily satisfied, and strongest where mental life is the most vigorous. It is an attribute of great minds in proportion to their greatness. To be without it, would be to live a minor in point of

intellect, not much removed from imbecility. It is not a waste of energy, rather it furnishes the motive-power to all human volition. It comes of the natural working of the understanding that discerns good, and other good above that, and so still higher and higher good without limit; and of the natural working of the will, following up and fastening upon what the understanding discerns as good. The desire in question, then, is by no means a necessary evil, or natural flaw, in the human constitution.

10. It follows that the desire of perfect happiness is in man by the normal growth of his nature, and for the better. But it would be a vain desire, and objectless, if it were essentially incapable of satisfaction: and man would be a made and abiding piece of imperfection, if there were no good accessible to his intellectual nature sufficient to meet its proper exigence of perfect happiness. But no such perfect happiness is attainable in this world. Therefore there must be a world to come, in which he who was man, now a disembodied spirit, but still the same person, shall under due conditions find a perfect good, the adequate object of his natural desire. Else is the deepest craving of human nature in vain, and man himself is vanity of vanities.

11. It may be objected that there is no need to go beyond this world to explain how the desire of perfect happiness is not in vain. It works like the desire of the philosopher's stone among the old alchemists. The thing they were in search of was a chimera, but in looking for it they found a real good, modern chemistry. In like manner, it is

contended, though perfect happiness is not to be
had anywhere, yet the desire of it keeps men from
sitting down on the path of progress; and thus
to that desire we owe all our modern civilization,
and all our hope and prospect of higher civilization
to come. Without questioning the alleged fact
about the alchemists, we may reply that modern
chemistry has dissipated the desire of the philosopher's stone, but modern civilization has not dissipated the desire of perfect happiness: it has deepened
it, and perhaps rather obscured the prospect of its
fulfilment. A desire that grows with progress certainly cannot be satisfied by progressing. But if it
is never to be satisfied, what is it? A goad thrust
into the side of man, that shall keep him coursing
along from century to century, like Io under the
gadfly, only to find himself in the last century as far
from the mark as in the first. Apart from the hope
of the world to come, is the Italy of to-day happier
than the Italy of Antoninus Pius? Here is a modern
Italian's conclusion: " I have studied man, I have
examined nature, I have passed whole nights observing the starry heavens. And what is the result
of these long investigations? Simply this, that the
life of man is nothing; that man himself is nothing;
that he will never penetrate the mystery which surrounds the universe. With this comfortless conviction I descend into the grave, and console myself
with the hope of speedy annihilation. The lamp
goes out; and nothing, nothing can rekindle it. So,
Nature, I return to thee, to be united with thee for
ever. Never wilt thou have received into thy bosom

a more unhappy being." (*La Nullità della Vita.* By G. P., 1882.)

This is an extreme case, but much of modern progress tends this way. Civilization is not happiness, nor is the desire for happiness other than vain, if it merely leads to increased civilization.

Readings.—St. Thomas, *C. G.*, iii., 48; Newman's *Historical Sketches—Conversion of Augustine;* Mill's *Autobiography*, pp. 133—149.

SECTION IV.—*Of the Object of Perfect Happiness.*

1. As happiness is an act of the speculative intellect contemplating (s. ii., n. 6, p. 9), so the thing thus contemplated is the *object of happiness.* As happiness is the *subjective last end,* so will this object, inasmuch as the contemplation of it yields perfect happiness, be the *objective last end* of man. (s. i., nn. 3. 4, p. 4.) As perfect happiness is possible, and intended by nature, so is this objective last end attainable, and should be attained. But attained by man? Aye, there's the rub. It cannot be attained in this life, and after death man is no more: a soul out of the body is not man. About the resurrection of the body philosophy knows nothing. Nature can make out no title to resurrection. That is a gratuitous gift of God in Christ. When it takes effect, *stupebit natura.* Philosophy deals only with the natural order, with man as man, leaving the supernatural order, or the privileges and *status* of man as a child of God, to the higher science of Scholastic Theology. Had God so willed it, there might have been no supernatural at all. Philosophy shows the world as it would

have been on that hypothesis. In that case, then, man would have been, as Aristotle represents him, a being incapable of perfect happiness; but *he who is man* could have become perfectly happy in a state other than human, that is, as a disembodied spirit. Peter is man: the soul of Peter, after separation, is man no longer; but Peter is not one person, and Peter's soul out of the body another person; there is but one person there, with one personal history and liabilities. The soul of Peter is Peter still: therefore the person Peter, or he *who is Peter*, attains to happiness, but not the man Peter, as man, apart from the supernatural privilege of the resurrection. Hence Aristotle well said, though he failed to see the significance of his own saying, that man should aim at a life of happiness too good for man. (s. ii., nn. 7, 8, p. 9.)

2. The object of happiness,—the objective last end of man,—will be that which the soul contemplating in the life to come will be perfectly happy by so doing. The soul will contemplate all intellectual beauty that she finds about her, all heights of truth, all the expanse of goodness and mystery of love. She will see herself: a vast and curious sight is one pure spirit: but that will not be enough for her, her eye travels beyond. She must be in company, live with myriads of pure spirits like herself,—see them, study them, and admire them, and converse with them in closest intimacy. Together they must explore the secrets of all creation even to the most distant star: they must read the laws of the universe, which science laboriously spells

out here below : they must range from science to art, and from facts to possibilities, till even their pure intellect is baffled by the vast intricacy of things that might be and are not : but yet they are not satisfied. A point of convergency is wanted for all these vistas of being, whence they may go forth, and whither they may return and meet : otherwise the soul is distracted and lost in a maze of incoherent wandering, crying out, Whence all this? and what is it for? and above all, whose is it? These are the questions that the human mind asks in her present condition : much more will she ask them then, when wonders are multiplied before her gaze : for it is the same soul there and here. Here men are tormented in mind, if they find no answer to these questions. Scientific men cannot leave theology alone. They will not be happy there without an answer. Their contemplation will still desiderate something beyond all finite being, actual or possible. Is that God? It is nothing else. But God dwells in light inaccessible, where no creature, as such, can come near Him nor see Him. The beauties of creation, as so many streams of tendency, meet at the foot of His Throne, and there are lost. Their course is towards Him, and is, so far as it goes, an indication of Him : but He is infinitely, unspeakably above them. No intelligence created, or creatable, can arrive by its own natural perception to see Him as He is : for mind can only discern what is proportionate to itself : and God is out of proportion with all the being of all possible creatures. It is only by analogy that the word *being*, or any other word whatever can be applied to Him. As Plato says, "the First Good is not Being, but over and beyond Being in dignity and power." (*Rep.* 509, B.)

3. To see God face to face, which is called the beatific vision, is not the natural destiny of man, nor of any possible creature. Such happiness is not the happiness of man, nor of angel, but of God Himself, and of any creature whom He may deign by an act of gratuitous condescension to invite to sit as guest at His own royal table. That God has so invited men and angels, revelation informs us. Scholastic theology enlarges upon that revelation, but it is beyond philosophy. Like the resurrection of the body, and much more even than that, the Beatific Vision must be relegated to the realm of the Supernatural.

4. But even in the natural order *the object of perfect happiness* is God. The natural and supernatural have the same object, but differ in the mode of attainment. By supernatural grace, bearing perfect fruit, man sees God with the eyes of his soul, as we see the faces of our friends on earth. In perfect happiness of the natural order, creatures alone are directly apprehended, or seen, and from the creature is gathered the excellence of the unseen God. The process is an ascent, as described by Plato, from the individual to the universal, and from bodily to moral and intellectual beauty, till we reach a Beauty eternal, immutable, absolute, substantial, and self-existent, on which all other beauties depend for their being, while it is independent of

them. (Plato, *Symposium*, 210, 211.) Unless the ascent be prosecuted thus far, the contemplation is inadequate, the happiness incomplete. The mind needs to travel to the beginning and end of things, to the Alpha and Omega of all. The mind needs to reach some perfect good : some object, which though it is beyond the comprehension, is nevertheless understood to be the very good of goods, unalloyed with any admixture of defect or imperfection. The mind needs an infinite object to rest upon, though it cannot grasp that object positively in its infinity. If this is the case even with the human mind, still wearing "this muddy vesture of decay," how much more ardent the longing, as how much keener the gaze, of the pure spirit after Him who is the centre and rest of all intellectual nature ?

5. Creatures to contemplate and see God in, are conditions and secondary objects of natural happiness. They do not afford happiness finally of themselves, but as manifesting God, even as a mirror would be of little interest except for its power of reflection.

6. In saying that God is the object of happiness, we must remember that He is no cold, impersonal Beauty, but a living and loving God, not indeed in the order of nature our Father and Friend, but still our kind Master and very good Lord, who speaks to His servants from behind the clouds that hide His face, and assures them of His abiding favour and approving love. More than that, nature cannot look for : such aspiration were unnatural, unreason-

able, mere madness : it is enough for the creature,
as a creature, in its highest estate to stand before
God, hearing His voice, but seeing not His coun-
tenance, whom, without His free grace, none can
look upon and live.

Reading.—St. Thos., 1a 2æ, q. 2, art. 8.

SECTION V.—*Of the use of the present life.*

1. Since perfect happiness is not to be had in
this mortal life, and is to be had hereafter ; since
moreover man has free will and the control of his
own acts ; it is evidently most important for man in
this life so to control and rule himself here as to
dispose himself for happiness there.   Happiness
rests upon a habit of contemplation (s. ii., n. 9, p. 10),
rising to God. (s. iv., n. 4, p. 24.)   But a habit, as will
be seen, is not formed except by frequent acts, and
may be marred and broken by contrary acts.   It is,
then, important for man in this life so to act as to
acquire a habit of lifting his mind to God.   There
are two things here, to lift the mind, and to lift it to
God.   The mind is not lifted, if the man lives not
an intellectual life, but the life of a swine wallowing
in sensual indulgences ; or a frivolous life, taking
the outside of things as they strike the senses, and
flitting from image to image thoughtlessly ; or a
quarrelsome life, where reason is swallowed up in
anger and hatred.   Again, however sublime the
speculation and however active the intellect, if God
is not constantly referred to, the mind is lifted
indeed, but not to God.   It is wisdom, then, in
man during this life to look to God everywhere,

and ever to seek His face; to avoid idleness, anger, intemperance, and pride of intellect. For the mind will not soar to God when the heart is far from Him.

CHAPTER III.

OF HUMAN ACTS.

SECTION I.—*What makes a human act less voluntary.*

1 See c. i., nn. 2, 3, 4.

2. An act is more or less voluntary, as it is done with more or less knowledge, and proceeds more or less fully and purely from the will properly so called. Whatever diminishes knowledge, or partially supplants the will, takes off from the voluntariness of the act. *An act is rendered less voluntary by ignorance, by passionate desire, and by fear.*

3. If a man has done something in ignorance either of the law or of the facts of the case, and would be sorry for it, were he to find out what he has done, that act is *involuntary*, so far as it is traceable to ignorance alone. Even if he would not be sorry, still the act must be pronounced *not voluntary*, under the same reservation. Ignorance, sheer ignorance, takes whatever is done under it out of the region of volition. Nothing is willed but what is known. An ignorant man is as excusable as a drunken one, as such,—no more and no less.

The difference is, that drunkenness generally is
voluntary; ignorance often is not. But ignorance
may be voluntary, quite as voluntary as drunkenness.
It is a capital folly of our age to deny the possibility
of voluntary intellectual error. Error is often
voluntary, and (where the matter is one that the
person officially or otherwise is required to know)
immoral too. A strange thing it is to say that "it
is as unmeaning to speak of the immorality of an
intellectual mistake as it would be to talk of the
colour of a sound." (Lecky, *European Morals*, ii.,
202.)

4. There is an ignorance that is sought on
purpose, called *affected ignorance* (in the Shakspearian
sense of the word *affect*), as when a man will not
read begging-letters, that he may not give anything
away. Such ignorance does not hinder voluntariness.
It indicates a strong will of doing or omitting, come
what may. There is yet another ignorance called
crass, which is when a man, without absolutely
declining knowledge, yet takes no pains to acquire
it in a matter where he is aware that truth is
important to him. Whatever election is made in
consequence of such ignorance, is less voluntary,
indeed, than if it were made in the full light, still
it is to some extent voluntary. It is *voluntary in its
cause*, that is, in the voluntary ignorance that led to
it. Suppose a man sets up as a surgeon, having
made a very imperfect study of his art. He is
aware, that for want of knowledge and skill, he
shall endanger many lives : still he neglects opportunities of making himself competent, and goes

audaciously to work. If any harm comes of his bungling, he can plead intellectual error, an error of judgment for the time being ; he did his best as well as he knew it. Doubtless he did, and in that he is unlike the malicious maker of mischief: still he has chosen lightly and recklessly to hazard a great evil. To that extent his will is bound to the evil: he has chosen it, as it were, at one remove.

5. Another instance. A man is a long way on to seeing, though he does not quite see, the claims of the Church of Rome on his allegiance and sub-mission. He suspects that a little more prayer and search, and he shall be a Roman Catholic. To escape this, he resolves to go travelling and give up prayer. This is *affected ignorance*. Another has no such perception of the claims of Catholicism. He has no religion that satisfies him. He is aware speculatively of the importance of the religious question ; but his heart is not in religion at all. With Demas, he loves the things of this world. Very attractive and interesting does he find this life ; and for the life to come he is content to chance it. This is *crass ignorance* of religious truth. Such a man is not a formal heretic, for he is not altogether wilful and contumacious in his error. Still neither is it wholly involuntary, nor he wholly guiltless.

6. *Passionate desire* is not an affection of the will, but of the sensitive appetite. The will may co-operate, but the passion is not in the will. The will may neglect to check the passion, when it might : it may abet and inflame it : in these ways an act done in passion is a voluntary act. Still it

becomes voluntary only by the influx of the will,
positively permitting or stimulating : it is not voluntary precisely as it proceeds from passion : for
voluntary is that which is of the will. It belongs
to passion to bring on a momentary darkness in the
understanding : where such darkness is, there is so
much the less of a human act. But passion in an
adult of sane mind is hardly strong enough, of
itself and wholly without the will, to execute any
considerable outward action, involving the voluntary
muscles. Things are often said and done, and put
down to passion : but that is not the whole account
of the matter. The will has been for a long time
either feeding the passions, or letting them range
unchecked : that is the reason of their present
outburst, which is voluntary at least *in its cause*.
Once this evil preponderance has been brought
about, it is to be examined whether the will, in
calm moods, is making any efforts to redress the
evil. Such efforts, if made, go towards making the
effects of passion, when they come, involuntary, and
gradually preventing them altogether.

7. What a man does *from fear*, he is said to do
under compulsion, especially if the fear be applied
to him by some other person in order to gain
a purpose. Such *compulsory action* is distinguished
in ordinary parlance from voluntary action. And
it is certainly less voluntary, inasmuch as the will is
hedged in to make its choice between two evils, and
chooses one or other only as being the less evil of
the two, not for any liking to the thing in itself. Still,
all things considered, the thing is chosen, and the

action is so far voluntary. We may call it *voluntary in the concrete*, and *involuntary in the abstract*. The thing is willed as matters stand, but in itself and apart from existing need it is not liked at all. But as acts must be judged as they stand, by what the man wills now, not by what he would will, an act done under fear is on the whole voluntary. At the same time, fear sometimes excuses from the observance of a law, or of a contract, which from the way in which it was made was never meant to bind in so hard a case. Not all contracts, however, are of this accommodating nature ; and still less, all laws. But even where the law binds, the penalty of the law is sometimes not incurred, when the law was broken through fear.

Readings.—Ar., *Eth.*, III., i.; St. Thos., 1a 2æ, q. 6, art. 3 ; *ib.*, q. 6, art. 6, 8 ; *ib.*, q. 77, art. 6.

SECTION II.—*Of the determinants of morality in any given action.*

1. *The morality of any given action is determined by three elements, the end in view, the means taken, and the circumstances that accompany the taking of the said means.* Whoever knows this principle, does not thereby know the right and wrong of every action, but he knows how to go about the enquiry. It is a rule of diagnosis.

2. In order to know whether what a man does befits him as a man to do, the first thing to examine is that which he mainly desires and wills in his action. Now the end is more willed and desired than the means. He who steals to commit adultery,

says Aristotle, is more of an adulterer than a thief. The end in view is what lies nearest to a man's heart as he acts. On that his mind is chiefly bent; on that his main purpose is fixed. Though the end is last in the order of execution, it is first and foremost in the order of intention. Therefore the end in view enters into morality more deeply than any other element of the action. It is not, however, the most obvious determinant, because it is the last point to be gained; and because, while the means are taken openly, the end is often a secret locked up in the heart of the doer, the same means leading to many ends, as the road to a city leads to many homes and resting-places. Conversely, one end may be prosecuted by many means, as there are many roads converging upon one goal.

3. If morality were determined by the end in view, and by that alone, the doctrine would hold that the end justifies the means. That doctrine is false, because the moral character of a human act depends on the thing willed, or object of volition, according as it is or is not a fit object. Now the object of volition is not only the end in view, but likewise the means chosen. Besides the end, the means are likewise willed. Indeed, the means are willed more immediately even than the end, as they have to be taken first.

4. A good action, like any other good thing, must possess a certain requisite fulness of being, proper to itself. As it is not enough for the physical excellence of a man to have the bare essentials, a body with a soul animating it, but there is needed a

certain grace of form, colour, agility, and many accidental qualities besides; so for a good act it is not enough that proper means be taken to a proper end, but they must be taken by a proper person, at a proper place and time, in a proper manner, and with manifold other circumstances of propriety.

5. The end in view may be either *single*, as when you forgive an injury solely for the love of Christ: or *multiple co-ordinate*, as when you forgive both for the love of Christ and for the mediation of a friend, and are disposed to forgive on either ground separately; or *multiple subordinate*, as when you would not have forgiven on the latter ground alone, but forgive the more easily for its addition, having been ready, however, to forgive on the former alone: or *cumulative*, as when you forgive on a number of grounds collectively, on no one of which would you have forgiven apart from the rest.

6. Where there is no outward action, but only an internal act, and the object of that act is some good that is willed for its own sake, there can be no question of means taken, as the end in view is immediately attained.

7. The means taken and the circumstances of those means enter into the morality of the act, *formally* as they are seen by the intellect, *materially* as they are in themselves. (See what is said of ignorance, c. iii., s. i., nn. 3—5, p. 27.) This explains the difference between *formal* and *material* sin. A *material* sin would be *formal* also, did the agent know what he was doing. No sin is culpable that is not *formal*. But, as has been said, there may be a cul-

D

pable perversion of the intellect, so that the man is the author of his own obliquity or defect of vision. When Saul persecuted the Christians, he probably sinned materially, not formally. When Caiphas spoke the truth without knowing it, he said well materially, but ill formally.

8. In looking at the means taken and the circumstances that accompany those means, it is important to have a ready rule for pronouncing what particular belongs to the means and what to the circumstances. Thus Clytemnestra deals her husband Agamemnon a deadly stroke with an axe, partly for revenge, partly that she may take to herself another consort; is the deadliness of the blow part of the means taken or only an accompanying circumstance? It is part of the means taken. The means taken include every particular that is willed and chosen as making for the end in view. The fatal character of the blow does make to that end; if Agamemnon does not die, the revenge will not be complete, and life with Aegisthus will be impossible. On the other hand, the fact that Clytemnestra is the wife of the man whom she murders, is not a point that her will rests upon as furthering her purpose at all; it is an accompanying circumstance. This method of distinguishing means from circumstance is of great value in casuistry.

9. It is clear that not every attendant circumstance affects the morality of the means taken. Thus the blow under which Agamemnon sank was neither more nor less guiltily struck because it was dealt with an axe, because it was under pretence of

giving him a bath, or because his feet were entangled in a long robe. These circumstances are all irrelevant. Those only are relevant which attach some special reasonableness or unreasonableness to the thing done. Thus the provocation that Clytemnestra had from her husband's introduction of Cassandra into her house made her act of vengeance less unreasonable: on the other hand it was rendered more unreasonable by the circumstance of the dear and holy tie that binds wife to husband. The provocation and the relationship were two relevant circumstances in that case.

10. But it happens sometimes that a circumstance only affects the reasonableness of an action on the supposition of some previous circumstance so affecting it. Thus to carry off a thing in large or small quantities does not affect the reasonableness of the carrying, unless there be already some other circumstance attached that renders the act good or evil; as for instance, if the goods that are being removed are stolen property. Circumstances of this sort are called *aggravating*—or, as the case may be, *extenuating*—circumstances. Circumstances that of themselves, and apart from any previous supposition, make the thing done peculiarly reasonable or unreasonable, are called *specifying* circumstances. They are so called, because they place the action in some species of virtue or vice; whereas *aggravating* or *extenuating* circumstances add to, or take off from, the good or evil of the action in that species of virtue or vice to which it already belongs.

11. A variety of specifying circumstances may place one and the same action in many various

species of virtue or vice. Thus a religious robbing his parents would sin at once against justice, piety, and religion. A nun preferring death to dishonour practises three virtues, chastity, fortitude, and religion.

12. The means chosen may be of four several characters :—

(*a*) A thing *evil of itself* and inexcusable under all conceivable circumstances; for instance, blasphemy, idolatry, lying.

(*b*) *Needing excuse*, as the killing of a man, the looking at an indecent object. Such things are not to be done except under certain circumstances and with a grave reason. Thus indecent sights may be met in the discharge of professional duty. In that case indeed they cease to be indecent. They are then only indecent when they are viewed without cause. The absence of a good motive in a case like this commonly implies the presence of a bad one.

(*c*) *Indifferent*, as walking or sitting down.

(*d*) *Good of itself*, but liable to be vitiated by circumstances, as prayer and almsgiving; the good of such actions may be destroyed wholly or in part by their being done out of a vain motive, or unseasonably, or indiscreetly.

13. It is said, "If thy eye be single, thy whole body shall be lightsome." (St. Matt. vi., 22.) The eye is the intention contemplating the end in view. Whoever has placed a good end before him, and regards it steadily with a well-ordered love, never swerving in his affection from the way that reason would have him love, must needs take towards his

end those means, and those only, which are in themselves reasonable and just: as it is written : " Thou
shalt follow justly after that which is just." (Deut.
xvi., 20.)   Thus I am building a church to the glory
of God ; money runs short : I perceive that by
signing a certain contract that must mean grievous
oppression of the poor, I shall save considerable
expense, whereas, if I refuse, the works will have to
be abandoned for want of funds.   If I have purely
the glory of God before my eyes, I certainly shall
not sign that contract : for injustice I know can bear
no fruit of Divine glory.   But if I am bent upon
having the building up in any case, of course I shall
sign : but then my love for the end in view is no
longer pure and regulated by reason : it is not God
but myself that I am seeking in the work.   Thus an
end entirely just, holy, and pure, purifies and sanctifies the means, not formally, by investing with a
character of justice means in themselves unjust,
for that is impossible,—the leopard cannot change
his spots,—but by way of elimination, removing
unjust means as ineligible to my purpose, and
leaving me only those means to choose from which
are in themselves just.

14. With means in themselves indifferent, the
case is otherwise.   A holy and pious end does
formally sanctify those means, while a wicked end
vitiates them.   I beg the reader to observe what sort
of means are here in question.   There is no question
of means in themselves or in their circumstances
unjust, as theft, lying, murder, but of such indifferent things as reading, writing, painting, singing,

travelling. Whoever travels to commit sin at the
end of his journey, his very travelling, so far as it is
referred to that end, is part of his sin : it is a wicked
journey that he takes. And he who travels to
worship at some shrine or place of pilgrimage,
includes his journey in his devotion. The end in
view there sanctifies means in themselves indifferent.

15. As a great part of the things that we do are
indifferent as well in themselves as in the circumstances of the doing of them, the moral character of
our lives depends largely on the ends that we
habitually propose to ourselves. One man's great
thought is how to make money ; what he reads,
writes, says, where he goes, where he elects to
reside, his very eating, drinking and personal expenditure, all turns on what he calls making his fortune.
It is all to gain money—*quocunque modo rem.* Another
is active for bettering the condition of the labouring
classes : a third for the suppression of vice. These
three men go some way together in a common orbit
of small actions, alike to the eye, but morally unlike,
because of the various guiding purposes for which
they are done. Hence, when we consider such
pregnant final ends as the service of God and the
glory of a world to come, it appears how vast is the
alteration in the moral line and colouring of a man's
life, according to his practical taking up or setting
aside of these great ends.

16. We must beware however of an exaggeration
here. The final end of action is often latent, not
explicitly considered. A fervent worshipper of God
wishes to refer his whole self with all that he does

to the Divine glory and service. Yet such a one will eat, drink, and be merry with his friends, not thinking of God at the time. Still, supposing him to keep within the bounds of temperance, he is serving God and doing good actions. But what of a man who has entirely broken away from God, what of his eating, drinking, and other actions that are of their kind indifferent? We cannot call them sins : there is nothing wrong about them, neither in the thing done, nor in the circumstances of the doing, nor in the intention. Pius V. condemned the proposition : " All the works of infidels are sins." Neither must we call such actions indifferent in the individual who does them, supposing them to be true human acts, according to the definition, and not done merely mechanically. They are not indifferent, because they receive a certain measure of natural goodness from the good natural purpose which they serve, namely, the conservation and well-being of the agent. *Every human act is either good or evil in him who does it.* I speak of natural goodness only.

17. The *effect consequent* upon an action is distinguishable from the action itself, from which it is not unfrequently separated by a considerable interval of time, as the death of a man from poison administered a month before. The effect consequent enters into morality only in so far as it is either chosen as a means or intended as an end (nn. 2, 3, p. 31), or is annexed as a relevant circumstance to the means chosen (n. 9, p. 34.). Once the act is done, it matters nothing to morality whether the effect consequent actually ensues or not, provided no new

act be elicited thereupon, whether of commission or of culpable omission to prevent. It matters not to morality, but it does matter to the agent's claim to reward or liability to punishment at the hands of human legislators civil and ecclesiastical.

18. As soul and body make one man, so the inward and outward act—as the will to strike and the actual blow struck—are one human act. The outward act gives a certain physical completeness to the inward. Moreover the inward act is no thorough-going thing, if it stops short of outward action where the opportunity offers. Otherwise, the inward act may be as good or as bad morally as inward and outward act together. The mere wish to kill, where the deed is impossible, may be as wicked as wish and deed conjoined. It may be, but commonly it will not, for this reason, that the outward execution of the deed reacts upon the will and calls it forth with greater intensity; the will as it were expands where it finds outward vent. There is no one who has not felt the relative mildness of inward feelings of impatience or indignation, compared with those engendered by speaking out one's mind. Often also the outward act entails a long course of preparation, all during which the inward will is sustained and frequently renewed, as in a carefully planned burglary.

Readings.—St. Thos., 1a 2æ, q. 18, art. 1 ; *ib.*, q. 18, art. 2, in corp., ad 1 ; *ib.*, q. 18, art. 3, in corp., ad 2 ; *ib.*, q. 18, art. 4—6 ; *ib.*, q. 18, art. 8, in corp., ad

2, 3; *ib.*, q. 18, art. 9, in corp., ad 3; *ib.*, q. 18, art. 10, 3; *ib.*, q. 18, art. 11, in corp.; *ib.*, q. 20, art. 4, in corp.

CHAPTER IV.

OF PASSIONS.

SECTION I.—*Of Passions in General.*

1. A PASSION is defined to be : *A movement of the irrational part of the soul, attended by a notable altera- tion of the body, on the apprehension of good or evil.* The soul is made up of intellect, will, and sensible appetite. The first two are rational, the third irrational : the third is the seat of the passions. In a disembodied spirit, or an angel, there are no senses, no sensible appetite, no passions. The angel, or the departed soul, can love and hate, fear and desire, rejoice and grieve, but these are not passions in the pure spirit, they are acts of intellect and will alone. So man also often loves and hates, and does other acts that are synonymous with cor- responding passions, and yet no passion is there. The man is working with his calm reason : his irrational soul is not stirred. To an author, when he is in the humour for it, it is a delight to be writing, but not a passionate delight. The will finds satisfaction in the act : the irrational soul is not affected by it. Or a penitent is sorry for his sin : he sincerely regrets it before God : his will is heartily turned away, and wishes that that sin had

never been : at the same time his eye is dry,
his features unmoved, not a sigh does he utter,
and yet he is truly sorry. It is important to
bear these facts in mind : else we shall be continually mistaking for passions what are pure acts
of will, or *vice versa,* misled by the identity of
name.

2. The great mark of a passion is its sensible
working of itself out upon the body,—what Dr. Bain
calls "the diffusive wave of emotion." Without
this mark there is no passion, but with it are other
mental states besides passions, as we define them.
All strong emotion affects the body sensibly, but not
all emotions are passions. There are emotions that
arise from and appertain to the rational portion
of the soul. Such are Surprise, Laughter, Shame.
There is no sense of humour in any but rational
beings ; and though dogs look ashamed and horses
betray curiosity, that is only inasmuch as in these
higher animals there is something analogous to what
is reason in man. Moreover passions are conversant
with good and evil affecting sense, but the objects
of such emotions as those just mentioned are not
good and evil as such, common parlance notwithstanding, whereby we are said to laugh at a *bon mot,*
or "a good thing."

3. *Love* is a generic passion, having for its
species *desire* and *delight,* the contraries of which
are *abhorrence* and *pain.* Desire is of absent good ;
abhorrence is of absent evil ; delight is in present
good ; pain is at present evil. The good and the evil
which is the object of any passion must be appre-

hended by sense, or by imagination in a sensible way, whether itself be a thing of sense or not.

4. Desire and abhorrence, delight and pain, are conversant with good and evil simply. But good is often attainable only by an effort, and evil avoidable by an effort. The effort that good costs to attain casts a shade of evil or undesirableness over it: we may shrink from the effort while coveting the good. Again, the fact of evil being at all avoidable is a good thing about such evil. If we call evil black, and good white, avoidable evil will be black just silvering into grey: and arduous good will be white with a cloud on it. And if the white attracts, and the black repels the appetite, it appears that arduous good is somewhat distasteful, to wit, to the faint-hearted; and avoidable, or vincible, evil has its attraction for the man of spirit. About these two objects, good hard of getting and evil hard of avoidance, arise four other passions, *hope* and *despair* about the former, *fear* and *daring* about the latter. Hope goes out towards a difficult good: despair flies from it, the difficulty here being more repellent than the good is attractive. Fear flies from a threatening evil: while daring goes up to the same, drawn by the likelihood of vanquishing it. *Desire* and *abhorrence, delight* and *pain, hope* and *despair, fear* and *daring,* with *anger* and *hatred* (of which presently), complete our list of passions.

5. Aristotle and his school of old, called Peripatetics, recommended the moderation of the passions, not their extirpation. The Stoics on the other hand contended that the model man, the sage,

should be totally devoid of passions. This celebrated dispute turned largely on the two schools
not understanding the same thing by the word
passion. Yet not entirely so. There was a residue of
real difference, and it came to this. If the sensitive
appetite stirs at all, it must stir in one or other of
nine ways corresponding to the nine passions which
we have enumerated. Such an emotion as Laughter
affects the imagination and the sensitive part of
man, and of course the body visibly, but it does not
stir the sensitive appetite, since it does not prompt
to action. To say then that a man has no passions,
means that the sensitive appetite never stirs within
him, but is wholly dead. But this is impossible, as
the Stoic philosopher was fain to confess when
he got frightened in a storm at sea. Having no
passions cannot in any practical sense mean having
no movements of the sensitive appetite, for that will
be afoot of its own proper motion independent of
reason : but it may mean cherishing no passions,
allowing none to arise unresisted, but suppressing
their every movement to the utmost that the will can.
In that sense it is a very intelligible and practical
piece of advice, that the wise man should labour to
have no passions. It is the advice embodied in
Horace's *Nil admirari*, Talleyrand's "No zeal,"
Beaconsfield's " Beware of enthusiasm." It would
have man to work like a scientific instrument, calm as
a chronometer, regulated by reason alone. This was
the Stoic teaching, this the perfection that they
inculcated, quite a possible goal to make for, if not
to attain. And it is worth a wise man's while to

consider, whether he should bend his efforts in this direction or not. The determination here taken and acted upon will elaborate quite a different character of man one way or the other. The effort made as the Stoics direct, would mean no yielding to excitement, no poetry, no high-strung devotion, no rapture, no ecstasy, no ardour of love, no earnest rhetoric spoken or listened to, no mourning, no rejoicing other than the most conventional, to the persistent smothering of whatever is natural and really felt, no tear of pity freely let flow, no touch of noble anger responded to, no scudding before the breeze of indignation,—all this, that reason may keep on the even tenour of her way undisturbed.

6. The fault in this picture is that it is not the picture of a man, but of a spirit. He who being man should try to realize it in himself, would fall short of human perfection. For though the sensitive appetite is distinguished from the will, and the two may clash and come in conflict, yet they are not two wholly independent powers, but the one man is both will and sensitive appetite, and he rarely operates according to one power without the other being brought into corresponding play. There is a similar concomitance of the operations of intellect and imagination. What attracts the sensitive appetite, commonly allures also the *affective* will, though on advertence the *elective* will may reject it. On the other hand, a strong affection and election of the will cannot be without the sensitive appetite being stirred, and that so strongly that the motion is notable in the body,—in other words, is a passion.

Passion is the natural and in a certain degree the inseparable adjunct of strong volition. To check one is to check the other. Not only is the passion repressed by repressing the volition, but the repression of the passion is also the repression of the volition. A man then who did his best to repress all movements of passion indiscriminately, would lay fetters on his will, lamentable and cruel and impolitic fetters, where his will was bent on any object good and honourable and well-judged.

7. Again, man's will is reached by two channels, from above downwards and from below upwards : it is reached through the reason and through the imagination and senses. By the latter channel it often receives evil impressions, undoubtedly, but not unfrequently by the former also. Reason may be inconsiderate, vain, haughty, mutinous, unduly sceptical. The abuse is no justification for closing either channel. Now the channel of the senses and of the imagination is the wider, and in many cases affords the better passage of the two. The will that is hardly reached by reason, is approached and won by a pathetic sight, a cry of enthusiasm, a threat that sends a tremor through the limbs. Rather I should say the affective will is approached in this way : for it remains with the elective will, on ad-vertence and consultation with reason, to decide whether or not it shall be won to consent. But were it not for the channel of passion, this will could never have been approached at all even by reasons the most cogent. Rhetoric often succeeds, where mere dry logic would have been thrown away. God

help vast numbers of the human race, if their wills were approachable only through their reasons! They would indeed be fixtures.

8. Another fact to notice is the liability of reason's gaze to become morbid and as it were inflamed by unremitting exercise. I do not here allude to hard study, but to overcurious scanning of the realities of this life, and the still greater realities and more momentous possibilities of the world to come. There is a sense of the surroundings being too much for us, an alarm and a giddiness, that comes of sober matter-of-fact thought over-much prolonged. Then it happens that one or more undeniable truths are laid hold of, and considered in strong relief and in isolation from the rest: the result is a distorted and partial view of truth as a whole, and therewith the mind is troubled. Here the kindlier passions, judiciously allowed to play, come in to soothe the wound and soreness of pure intellect, too keen in its workings for one who is not yet a pure spirit.

9. Moral good and evil are predicable only of *human acts*, in the technical sense of the term. (c. i., nn. 2—4, p. 41.) As the passions by definition (c. iv., s. i., n. 1, p. 41) are not human acts, they can never be morally evil of themselves. But they are an occasion of moral evil in this way. They often serve to wake up the slumbering Reason. To that end it is necessary that they should start up of themselves without the call of Reason. This would be no inconvenience, if the instant Reason awoke, and adverted to the tumult and stir of Passion, she could

take command of it, and where she saw fit, quell it.
But Reason has no such command, except in cases
where she has acquired it by years of hard fighting.
Passion once afoot holds on her course against the
dictate of Reason. True, so long as it remains mere
Passion, and Reason is not dragged away by it, no
consent of the will given, no voluntary act elicited,
still less carried into outward effect,—so long as
things remain thus, however Passion may rage,
there is no moral evil done. But there is a great
temptation, and in great temptation many men fall.
The evil is the act of free will, but the pressure on
the will is the pressure of Passion. But Passion
happily is a young colt amenable to discipline.
Where the assaults of Passion are resolutely and
piously withstood, and the incentives thereto
avoided—unnatural and unnecessary incentives I
mean—Passion itself acquires a certain habit of
obedience to Reason, which habit is moral virtue.
Of that presently.

10. In a man of confirmed habits of moral
virtue, Passion starts up indeed independently of
Reason, but then Reason ordinarily finds little difficulty in regulating the Passion so aroused. In a
certain high and extraordinary condition of human
nature, not only has Reason entire mastery over
Passion wherever she finds it astir, but Passion
cannot stir in the first instance, without Reason
calling upon it to do so. In this case the torpor of
the will deprecated above (n. 7) is not to be feared,
because Reason is so vigorous and so masterful as to
be adequate to range everywhere and meet all emer-

gencies without the goad of Passion. This state is called by divines the *state of integrity*. In it Adam was before he sinned. It was lost at the Fall, and has not been restored by the Redemption. It is not a thing in any way due to human nature: nothing truly natural to man was forfeited by Adam's sin. It is no point of holiness, no guerdon of victory, this state of integrity, but rather a being borne on angel's wings above the battle. But one who has no battle in his own breast against Passion, may yet suffer and bleed and die under exterior persecution: nay, he may, if he wills, let in Passion upon himself, to fear and grieve, when he need not. So did the Second Adam in the Garden of Gethsemane.

Readings.—St. Thos., 1a, q. 81, art. 2, in corp.; *id.*, 1a 2æ, q. 23, art. 1, in corp.; *ib.*, q. 23, art. 2, in corp.; Cicero, *Tusc. Disp.*, iv., cc. 17—26; St. Aug., *De Civitate Dei*, ix., cc. 4, 5; Ar, *Eth.*, III., v., 3, 4; *ib.*, I., xiii., 15—17; St. Thos., 3a, q. 15, art. 4; *id.*, 1a 2æ, q. 59, art. 5; Plato, *Timæus*, 69, B, E: 70, A.

SECTION II.—*Of Desire.*

1. Desires are either *physical* cravings, by moderns called *appetites;* or ~~physical~~ desires or *tastes*, called *desires* proper. The appetites have their beginning in bodily uneasiness. They are felt needs of something required for the animal maintenance of the individual or of the race. The objects of the several appetites are Meat and Drink, Warmth or Coolness, Exercise and Repose, Sleep, Sex. The object of mere appetite is marked by quantity only, not by quality. That is to say, the thing is sought

E

for in the vague, in a certain amount sufficient to supply the want, but not this or that variety of the thing. The cry of a hungry man is, " Give me to eat," if very hungry, " Give me much:" but so far as he is under the mere dominion of appetite he does not crave any particular article of food, vegetable or animal: he wants quantity merely. So of thirst, so of all the appetites, where there is nothing else but appetite present.

2. But if a thirsty man cries for champagne, or a hungry man fancies a venison pasty, there is another element beyond appetite in that demand. On the matter of the physical craving there is stamped the form of a psychical desire. The psychical element prescribes a quality of the objects sought. The thirsty man thus prompted no longer wants drink but wine: the man mewed up within doors no longer calls for exercise, but for a horse or a bicycle. It is obvious that in man the appetites generally pass into the further shape of psychical desire. It is when the appetite is vehement, or the man is one who makes slight study of his animal wants, that pure appetite, sheer physical craving, is best shown. Darius flying before his conqueror is ready to drink at any source, muddy or clear, a drink is all that he wants: it is all that is wanted by St. Paul the first Hermit. But your modern lounger at the clubs, what variety of liquors are excogitated to please his palate!

3. Not all psychical desires are on the matter of appetite ; they may be fixed on any good whatsoever of body or of mind. Many psychical desires are

not passions at all, but reside exclusively in the superior part of the soul, in the will prompted by the understanding, and do not affect the body in any sensible way. Such for instance is the great desire of happiness. Those desires that are passions are prompted, not by the understanding, but by the imagination or fancy, imaging to itself some particular good, not good in general, for that the understanding contemplates. Fancy paints the picture; or if sense presents it, fancy appropriates and embellishes it: the sensitive appetite fastens upon the representation: the bodily organs sensibly respond; and there is the passion of psychical desire.

4. *Physical cravings, or appetites, have limited objects: the objects of psychical desires may be unlimited.* A thirsty man thirsts not for an ocean, but for drink *quantum sufficit*: give him that and the appetite is gone. But the miser covets all the money that he can get: the voluptuary ranges land and sea in search of a new pleasure: the philosopher ever longs for a higher knowledge: the saint is indefatigable in doing good. Whatever a man takes to be an end in itself, not simply a means, that he desires without end or measure. What he desires as a means, he desires under a limitation, so far forth as it makes for the end, so much and no more. As Aristotle says of the processes of art, "the end in view is the limit," πέρας τὸ τέλος (cf. c. ii., s. iii., n. 3, p. 15). Whatever is desired as an end in itself, is taken to be a part of happiness, or to represent happiness. Happiness and the object that gives happiness is the one thing that man desires for itself, and desires

without end or measure. Unfortunately he is often mistaken in the choice of this object. He often takes for an end what is properly only a means. They "whose god is their belly," have made this mistake in regard of the gratification of appetite. It is not appetite proper that has led to this perversion, but psychical desire, or appetite inflamed by the artificial stimulus of imagination. For one who would be temperate, it is more important to control his imagination than to trouble about his appetite. Appetite exhausts itself, sometimes within the bounds of what is good for the subject, sometimes beyond them, but still within some bounds; but there is no limit to the cravings bred of imagination.

5. By this canon a man may try himself to discover whether or not a favourite amusement is gaining too much upon him. An amusement is properly a means to the end, that a man may come away from it better fitted to do the serious work of his life. Pushed beyond a certain point, the amusement ceases to minister to this end. The wise man drops it at that point. But if one knows not where to stop : or if when stopped in spite of himself, he is restless till he begin again, and never willingly can forego any measure of the diversion that comes within his reach, the means in that case has passed into an end : he is enslaved to that amusement, inasmuch as he will do anything and everything for the sake of it. Thus some men serve pleasure, and other men money.

6. Hence is apparent the folly of supposing that crimes against property are preventible simply by

placing it within the power of all members of the
community easily to earn an honest livelihood, and
therewith the satisfaction of all their natural needs.
It is not merely to escape cold and hunger that men
turn to burglary or fraudulent dealing: it is more
for the gratification of a fancy, the satisfaction of
an inordinate desire. Great crimes are not committed "to keep the wolf from the door," but
because of the wolf in the heart, the overgrown
psychical desire, which is bred in many a well-
nourished, warmly clad, comfortably housed, highly
educated citizen. There is a sin born of "fulness
of bread."

Readings.—St. Thos., 1a 2æ, q. 30, art. 3, in
corp.; *ib.*, q. 30, art. 4, in corp.; Ar., *Eth.*, III., xi.,
1—4: Ar., *Pol.*, I., ix., 13; *ib.*, II., vii., 11—13.

N.B.—The division of desires into *physical* and
psychical is first suggested by Plato, who (*Rep.* 558
D to 559 C) divides them as *necessary* and *unnecessary*. Unnecessary desires he treats as evil.
What Plato calls a *necessary*, Aristotle calls a *physical*,
and St. Thomas a *natural* desire. Unfortunately,
Aristotle and St. Thomas had but one word for our
English two, *physical* and *natural*. Desires that are
not physical, not natural nor necessary to man in
his animal capacity, may be highly natural and
becoming to man as he is a reasonable being, or
they may be highly unbecoming. These psychical
desires, called by St. Thomas *not natural*, take in
at once the noblest and the basest aspirations of
humanity.

Section III.—*Of Delight.*

1. Delight like desire may be either physical or
psychical. All that has been said above of desire
under this division applies also to delight, which is
the realization of desire. This division does not
altogether fall in with that into *sensual* delights and
intellectual delights. A professional wine-taster could
hardly be said to find intellectual delight in a
bottle of good Champagne, real *Veuve-Clicquot :* yet
certainly his is a psychical delight, no mere un-
sophisticated gratification of appetite. Sensual
delights then are those delights which are founded
on the gratification of appetite, whether simple—
in which case the delight is physical—or studied
and fancy-wrought appetite, the gratification of
which is psychical delight. Intellectual delights on
the other hand are those that come of the exercise
of intellect, not unsupported by imagination, but
where appetite enters not at all, or only as a remote
adjunct, albeit the delight may turn upon some
sight or sound, as of music, or of a fine range of
hills. Or the object may be a thing of intellect,
pure and removed from sense as far as an object
of human contemplation can be, for instance, the
first elements of matter, freewill, the immensity of
God. The study of such objects yields a purer
intellectual delight than that of the preceding. But
this is a high ground and a keen upper air, where
few can tread and breathe.

2. A man has more complacency in himself upon
attaining to some intellectual delight than upon a

sensual satisfaction : he is prouder to have solved a
problem than to have enjoyed his dinner. Also,
he would rather forego the capacity of sensual enjoyment than that of intellectual pleasure ; rather lose
his sense of taste than his science or his scholar-
ship, if he has any notable amount of either.
Again, put sensual delight in one scale, and in the
other the intellectual delight of honour, no worthy
specimen of a man will purchase the pleasure at
the price of honour. The disgrace attaching to
certain modes of enjoyment is sufficient to make
men shun them, very pleasant though they be to
sense. Again, sensual delight is a passing thing,
waxing and waning : but intellectual delight is steady,
grasped and held firmly as a whole. But sensual
delight comes more welcome of the two in this
that it removes a pre-existing uneasiness, as hunger,
weariness, nervous prostration, thus doing a medicinal office : whereas no such office attaches in the
essential nature of things to intellectual delight,
as that does not presuppose any uneasiness ; and
though it may remove uneasiness, the removal is
difficult, because the uneasiness itself is an obstacle
to the intellectual effort that must be made to derive
any intellectual delight. Sensual enjoyment is the
cheaper physician, and ailing mortals mostly resort
to that door.

3. " I will omit much usual declamation on the
dignity and capacity of our nature : the superiority
of the soul to the body, of the rational to the
animal part of our constitution ; upon the worthi-
ness, refinement, and delicacy of some satisfactions,

or the meanness, grossness, and sensuality of others: because I hold that pleasures differ in nothing but in continuance and intensity." (Paley, *Moral Philosophy,* bk. i., c. vi.)

In opposition to the above it is here laid down that *delights do not differ in continuance and intensity, that is, in quantity, alone, but likewise in quality,* that is, some are nobler, better, and more becoming a man than others, and therefore preferable on other grounds than those of mere continuance and intensity. I wish to show that the more pleasant pleasure is not always the better pleasure; that even the pleasure which is more durable, and thereby more pleasant in the long run, is not the better of the two simply as carrying the greater *cumulus* of pleasure. If this is shown, it will follow that pleasure is not identical with good; or that pleasure is not happiness, not the last end of man.

4. Delight comes of activity, not necessarily of change, except so far as activity itself involves change, as it always does in mortal man. Delight sits upon activity, as the bloom upon youth. Bloom is the natural sign of maturity; and the delight that we come to take in doing a thing shows that we are at least beginning to do it well : our activity is approaching perfection. In this sense it is said that *delight perfects activity.* As the activity, so will be the delight. But the activity will be as the power of which it is an exercise. Powers like in kind will supply like activities, and these again will yield delights alike in kind. There is no difference of quality in such delights, they differ in quantity

What R. wants to do is to get hold of a mans will by showing him that to be rational he must submit to a rational habit of life.

OF DELIGHT. 57

alone. Thus taste and smell are two senses: the difference between them can hardly be called one of kind: therefore the delights of smelling and of tasting fall under one category. We may exchange so much smell for an equal amount of taste: it is a mere matter of quantity. But between sight and hearing on the one hand, and taste and smell and touch on the other, there is a wider difference, due to the fact that intellect allies itself more readily to the operation of the two former senses.

5. Widest of all differences is that between sense and intellect. To explain this difference in full belongs to Psychology. Enough to say here that the object of sense is always particular, bound up in circumstances of present time and place, as *this horse*: while the object of intellect is universal, as *horse* simply. The human intellect never works without the concurrence either of sense or of imagination, which is as it were sense at second hand. As pure intellectual operation is never found in man, so neither is pure intellectual delight, like that of an angel. Still, as even in man sense and intellect are two powers differing in kind, so must their operations differ in kind, and the delights consequent upon those operations. Therefore, unless Paley would have been willing to allow that the rational and animal parts of our nature differ only as *more* and *less*—which is tantamount to avowing that man is but a magnified brute—he ought not to have penned his celebrated utterance, that pleasures differ only in continuance and intensity: he should have admitted that they differ likewise

in kind; or in other words, that pleasures differ in quality as well as in quantity. The goodness of a pleasure, then, is not the mere amount of it. To repeat St. Augustine's reflection on the drunken Milanese : " It makes a difference what source a man draws his delight from." * As in man reason is nobler than sense, preferable, and a better good to its possessor—for reason it is that makes him man and raises him above the brute—so the use of the reason and the delight that comes thereof is nobler, preferable, and a better good to him than the pleasure that is of the mere operation of his animal nature. A little of the nobler delight outweighs a vast volume of the baser : not that the nobler is the pleasanter, but because it is the nobler. Nor can it be pretended that the nobler prevails as being the more durable, and thereby likely to prove the pleasanter in the long run. The nobler is better at the time and in itself, because it is the more human delight and characteristic of the higher species. I have but to add that what is better in itself is not better under all circumstances. The best life of man can only be lived at intervals. The lower operations and the delights that go with them have a medicinal power to restore the vigour that has become enfeebled by a lengthened exercise of the higher faculties. At those " dead points " food and fiddling are better than philosophy.

6. This medicinal or restorative virtue of delight is a fact to bear in mind in debating the question how far it is right to act for the pleasure that the

* *Interest unde quis gaudeat.* (S. Aug., *Confess.*, **vi., 6.**)

action gives. It is certainly wrong to act for mere animal gratification. Such gratification is a stimulus to us to do that which makes for the well-being of our nature : to fling away all intention of any good other than the delight of the action, is to mistake the incentive for the end proposed. But this is a doctrine easily misunderstood. An example may save it from being construed too rigidly. Suppose a man. has a vinery, and being fond of fruit he goes there occasionally, and eats, not for hunger, but as he says, because he likes grapes. He seems to act for mere pleasure : yet who shall be stern enough to condemn him, so that he exceed not in quantity? If he returns from the vinery in a more amiable and charitable mood, more satisfied with Providence, more apt to converse with men and do his work in the commonwealth, who can deny that in acting in view of these ends, at least implicitly, he has taken lawful means to a proper purpose? He has not been fed, but recreated : he has not taken nourishment, but medicine, preventive or remedial, to a mind diseased. It is no doubt a sweet and agreeable medicine : this very agreeableness makes its medical virtue. It is a sweet antidote to the bitterness of life. But though a man may live by medicine, he does not live for it. So no man by rights lives for pleasure. The pleasure that a man finds in his work encourages him to go on with it. The pleasure that a man finds by turning aside to what is not work, picks him up, rests and renovates him, that he may go forth as from a wayside inn, or *diverticulum,* refreshed to resume the road of labour. Hence we gather the solution of the question as to the lawfulness of acting for pleasure. If a man does a thing because it is pleasant, and takes the pleasure as an incentive to carry on his labour, or as a remedy to enable him to resume it, he acts for pleasure rightly. For this it is not necessary that he should expressly think of the pleasure as being helpful to labour: it is enough that he accepts the subordination of pleasure to work as nature has ordained it; and this ordinance he does accept, if he puts forth no positive volition the other way, whether expressly, as none but a wrong-headed theologian is likely to do, or virtually, by taking his pleasure with such greediness that the motion of his will is all spent therein as in its last end and terminus, so that the pleasure ceases to be referable to aught beyond itself, a case of much easier occurrence. Or lastly, the natural subordination of pleasure to work may be set aside, defeated, and rendered impossible by the whole tenour of an individual's life, if he be one of those giddy butterflies who flit from pleasure to pleasure and do no work at all. Till late in the morning he sleeps, then breakfasts, then he shoots, lunches, rides, bathes, dines, listens to music, smokes, and reads fiction till late at night, then sleeps again; and this, or the like of this is his day, some three hundred days at least in the year. This is not mere acting for pleasure, it is living for pleasure, or acting for pleasure so continuously as to leave no scope for any further end of life. It may be hard to indicate the precise hour in which this man's pleasure-seeking passes into sin : still this is clear, his life is not innocent. Clear him of gluttony and lust, there remains upon him the sin of sloth and of a wasted existence.

7. Even the very highest of delights, the delight of contemplation, is not the highest of goods, but a concomitant of the highest good. The highest good is the final object of the will : but the object of the will is not the will's own act : we do not will willing, as neither do we understand understanding, not at least without a reflex effort. What we will in contemplating is, not to be delighted, but to see. This is the subjective end and happiness of man, to see, to contemplate. Delight is not anything objective : neither is it the subjective last end of humanity. In no sense then is delight, or pleasure, the highest good.

Readings.—Ar., *Eth.*, X., iv., 8 ; *ib.*, X., iii., 8—13, *ib.*, X., v., 1—5 ; Plato, *Gorgias*, pp. 494, 495 ; Mill, *Utilitarianism*, 2nd. edit., pp. 11—16 ; St. Thos., 1a 2æ, q. 31, art. 5 ; *id.*, *Contra Gentiles*, iii., 26, nn. 8, 10, 11, 12.

Section IV.—*Of Anger.*

1. Anger is a compound passion, made up of displeasure, desire, and hope : displeasure at a slight received, desire of revenge and satisfaction, and hope of getting the same, the getting of it being a matter of some difficulty and calling for some exertion, for we are not angry with one who lies wholly in our power, or whom we despise. Anger then is conversant at once with the good of vengeance

and with the evil of a slight received : the good
being somewhat difficult to compass, and the evil
not altogether easy to wipe out. (Cf. s. i., n. 4, p. 43.)

2. Anger is defined : *A desire of open vengeance
for an open slight, attended with displeasure at the same,
the slight being put upon self, or upon some dear one,
unbefittingly.* The vengeance that the angry man
craves is a vengeance that all shall see. " No, ye
unnatural hags," cries Lear in his fury, " I will do
such things,—what they shall be yet I know not,
but *they shall be the terror of the earth.*" When we
are angry, we talk of "making an example" of the
offender. The idea is that, as all the world has
seen us slighted and set at naught, so all the world,
witnessing the punishment of the offending party,
may take to heart the lesson which we are enforcing
upon him, namely, that we are men of might and
importance whom none should despise. Whoever
is angry, is angry at being despised, flouted to his
face and set at naught, either in his own person, or
in the person of one whom he venerates and loves,
or in some cause that lies near to his heart. Anger
is essentially a craving for vengeance on account of
a wrong done. If then we have suffered, but think
we deserve to suffer, we are not angry. If we have
suffered wrong, but the wrong seems to have been
done in ignorance, or in the heat of passion, we are
not angry, or we are not so very angry. " If he
had known what he was about," we say, or, " if he
had been in his right mind, he could not have
brought himself to treat me so." But when one
has done us cool and deliberate wrong, then we are

angry, because the slight is most considerable.
There is an appearance of our claims to considerations having been weighed, and found wanting.
We call it, "a cool piece of impertinence," "spiteful
malevolence," and the like. Any other motive to
which the wrong is traceable on the part of the
wrong-doer, lessens our anger against him: but the
motive of contempt, and that alone, if we seem to
discover it in him, invariably increases it. To this
all other points are reducible that move our anger,
as forgetfulness, rudely delivered tidings of misfortune, a face of mirth looking on at our distress,
or getting in the way and thwarting our purpose.

3. Anger differs from hatred. Hatred is a chronic
affection, anger an acute one. Hatred wishes evil
to a man as it is evil, anger as it is just. Anger
wishes evil to fall on its object in the sight of all
men, and with the full consciousness of the sufferer:
hatred is satisfied with even a secret mischief, and,
so that the evil be a grievous one, does not much
mind whether the sufferer be conscious of it or no.
Thus an angry man may wish to see him who has
offended brought to public confession and shame:
but a hater is well content to see his enemy spending
his fortune foolishly, or dead drunk in a ditch on
a lonely wayside. The man in anger feels grief and
annoyance, not so the hater. At a certain point of
suffering anger stops, and is appeased when full
satisfaction seems to have been made: but an
enemy is implacable and insatiate in his desire of
your harm. St. Augustine in his Rule to his brethren
says: "For quarrels, either have them not, or end

them with all speed, lest anger grow to hatred, and of a mote make a beam."

4. Anger, like vengeance, is then only a safe course to enter on, when it proceeds not upon personal but upon public grounds. And even by this maxim many deceive themselves.

Readings.—Ar., *Rhet.*, ii., 2; *ib.*, 4, ad fin.; St. Thos., 1a 2æ, q. 46, art. 2, in corp.; *ib.*, q. 46, art. 3, in corp.; *ib.*, q. 46, art. 6; *ib.*, q. 47, art. 2.

CHAPTER V.

OF HABITS AND VIRTUES.

Section I.—*Of Habit.*

1. *A habit is a quality difficult to change, whereby an agent whose nature it was to work one way or another indeterminately, is disposed easily and readily at will to follow this or that particular line of action.* Habit differs from *disposition*, as disposition is a quality easily changed. Thus one in a good humour is in a *disposition* to be kind. Habit is a part of character: disposition is a passing fit. Again, habit differs from *faculty*, or power: as power enables one to act; but habit, presupposing power, renders action easy and expeditious, and reliable to come at call. We have a power to move our limbs, but a habit to walk or ride or swim. Habit then is the determinant of power. One and the same power works well or ill, but not one and the same habit.

2. A power that has only one way of working, set and fixed, is not susceptible of habit. Such powers are the forces of inanimate nature, as gravitation and electricity. A thing does not gravitate better for gravitating often. The moon does not obey the earth more readily to-day than she did in the days of Ptolemy, or of the Chaldean sages. Some specious claim to habit might be set up on behalf of electricity and magnetism. A glass rod rubbed at frequent intervals for six months, is a different instrument from what it would have been, if left all that time idle in a drawer. Then there are such cases as the gradual magnetising of an iron bar. Still we cannot speak of electrical habits, or magnetic habits, not at least in things without life, because there is no will there to control the exercise of the quality. As well might we speak of a "tumble-down" habit in a row of houses, brought on by locomotives running underneath their foundations. It is but a case of an accumulation of small effects, inducing gradually a new molecular arrangement, so that the old powers act under new material conditions. But habit is a thing of life, an appurtenance of will, not of course independent of material conditions and structural alterations, in so far forth as a living and volitional is also a material agent, but essentially usable *at will*, and brought into play and controlled in its operation by free choice, Therefore a habit that works almost automatically has less of the character of a true habit, and passes rather out of morality into the region of physics. Again, bad habits, vices to which a man is become

F

a slave against his better judgment, are less properly called habits than virtues are; for such evil habits do not so much attend on volition (albeit volition has created them) as drag the will in their wake. For the like reason, habit is less properly predicable of brute animals than of men: for brutes have no intelligent will to govern their habits. The highest brutes are most susceptible of habit. They are most like men in being most educable. And, of human progeny, some take up habits, in the best and completest sense of the term, more readily than others. They are better subjects for education: education being nothing else than the formation of habits.

3. Knowledge consists of intellectual habits. But the habits of most consequence to the moralist lie in the will, and in the sensitive appetite as amenable to the control of the will. In this category come the virtues, in the ordinary sense of that name, and secondarily the vices.

4. A habit is acquired by acts. Whereupon this difficulty has been started:—If the habit, say of mental application, comes from acts of study, and again the acts from the habit, how ever is the habit originally acquired? We answer that there are two ways in which one thing may come from another. It may come in point of its very existence, as child from parent; or in point of some mode of existence, as scholar from master. A habit has its very existence from acts preceding: but those acts have their existence independent of the habit. The acts which are elicited after the habit is formed, owe to

the habit, not their existence, but the mode of their existence: that is to say, because of the habit the acts are now formed readily, reliably, and artistically, or virtuously. The primitive acts which gradually engendered the habit, were done with difficulty, fitfully, and with many failures,—more by good luck than good management, if it was a matter of skill, and by a special effort rather than as a thing of course, where it was question of moral well-doing. (See c. ii., s. ii., n. 9, p. 10.)

5. A habit is a living thing: it grows and must be fed. It grows on acts, and acts are the food that sustain it. Unexercised, a habit pines away: corruption sets in and disintegration. A man, we will say, has a habit of thinking of God during his work. He gives over doing so. That means that he either takes to thinking of everything and nothing, or he takes up some definite line of thought to the exclusion of God. Either way there is a new formation to the gradual ruin of the old habit.

6. *Habit* and *custom* may be distinguished in philosophical language. We may say that custom makes the habit. Custom does not imply any skill or special facility. A habit is a channel whereby the energies flow, as otherwise they would not have flowed, freely and readily in some particular direction. A habit, then, is a determination of a faculty for good or for evil. It is something intrinsic in a man, a real modification of his being, abiding in him in the intervals between one occasion for its exercise and another: whereas custom is a mere denomination, expressive of frequent action and no

more. Thus it would be more philosophical to speak of a *custom* of early rising, and of a *custom* of smoking, rather than of a *habit* of smoking, except so far as, by the use of the word *habit*, you may wish to point to a certain acquired skill of the respiratory and facial muscles, and a certain acquired temper of the stomach, enabling one to inhale tobacco fumes with impunity.

7. Habits are acquired, but it is obvious that the rate of acquisition varies in different persons. This comes from one person being more predisposed by nature than another to the acquiring of this or that habit. By *nature*, that is by the native temper and conformation of his body wherewith he was born, this child is more prone to literary learning, that to mechanics, this one to obstinacy and contentiousness, that to sensuality, and so of the rest. For though it is by the soul that a man learns, and by the act of his will and spiritual powers he becomes a glutton or a zealot, nevertheless the bodily organs concur and act jointly towards these ends. The native dispositions of the child's body for the acquisition of habits depend to an unascertained extent upon the habits of his ancestors. This is the fact of *heredity*.

8. Man is said to be "a creature of habits." The formation of habits in the will saves the necessity of continually making up the mind anew. A man will act as he has become habituated, except under some special motive from without, or some special effort from within. In the case of evil habits, that effort is attended with immense difficulty. The

habit is indeed the man's own creation, the outcome of his free acts.   But he is become the bondslave of his creature, so much so that when the occasion arrives, three-fourths of the act is already done, by the force of the habit alone, before his will is awakened, or drowsily moves in its sleep.   The only way for the will to free itself here is not to wait for the occasion to come, but be astir betimes, keep the occasion at arm's length, and register many a determination and firm protest and fervent prayer against the habit.   He who neglects to do this in the interval has himself to blame for being overcome every time that he falls upon the occasion which brings into play the evil habit.

Readings.—St. Thos., 1a 2æ, q. 49, art. 4, ad 1, 2 ; *ib.*, q. 50, art. 3, in corp., ad. 1, 2 ; *ib.*, q. 51, art. 1, in corp. ; *ib.*, q. 53, art. 3, in corp. ; Ar., *Eth.*, II., i. ; *ib.*, III., v., 10—14 ; *ib.*, II., iv., 1, 2, 4.

Section II.—*Of Virtues in General.*

1. Virtue in its most transcendental sense means the excellence of a thing according to its kind. Thus it is the virtue of the eye to see, and of a horse to be fleet of foot.   Vice is a *flaw* in the make of a thing, going to render it useless for the purpose to which it was ordained.   From the ethical stand-point, virtue is a habit that a man has got of doing moral good, or doing that which it befits his rational nature to do : and vice is a habit of doing moral evil. (See c. 1., n. 5.)   It is important to observe that virtue and vice are not acts but habits.   Vices do not make a man guilty, nor do virtues make him

innocent.   A man is guilty or innocent according to
his acts, not according to his habits.   A man may
do a wicked thing and not be vicious, or a good
action and not be virtuous.   But no man is vicious
who has not done one, two, aye, many wicked
things : and to be virtuous, a man must have
performed many acts of virtue.   Children do right
and wrong, but they have neither virtues nor vices
except in a nascent state : there has not yet been
time in them for the habits to be formed.   When
sin is taken away by God and pardoned, the vice,
that is, the evil habit, if any such existed before, still
remains, and constitutes a danger for the future.
The habit can only be overcome by watchfulness
and a long continuance of contrary acts.   But vice
is not sin, nor is sin vice, nor a good deed a virtue.

   2. The name of virtue is given to certain habits
residing in the intellect, as *intuition* or *insight* (into
self-evident truths), *wisdom* (regarding conclusions
of main application), *science* (of conclusions in special
departments), and *art*.   These are called *intellectual
virtues*.

   It was a peculiarity of Socrates' teaching, largely
shared by Plato, to make all virtue intellectual, a
doctrine expressed in the formula, *Virtue is knowledge;* which is tantamount to this other, *Vice is
ignorance,* or *an erroneous view*.   From whence the
conclusion is inevitable : *No evil deed is wilfully done;*
and therefore, *No man is to blame for being wicked.*

   3. Undoubtedly there is a certain element of
ignorance in all vice, and a certain absence of
will about every vicious act.   There is likewise an

intellectual side to all virtue. These positions we willingly concede to the Socratics. Every morally evil act is borne of some voluntary inconsiderateness. The agent is looking the wrong way in the instant at which he does wrong. Either he is regarding only the solicitations of his inferior nature to the neglect of the superior, or he is considering some rational good indeed, but a rational good which, if he would look steadily upon it, he would perceive to be unbefitting for him to choose. No man can do evil in the very instant in which his understanding is considering, above all things else, that which it behoves him specially to consider in the case. Again, in every wrong act, it is not the sheer evil that is willed, but the good through or with the evil. Good, real or supposed, is sought for : evil is accepted as leading to good in the way of means, or annexed thereto as a circumstance. Moreover, no act is virtuous that is elicited quite mechanically, or at the blind instance of passion. To be virtuous, the thing must be done *on principle,* that is, at the dictate of reason and by the light of intellect.

4. Still, virtue is not knowledge. There are other than intellectual habits needed to complete the character of a virtuous man. "I see the better course and approve it, and follow the worse," said the Roman poet.* " The evil which I will not, that I do," said the Apostle. It is not enough to have an intellectual discernment of and preference for

* Video meliora proboque,
Deteriora sequor.

(Ovid, *Metamorph.*, vii., 21.)

what is right : but the will must be habituated to embrace it, and the passions too must be habituated to submit and square themselves to right being done. In other words, a virtuous man is made up by the union of enlightened intellect with the moral virtues. The addition is necessary for several reasons.

(*a*) Ordinarily, the intellect does not necessitate the will. The will, then, needs to be clamped and set by habit to choose the right thing as the intellect proposes it.

(*b.*) Intellect, or Reason, is not absolute in the human constitution. As Aristotle (*Pol.*, I., v., 6) says : " The soul rules the body with a despotic command : but reason rules appetite with a command constitutional and kingly " : that is to say, as Aristotle elsewhere (*Eth.*, I., xiii., 15, 16) explains, passion often " fights and resists reason, opposes and contradicts " : it has therefore to be bound by ordinances and institutions to follow reason's lead : these institutions are good habits, moral virtues, resident there where passion itself is resident, in the inferior appetite. It is not enough that the rider is competent, but the horse too must be broken in.

(*c.*) It is a saying, that " no mortal is always wise." There are times when reason's utterance is faint from weariness and vexation. Then, unless a man has acquired an almost mechanical habit of obeying reason in the conduct of his will and passions, he will in such a conjuncture act inconsiderately and do wrong. That habit is moral virtue. Moral virtue is as the fly-wheel of an engine, a reservoir of force to carry the machine past the " dead points " in its working.   Or again, moral virtue is as discipline to troops suddenly attacked, or hard pressed in the fight.

5. Therefore, besides the habits in the intellect that bear the name of *intellectual virtues*, the virtuous man must possess other habits, as well in the will, that this power may readily embrace what the understanding points out to be good, as in the sensitive appetite in both its parts, concupiscible and irascible, so far forth as appetite is amenable to the control of the will, that it may be so controlled and promptly obey the better guidance. These habits in the will and in the sensitive appetite are called *moral virtues*, and to them the name of *virtue* is usually confined.

Readings.—St. Thos., 1a 2æ, q. 71, art. 1, in corp.; *ib.*, q. 58, art. 2; *ib.*, q. 58, art. 3, in corp., ad 3; *ib.*, q. 56, art. 4, in corp., ad 1—3.

SECTION III.—*Of the Difference between Virtues Intellectual and Moral.*

1. St. Thomas* (1a 2æ, q. 56, art. 3, in corp.) draws this difference, that an intellectual virtue gives one a facility in doing a good act; but a moral virtue not only gives facility, but makes one put the facility in use.   Thus a habit of grammar

---

* By *doing good* St. Thomas means the determination of the appetite, rational or sensitive, to good. He says that intellectual virtue does not prompt this determination of the appetite. Of course it does not: it prompts only the act of the power wherein it resides: now it resides in the intellect, not in the appetite; and it prompts the act of the intellect, which however is not always followed by an act of appetite in accordance with it.

he says, enables one readily to speak correctly, but
does not ensure that one always shall speak correctly, for a grammarian may make solecisms on
purpose : whereas a habit of justice not only makes
a man prompt and ready to do just deeds, but
makes him actually do them. Not that any habit
necessitates volition. Habits do not necessitate,
but they facilitate the act of the will. (s. i., nn. 1,
2, 8, pp. 64, 68.)

2. Another distinction may be gathered from
St. Thomas (1a 2æ, q. 21, art. 2, ad 2), that the special
intellectual habit called *art* disposes a man to act
correctly towards some particular end, but a moral
habit towards the common end, scope and purpose
of all human life. Thus medical skill ministers to
the particular end of healing : while the moral habit
of temperance serves the general end, which is final
happiness and perfection. So to give a wrong
prescription through sheer antecedent ignorance, is
to fail as a doctor : but to get drunk wittingly and
knowingly is to fail as a man.

3. The grand distinction between intellectual
and moral habits seems to be this, that moral habits
reside in powers which may act against the dictate
of the understanding,—the error of Socrates, noticed
above (c. v., s. ii., n. 2, p. 70), lay in supposing that
they could not so act : whereas the power which is
the seat of the intellectual habits, the understanding,
cannot possibly act against itself. Habits dispose
the subject to elicit acts of the power wherein they
reside. Moral habits induce acts of will and sensitive appetite : intellectual habits, acts of intellect.

Will and appetite may act against what the agent knows to be best : but intellect cannot contradict intellect. It cannot judge that to be true and beautiful which it knows to be false and foul. If a musician strikes discords on purpose, or a grammarian makes solecisms wilfully, he is not therein contradicting the intellectual habit within him, for it is the office of such a habit to aid the intellect to judge correctly, and the intellect here does correctly judge the effect produced. On the other hand, if the musician or grammarian blunders, the intellect within him has not been contradicted, seeing that he knew no better : the habit of grammar or music has not been violated, but has failed to cover the case. Therefore the intellectual habit is not a safe-guard to keep a man from going against his in-telligent self. No such safeguard is needed : the thing is impossible, in the region of pure intellect. In a region where no temptation could enter, in-tellectual habits would suffice alone of themselves to make a perfectly virtuous man. To avoid evil and choose good, it would be enough to know the one and the other. But in this world seductive reason-ings sway the will, and fits of passion the sensitive appetite, prompting the one and the other to rise up and break away from what the intellect knows all along to be the true good of man. Unless moral virtue be there to hold these powers to their allegiance, they will frequently disobey the under-standing. Such disobedience is more irrational than any mere intellectual error. In an error purely intellectual, where the will has no part, the objective truth indeed is missed, but the intelligence that dwells within the man is not flouted and gainsayed. It takes two to make a contradiction as to make a quarrel. But an intellectual error has only one side. The intellect utters some false pronouncement, and there is nothing within the man that says otherwise. In the moral error there is a contradiction within, an intestine quarrel. The intellect pronounces a thing not good, not to be taken, and the sensitive appetite will throw a veil over the face of intellect, and seize upon the thing. That amounts to a contradiction of a man's own intelligent self.

4. It appears that, absolutely speaking, intellectual virtue is the greater perfection of a man: indeed in the act of that virtue, as we have seen, his crowning perfection and happiness lies. But moral virtue is the greater safeguard. The breach of moral virtue is the direr evil. Sin is worse than ignorance, and more against reason, because it is against the doer's own reason. Moral virtue then is more necessary than intellectual in a world where evil is rife, as it is a more vital thing to escape grievous disease than to attain the highest development of strength and beauty. And as disease spoils strength and beauty, not indeed always taking them away, but rendering them valueless, so evil moral habits subvert intellectual virtue, and turn it aside in a wrong direction. The vicious will keeps the intellect from contemplating the objects which are the best good of man: so the contemplation is thrown away on inferior things, often on base things, and an overgrowth of folly ensues on those

points whereupon it most imports a man to be wise.

To sum up all in a sentence, not exclusive but dealing with characteristics : *the moral virtues are the virtues for this world, intellectual virtue is the virtue of the life to come.*

Readings.—St. Thos., 1a 2æ, q. 58, art. 2, in corp.; Ar., *Eth.*, I., xiii., 15—19 ; St. Thos., 1a 2æ, q. 66, art. 3.

Section IV.—*Of the Mean in Moral Virtue.*

1. Moral virtue is a habit of doing the right thing in the conduct of the will and the government of the passions. Doing right is opposed to overdoing the thing, and to underdoing it. Doing right is taking what it suits a rational nature to desire, and eschewing what is unsuitable under the circumstances. (c. i., n. 5.)

But a thing may be unsuitable in two ways, by excess, and by defect : the rational choice is in the mean between these two. The moral order here is illustrated from the physical. Too much exercise and too little alike impair the strength ; so of meat and drink in regard to health ; but diet and exercise in moderation, and in proportion to the subject create, increase, and preserve both health and strength. So it is with temperance, and fortitude, and all varieties of moral virtue. He who fights shy of everything, and never stands his ground, becomes a coward ; while he who never fears at all, but walks boldly up to all danger, turns out rash. The enjoyer of every pleasure, who knows not what it is to deny himself aught, is a libertine and loose liver; while to throw over all the graces and delicious things of life, not as St. Paul did, who counted all things dross, that he might gain Christ, but absolutely, as though such things were of themselves devoid of attraction, is boorishness and insensibility. Thus the virtues of temperance and fortitude perish in excess and defect, and live in the mean. It is to be noticed in this illustration that the mean of health is not necessarily the mean of virtue. What is too little food, and too much exercise, for the animal well-being of a man, may be the right amount of both for him in some higher relation, inasmuch as he is more than a mere animal; as for a soldier in a hard campaign, where a sufficiency of food and rest is incompatible with his serving his country's need.

2. The taking of means to an end implies the taking them in moderation, not in excess, or we shall overshoot the mark, nor again so feebly and inadequately as to fall short of it. No mere instrument admits of an unlimited use; but the end to be gained fixes limits to the use of the instrument, thus far, no more, and no less. Wherever then reason requires an end to be gained, it requires a use of means proportionate to the end, not coming short of it, nor going so far beyond as to defeat the purpose in view. The variety of good that is called the Useful lies within definite limits, between two wildernesses, so to speak, stretching out undefined into the distance, wilderness of Excess on the one side, and wilderness of Defect on the other.

3. A true work of art cannot be added to or taken from without spoiling it. A perfect church would be spoiled by a lengthening of the chancel or raising the tower, albeit there are buildings, secular and ecclesiastical, that might be drawn out two miles long and not look any worse. The colouring of a picture must not be too violent and positive; but artistic colouring must be chaste, and artistic utterance gentle, and artistic action calm and indicative of self-command. Not that voice and action should not be impassioned for a great emergency, but the very passion should bear the mark of control : in the great master's phrase, you must not "tear a passion to tatters." It is by moderation sitting upon power that works of art truly masculine and mighty are produced ; and by this sign they are marked off from the lower host of things, gorgeous and redundant, and still more from the order of "the loose, the lawless, the exaggerated, the insolent, and the profane."

4. On these considerations Aristotle framed his celebrated definition of moral virtue : *the habit of fixing the choice in the golden mean in relation to ourselves, defined by reason, as a prudent man would define it.* All virtue is a *habit,* as we have seen—a habit of doing that which is the proper act of the power wherein the habit resides. One class of moral virtues is resident in the will, the act of which power is properly called *choice.* The rest of the moral virtues reside in the sensitive appetite, which also may be said to *choose* that object on which it fastens. Thus moral virtue is a habit of *fixing the choice.* The

golden mean between two extremes of excess and defect respectively has been already explained, and may be further shown by a review of the virtues. Besides fortitude and temperance, already described, *liberality* is a mean between prodigality and stinginess; *magnificence* between vulgar display and pettiness : *magnanimity* between vainglory and pusillanimity; *truthfulness* between exaggeration and dissimulation ; *friendship* between complaisance, or flattery, and frowardness,—and so of the rest. The golden mean must be taken *in relation to ourselves*, because in many matters of behaviour and the management of the passions the right amount for one person would be excessive for another, according to varieties of age, sex, station, and disposition. Thus anger that might become a layman might be unbefitting in a churchman ; and a man might be thought loquacious if he talked as much as a discreet matron.* The golden mean, then, must be *defined by reason* according to the particular circumstances of each case. But as Reason herself is to seek where she is not guided by Prudence, the mean of virtue must be defined, not by the reason of the buffoon Pantolabus, or of Nomentanus the spendthrift, but *as a prudent man* would define it, given an insight into the case.

5. The "golden mean," as Horace named it (*Od.*, ii., 10), obtains principally, if not solely, in living things, and in what appertains to living things, and in objects of art.   A lake, as such, has no natural

---

* Ar., *Pol.*, III., iv., 17, says just the converse, which marks the altered position of woman in modern society.

dimensions : it may be ten miles long, it may be a hundred ; but an elephant or an oak-tree cannot go beyond a certain growth.   There is a vast range between the temperature of a blast-furnace and the temperature of the ice-pack on the Polar Sea, but very limited is the range possible in the blood of a living man.   Viewed artistically, a hill may be too low, or a lake want width, for man's eye to rest upon it with perfect satisfaction.   The golden mean, then, is an artistic conception, and what I may call an *anthropological* conception : it suits man, and is required by man, though Nature may spurn and over-ride it.   The earthquake, the hurricane, and the angry ocean are not in the golden mean, not at least from a human point of view.   If man chooses to personify and body forth the powers of nature, he creates some monstrous uncouth figure, like the Assyrian and Egyptian idols ; but if man makes a study of man, and brings genius and patient elaboration to bear on his work, there emerges the symmetry and perfect proportion of the Greek statue.   No people ever made so much of the beauty of the human form as the ancient Greeks : they made it the object of a passion that marked their religion, their institutions, their literature, and their art. Their virtues and their vices turned upon it.   Hence the golden mean is eminently a Greek conception, a leading idea of the Hellenic race.   The Greek hated a thing overdone, a gaudy ornament, a proud title, a fulsome compliment, a high-flown speech, a wordy peroration.   *Nothing too much* was the inscription over the lintel of the national sanctuary

G

at Delphi. It is the surpassing grace of Greek art of the best period, that in it there shines out the highest power, with *nothing too much* of straining after effect. The study of Greek literary models operates as a corrective to redundancy, and to what ill-conditioned minds take to be fine writing. The Greek artist knew just how far to go, and when to stop. That point he called, in his own unsurpassed tongue, the καιρός. "The right measure (καιρός) is at the head of all," says Pindar. "Booby, not to have understood by how much the half is more than the whole," is the quaint cry of Hesiod. Æschylus puts these verses in the mouth of his *Furies :*

> The golden mean is God's delight :
> Extremes are hateful in His sight.
> Hold by the mean. and glorify
> Nor anaɩɕhy nor slavery.

Characteristic of Socrates was his *irony,* or way of understating himself, in protest against the extra-vagant professions of the Sophists. In the reckoning of the Pythagoreans, the Infinite, thc Unlimited, or Unchecked, was marked as evil, in opposition to good, which was the Limited. From thence, Plato, taking up his parable, writes : "The goddess of the Limit, my fair Philebus, seeing insolence and all manner of wickedness breaking loose from all limit in point of gratification and gluttonous greed, estab-lished a law and order of limited being ; and you say this restraint was the death of pleasure ; I say it was the saving of it." Going upon the tradition of his countrymen, upon their art and philosophy, their poetry, eloquence, politics, and inmost senti

ment., Aristotle formulated the law of moral virtue,
to hold by the *golden mean*, as discerned by the
prudent in view of the present circumstances, between the two extremes of excess and defect.

6. There is only one object on which man may
throw himself without reserve, his last end, the
adequate object of his happiness, God. God is
approached by faith, hope, and charity; but it
belongs not to philosophy to speak of these supernatural virtues. There remains to the philosopher
the natural virtue of religion, which is a part of
justice. Religion has to do with the inward act of
veneration and with its outward expression. To
the latter the rule of the mean at once applies.
Moderation in religion is necessary, so far as ex-
ternals are concerned. Not that any outward
assiduity, pomp, splendour, or costliness, can be
too much in itself, or anything like enough, to
worship God with, but it may be too much for our
limited means, which in this world are drawn on by
other calls. But our inward veneration for God
and desire to do Him honour, can never be too
intense : " Blessing the Lord, exalt Him as much as
you can : for He is above all praise." *

7. The rule of the mean, then, is a human rule,
for dealing with men, and with human goods considered as means. It is a Greek rule : for the
Greeks were of all nations the fondest admirers of
man and the things of man. But when we ascend
to God, we are out among the immensities and
eternities. The vastness of creation, the infinity

* Ecclus. xliii. 33.

of the Creator,—there is no mode or measure there.
In those heights the Hebrew Psalmist loved to soar.
Christianity, with its central dogma of the Incarnation, is the meeting of Hebrew and Greek. That
mystery clothes the Lord God of hosts with the
measured beauty, grace, and truth, that man can
enter into. But enough of this. Enough to show
that the Aristotelian doctrine of the mean is a highly
suggestive and wide-reaching doctrine beyond the
sphere of Morals. It throws out one great branch
into Art, another into Theology.

8. The vicious extremes, on this side and on
that of a virtue, are not always conterminous with
the virtue itself, but sometimes another and more
excellent virtue intervenes; as in giving we may
pass from justice to liberality, and only through
passing the bounds of liberality, do we arrive at the
vicious extreme of prodigality. So penitential fasting
intervenes between temperance in food and undue
neglect of sustenance. But it is to be noted that
the *central virtue*, so to speak, as justice, sobriety,
chastity, is for all persons on all occasions: the
more excellent *side-virtue*, as liberality, or total
abstinence, is for special occasions and special
classes of persons.

Readings.—Ar., *Eth.*, II., ii., 6, 7; *ib.*, II., cc. 6—9;
Hor., *Odes*, II., 10; Ruskin, *Modern Painters*, p. 3, s. i.,
c. x.

Section V.—*Of Cardinal Virtues.*

1. The enumeration of cardinal virtues is a piece
of Greek philosophy that has found its ways into the

catechism. Prudence, justice, fortitude, and temperance are mentioned by Plato as recognised heads of
virtue. They are recognised, though less clearly, by
Xenophon, reporting the conversations of Socrates.
It does not look as though Socrates invented the
division: he seems to have received it from an
earlier source, possibly Pythagoras. They are mentioned in Holy Scripture (Wisdom viii., 7, which is
however a Greek book), and Proverbs viii., 14. They
make no figure in the philosophies of India and
China.

2. The cardinal virtues are thus made out.—
Virtue is a habit that gives a man readiness in
behaving according to the reason that is in him.
Such a habit may be fourfold. (*a*) It may reside
in the reason, or intellect itself, enabling it readily
to discern the reasonable thing to do, according to
particular circumstances as they occur. That habit
is the virtue of *prudence*. (*b*) It may reside in the
rational appetite, otherwise called the will, disposing
a man to act fairly and reasonably in his dealings
with other men. That is *justice*. (*c*) It may reside
in the irrational, or sensitive, appetite, and that to
a twofold purpose; (*a*) to restrain the said appetite in its concupiscible part from a wanton and
immoderate eagerness after pleasure; that is *temperance*: (β) to incite the said appetite in its
irascible part not to shrink from danger, where
there is reason for going on in spite of danger; that
is *fortitude*.

3. Plato compares the rational soul in man to
a charioteer, driving two horses: one horse repre-

senting the concupiscible, the other the irascible part of the sensitive appetite. He draws a vivid picture of the resistance of the concupiscible part against reason, how madly it rushes after lawless pleasure, and how it is only kept in restraint by main force again and again applied, till gradually it grows submissive. This submissiveness, gradually acquired, is the virtue of temperance. Clearly the habit dwells in the appetite, not in reason: in the horse, not in the charioteer. It is that habitual state, which in a horse we call *being broken in.*

The concupiscible appetite is *broken in* to reason by temperance residing within it. Plato lavishes all evil names on the steed that represents the concupiscible part. But the irascible part, the other steed, has its own fault, and that fault twofold, sometimes of over-venturesomeness, sometimes of shying and turning tail. The habit engendered, in the irascible part, of being neither over-venturesome nor over-timorous, but going by reason, is termed fortitude.*

4. As the will is the rational appetite, the proper object of which is rational good, it does not need to be prompted by any habit to embrace rational good in what concerns only the inward administration of the agent's own self. There is no difficulty in that department, provided the sensitive appetite be kept in hand by fortitude and temperance. But

---

* It will help an Englishman to understand Plato's comparison, if instead of *concupiscible part* and *irascible part*, we call the one steed Passion and the other Pluck. Pluck fails, and Passion runs to excess, till Pluck is formed to fortitude, and Passion to temperance

where there is question of external relations with other men, it is not enough that the sensitive appetite be regulated, but a third virtue is necessary, the habit of justice, to be planted in the will, which would otherwise be too weak to attend steadily to points, not of the agent's own good merely, but of the good of other men.

5. Thus we have the four cardinal virtues: prudence, a habit of the intellect; temperance, a habit of the concupiscible appetite; fortitude, a habit of the irascible appetite; and justice, a habit of the will. Temperance and Fortitude in the Home Department; Justice for Foreign Affairs; with Prudence for Premier. Or, to use another comparison, borrowed from Plato, prudence is the health of the soul, temperance its beauty, fortitude its strength, and justice its wealth.

Readings.—St. Thos., 1a 2æ, q. 61, art. 2, in corp.; *ib.*, q. 56, art. 4, in corp., ad 1—3; *ib.*, q. 56, art. 6, in corp., ad 1, 3; *ib.*, q. 59, art. 4, in corp., ad 2; Plato, *Laws*, 631 B, C.

SECTION VI.—*Of Prudence.*

1. Prudence is *right reason applied to practice*, or more fully it may be defined, the habit of intellectual discernment that enables one to hit upon the golden mean of moral virtue and the way to secure that mean. Thus prudence tells one what amount of punishment is proper for a particular delinquent, and how to secure his getting it. It is to be observed that prudence does not will the golden mean in question, but simply indicates it. To will and

desire the mean is the work of the moral virtue
concerned therewith : as in the case given it is the
work of vindictive justice.

2. From the definition of moral virtue above
given (c. v., s. iv., n. 4, p. 79), it is clear that no
moral virtue can come into act without prudence :
for it is the judgment of the prudent man that must
define in each case the *golden mean* in relation to
ourselves, which every moral virtue aims at.   Thus,
without prudence, fortitude passes into rashness,
vindictive justice into harshness, clemency into
weakness, religion into superstition.

3. But may not one with no prudence to guide
him hit upon the *golden mean* by some happy
impulse, and thus do an act of virtue ?   We answer,
he may do a good act, and if you will, a virtuous act,
but not an act of virtue, not an act proceeding from
a pre-existent habit in the doer.   The act is like a
good stroke made by chance, not by skill ; and like
such a stroke, it cannot be readily repeated at the
agent's pleasure. (See c. v., s. i., n. 4, p. 66 ; and
Ar., *Eth.*, II., iv., 2.)

4. Prudence in its essence is an intellectual virtue,
being a habit resident in the understanding : but it
deals with the subject-matter of the moral virtues,
pointing out the measure of temperance, the bounds
of fortitude, or the path of justice.   It is the habit
of intellectual discernment that must enlighten every
moral virtue in its action.   There is no virtue that
goes blundering and stumbling in the dark.

5. He is a prudent man, that can give counsel to
others and to himself in order to the attainment of

ends that are worthy of human endeavour. If unworthy ends are intended, however sagaciously they are pursued, that is not prudence. We may call it *sagacity*, or *shrewdness*, being a habit of ready discernment and application of means to ends. Napoleon I. was conspicuous for this sagacity. It is the key to success in this world. But prudence discovers worthy ends only, and to them only does it provide means. The intellect is often blinded by passion, by desire and by fear, so as not to discern the proper end and term to make for in a particular instance and a practical case. The general rules of conduct remain in the mind, as that, " In anger be mindful of mercy: " but the propriety of mercy under the present provocation drops out of sight. The intellect does not discern the golden mean of justice and mercy in relation to the circumstances in which the agent now finds himself. In other words, the habit of prudence has failed ; and it has failed because of the excess of passion. Thus prudence is dependent on the presence of the virtues that restrain passion, namely, fortitude and temperance. A like argument would hold for the virtue of justice, that rectifies inordinate action in dealing with another. The conclusion is, that as the moral virtues cannot exist without prudence, so neither can prudence exist without them : for vice corrupts the judgment of prudence.

6. Hence we arrive at a settlement of the question, whether the virtues can be separated, or whether to possess one is to possess all. We must distinguish between the rudimentary forms of virtue and the

perfect habit. The rudimentary forms certainly can exist separate : they are a matter of temperament and inherited constitution : and the man whom nature has kindly predisposed to benevolence, she has perhaps very imperfectly prepared for prudence, fortitude, or sobriety. But one perfect habit of any one of the four cardinal virtues, acquired by repeated acts, and available at the call of reason, involves the presence, in a matured state, of the other three habits also. A man who acts irrationally upon one ground, will behave irrationally on other grounds also : or if his conduct be rational there, it will not be from regard for reason, but from impulse, temperament, or from some other motive than the proper motive of the virtue which he seems to be exercising.

Readings.—St. Thos., 1a 2æ, q. 54, art. 4 ; *ib.*, q. 58, art. 5, in corp. ; *ib.*, 2a 2æ, q. 47, art. 7, 12, 13 ; Λr., *Eth.*, VI., v. ; *ib.*, VI., xii., 9, 10 ; *ib.*, VI., xiii., 6 ; St. Francis of Sales, *Of the Love of God*, bk. xi., c. vii.

SECTION VII.—*Of Temperance.*

1. Temperance is a virtue which regulates by the judgment of reason those desires and delights which attend upon the operations whereby human nature is preserved in the individual and propagated in the species. Temperance is the virtue contrary to the two deadly sins of Gluttony and Lust. As against the former, it represents Abstinence, or moderation in solid food, and Sobriety, which is moderation in drink. As against the latter, it is the great virtue of

Chastity. The student must bear in mind that, to a philosopher, Temperance does not mean Total Abstinence, and Abstinence is quite independent of Fridays and flesh-meat. Temperance then is made up of Abstinence, Sobriety, and Chastity.

Aristotle writes : " Cases of falling short in the taking of pleasure, and of people enjoying themselves less than they ought, are not apt to occur : for such insensibility is not human : but if there be any one to whom nothing is pleasant, and all comes alike in the matter of taste, he must be far from the state and condition of humanity : such a being has no name, because he is nowhere met with." This is true, because where there is question of a virtue, such as Temperance, resident in the concupiscible appetite, we are not concerned with any sullenness or moroseness of will, nor with any scrupulosity or imbecility of judgment, refusing to gratify the reasonable cravings of appetite, but with the habitual leaning and lie of the appetite itself. Now the concupiscible appetite in every man, of its own nature, leans to its proper object of delectable good. No virtue is requisite to secure it from too little inclination that way : but to restrain the appetite from going out excessively to delight is the function, and the sole function, of Temperance. The measure of restraint is relative, as the golden mean is relative, and varies with different persons and in view of different ends. The training of the athlete is not the training of the saint.

3. Besides the primary virtue of Temperance, and its subordinate species (enumerated above, n. 1),

certain other virtues are brought under Temperance
in a secondary sense, as observing in easier matters
that moderation and self-restraint which the primary
virtue keeps in the matter that is most difficult of
all.   St. Thomas calls these *potential parts* of Temperance.   There is question here of what is most
difficult to man as an animal, not of what is most
difficult to him as a rational being. To rational man,
as such, ambition is harder to restrain than sensuality: which is proved by the fact that fewer men, who
have any ambition in them, do restrain that passion
than those who restrain the animal propensities that
are common to all.   But to man as an animal (and
vast numbers of the human race rise little above the
animal state), it is hardest of all things to restrain
those appetites that go with the maintenance and
propagation of flesh and blood.   These then are
the proper matter of Temperance : other virtues,
potential parts of Temperance, restrain other
cravings which are less animal.   Of these virtues
the most noticeable are humility, meekness, and
modesty.*

4. There is a thirst after honour and pre-
eminence, arising from self-esteem, and prevalent
especially where there is little thought of God, and
scant reverence for the present majesty of heaven.
A man who thinks little of his Maker is great in his
own eyes, as our green English hills are mountains
to one who has not seen the Alpine heights and

* This is St. Thomas's arrangement, placing Humility under
Temperance.   The connection of Humility with Magnanimity, and
thereby with Fortitude, is indicated pp. 100, 101.

snows. Apart from the consideration of God there
is no humility; and this is why Aristotle, who treats
of virtues as they minister to the dealings of man
with man, makes no mention of this virtue. There
are certain outward manifestations in words, acts,
and gestures, the demeanour of a humble man,
which is largely identified with modesty and with
submission to others as representing God.

5. Modesty is that outward comportment, style
of dress, conversation, and carriage, which indicates the presence of Temperance, "set up on
holy pedestal" (Plato, *Phædr.*, 254 B) in the heart
within.

6. Meekness is moderation in anger, and is or
should be the virtue of all men. Clemency is
moderation in punishment, and is the virtue of men
in office, who bear the sword or the rod.

7. As regards the vices opposite to Temperance,
an important distinction is to be drawn between
him who sins by outburst of passion and him whose
very principles are corrupt.* The former in doing
evil acknowledges it to be evil, and is prone to repent
of it afterwards: the latter has lost his belief in
virtue, and his admiration for it: he drinks in iniquity
like water, with no after-qualms; he glories in his
shame. The former is reclaimable, the latter is
reprobate: his intellect as well as his heart is
vitiated and gone bad. If there were no miracles,
he would be a lost man: but God can work miracles
in the moral as in the physical order: in that there
is hope for him.

* See the note in *Aquinas Ethicus,* Vol. I., pp. 170, 171.

8. A nation need not be virtuous in the great
bulk of her citizens, to be great in war and in
dominion, in laws, in arts, and in literature : but the
bulk of the people must possess at least the sense
and appreciation of virtue in order to such national
greatness. When that sense is lost, the nation
is undone and become impotent, for art no less
than for empire. Thus the Greece of Pericles and
of Phidias fell, to be "living Greece no more."

9. As in other moral matters, no hard and fast
line of division exists between sinning from passion
and sinning on principle, but cases of the one
shade into cases of the others, and by frequent
indulgence of passion principle is brought gradually
to decay.

Readings.—Ar., *Eth.*, III., x. ; St. Thos., 2a 2æ,
q. 141, art. 2; *ib.*, q. 141, art. 3, in corp.; *ib.*, q. 142,
art. 1; *ib.*, q. 143, art. 1, in corp., ad 2, 3; *ib.*, q. 161,
art. 1, ad 5; *ib.*, q. 161, art. 2, in corp.; *ib.*, q. 161, art.
6, in corp., ad 1; *ib.*, q. 157, art. 1, in corp., ad 3;
ib., q. 156, art. 3; Ar., *Eth.*, VII., viii.

Section VIII.—*Of Fortitude.*

1. As Temperance is a curb, restraining animal
nature in the pursuit of the good to which it goes out
most eagerly, namely, life and the means of its continuance, so Fortitude also is a curb, withholding that
nature from irrational flight from the evil which it
most dreads. Aristotle tells us what that evil is : "Most
dreadful of all things is death, for it is the limit, and
for the dead man there appears to be no further good
nor evil left." (*Eth.*, III., vi., 6.)   Death is truly the

limit to human existence: for, though the soul be
immortal, the being of flesh and blood, that we call
man, is dissolved in death, and, apart from supernatural hope of the resurrection, extinct for ever.
Death therefore is the direst of all evils in the animal
economy; and as such, is supremely abhorred by
the sensitive appetite, which is the animal part of
man. Fortitude moderates this abhorrence and fear
by the dictate of reason. Reason shows that there
are better things than life, and things worse than
death, for man in his spiritual capacity as an
intellectual and immortal being.

2. Fortitude is a mean between Cowardice
and Rashness, to which opposite extremes we are
carried by the contrary passions of Fear and
~~Daring~~ respectively. Fortitude thus is a two-
sided virtue, moderating two opposite tendencies:
while Temperance is one-sided, moderating Desire
alone. Life, rationally considered, bears undoubtedly a high value, and is not to be lightly
thrown away, or risked upon trivial or ignoble
objects. The brave man is circumspect in his
ventures, and moderate in his fears, which implies
that he does fear somewhat. He will fear superhuman visitations, as the judgments of God. He
will dread disgrace, and still more, sin. He will fear
death in an unworthy cause. And even in a good
cause, it has well been said: " The truly brave man
is not he who fears no danger, but the man whose
mind subdues the fear, and braves the danger that
nature shrinks from." The Duke of Marlborough is
said to have quaked in the saddle as he rode into

action, saying: "This poor body trembles at what
the mind within is about to do." Fortitude then is
the virtue that restrains fear and regulates venture-
someness by the judgment of reason, in danger
especially of a grand and glorious death.

3. To the ancients, there was no grander object
of devotion than the State, their native city: no
direr misfortune than its dissolution, or the loss of
its self-government: no nobler death than to die in
arms in its defence.   As old Tyrtæus sang:

> A noble thing it is to lie dead, fallen in the front ranks,
> A brave man in battle for his country.*

Such a death was taken to be the seal and stamp
of the highest fortitude.   Nor has Christianity
dimmed the glory that invests a soldier's death.
Only it points to a brighter glory, and a death in a
still nobler cause, the death of the martyr who dies
for the faith, and becomes valiant in battle for what
is more to him than any earthly city, the Church,
the City of God.   Nor must the martyr of charity,
who dies in succouring his neighbour, go without
the praise of fortitude: nor, in short, any one who
braves death, or other heavy affliction, in the discharge of duty, or when forwarding a good cause.

4. A man may brave death in a good cause, and
not be doing an act of fortitude.   So he may subscribe a large sum to a charitable purpose without
any exercise of the virtue of charity.   A virtue is
then only exercised, when its outward act is per-

τεθνάμεναι γὰρ καλόν, ἐνὶ προμάχοισι πεσόντα,
ἄνδρ ἀγαθὸν περὶ ᾗ πατρίδι μαρνάμενον.
(*Tyrtæus apud Lycurg.*)

formed from the proper motive of the virtue, and not
from any lower motive.   Thus the proper motive
of Fortitude is the conviction that death is an evil,
the risk of which is to be left out of count as a circumstance relatively inconsiderable, when there is
question of the defence of certain interests dearer to
a good man than life.   An improper motive would
be anger, which, however useful as an accessory, by
itself is not an intellectual motive at all, and therefore no motive of virtue.   The recklessness of an
angry man is not Fortitude.   It is not Fortitude to be
brave from ignorance or stupidity, not appreciating
the danger : nor again from experience, knowing
that the apparent danger is not real, at least to
yourself.   The brave man looks a real danger in the
face, and knows it, and goes on in spite of it, because
so it is meet and just, with the cause that he has, to
go on.

5. We may notice as *potential* parts of Fortitude
(s. vii., n. 3, p. 92), the three virtues of Magnificence, Magnanimity, and Patience.   It is the part of
Patience, philosophically to endure all sufferings short
of death.   It is the part of the former two, to dare
wisely, not in a matter of life and death, but in the
matter of expense, for Magnificence, and of honour,
for Magnanimity.   Magnificence, technically understood, observes the right measure in the expenditure
of large sums of money.   As being conversant with
large sums, it differs from Liberality.   A poor man
may be liberal out of his little store, but never
magnificent.   It is a virtue in the rich, not to be
afraid of spending largely and lavishly on a great

H

occasion, or a grand purpose. The expense may be
carried beyond what the occasion warrants : that is
one vicious extreme. The other extreme would be
to mar a costly work by sordid parsimony on a point
of detail. It is not easy to be magnificent : in the
first place, because not many are rich ; and then
because riches are seldom united with greatness of
soul and good judgment. Something analogous to
the virtue of Magnificence is shown in the generous
use of great abilities, or, in the supernatural order,
of great graces. The destinies of the world lie with
those men who have it in their power to be magnificent.

6. We are come to Magnanimity and the Magnanimous Man, the great creation of Aristotle. As
Magnanimity ranks under Fortitude, there must be
some fear to which the Magnanimous Man rises
superior, as the brave man rises superior to the fear
of death. What Magnanimity overcomes is the fear
of undeserved dishonour. The Magnanimous Man
is he who rates himself as worthy of great honours,
and is so worthy indeed. When honour is paid
to such a one, he makes no great account of it,
feeling that it is but his due, or even less than his
due. If he is dishonoured and insulted, he despises
the insult as an absurdity, offered to a man of his
deserts. He is too conscious of his real worth to
be much affected by the expression of his neighbour's view of him. For a man is most elated,
when complimented on an excellence which he was
not very sure of possessing : and most sensibly
grieved at an insult, where he half suspects himself

of really making a poor figure, whereas he would like to make a good one. It is doubtless the serene and settled conviction that Englishmen generally entertain of the greatness of their country, that enables them to listen with equanimity to abuse of England, such as no other people in Europe would endure levelled at themselves.

7. *Proud* is an epithet pretty freely applied to Englishmen abroad, and it seems to fit the character of the Magnanimous Man. He seems a Pharisee, and worse than a Pharisee. The Pharisee's pride was to some extent mitigated by breaking out into that disease of children and silly persons, vanity : he "did all his works to be seen of men." But here the disease is all driven inwards, and therefore more malignant. The Magnanimous Man is so much in conceit with himself as to have become a scorner of his fellows. He is self-sufficient, a deity to himself, the very type of Satanic pride. These are the charges brought against him.

8. To purify and rectify the character of the Magnanimous Man, we need to take a leaf out of the book of Christianity. Not that there is anything essentially Christian and supernatural in what we are about to allege : otherwise it would not belong to philosophy : it is a truth of reason, but a truth generally overlooked, till it found its exponent in the Christian preacher, and its development in the articles of the Christian faith. The truth is this. There is in every human being what theologians have called *man and man :* man as he is of himself, man again as he is by the gift and gracious mercy

of God.   The reasonably Magnanimous Man is
saved from pride by this distinction.   Of himself,
he knows that he is nothing but nothingness, meanness, sinfulness, and a walking sore of multitudinous
actual sins.   "I know that there dwelleth not in
me, that is, in my flesh, any good." (Rom. vii. 18.)
If he is insulted, he takes it as his due, not any
questionable due, for then he would resent the
insult, but as being undoubtedly what he deserves.
If he is honoured, he smiles at the absurdity of the
compliments paid to him.   It is as if an old gentleman, a prey to gout and rheumatism, were lauded
for his fleetness of foot.   He is then truly magnanimous on this side of his character by a kind of
obverse magnanimity, that bears insults handsomely,
as deserved, and honours modestly, as undeserved.

9. But let us go round to the other side of the
reasonably Magnanimous Man.   He was defined
to be, "one that deems himself worthy of great
honours, and is so worthy indeed."   Now, nothing is
truly worthy of honour but virtue.   He must then
be a good man, full of all virtues ; and all this goodness that he has, he recognises as being in him
of God.   He has "received God's Spirit "—or
something analogous in the natural order to the
gift of the Holy Ghost—"that he may know the
things that are given him of God." (2 Cor. ii. 12.)
It is told of St. Francis of Assisi, the humblest of
men, that on one occasion when he and his companions received from some persons extraordinary
marks of veneration, he, contrary to his usual wont,
took it not at all amiss : and said to his companions,

who wondered at his behaviour, "Let them alone: they cannot too much honour the work of God in us." This magnanimity bears honours gracefully, and insult unflinchingly, from a consciousness of internal worth, which internal worth and goodness however it takes not for its own native excellence, but holds as received from God, and unto God it refers all the glory.

10. Thus the genuine Magnanimous Man is a paradox and a prodigy. He despises an insult as undeserved, and he takes it as his due. He is conscious of the vast good that is in him; and he knows that there is no good in him. Highly honoured, he thinks that he gets but his due, while he believes that vials of scorn and ignominy may justly be poured upon him. He will bear the scorn, because he deserves it, and again, because it is wholly undeserved. The Magnanimous Man is the humble man. The secret of his marvellous virtue is his habit of practical discernment between the abyss of misery that he has within himself, as of himself, and the high gifts, also within him, which come of the mercy of God. Aristotle well says, "Magnanimity is a sort of robe of honour to the rest of the virtues: it both makes them greater and stands not without them: therefore it is hard to be truly magnanimous, for that cannot be without perfect virtue." We may add, that in the present order of Providence none can be magnanimous without supernatural aid, and supernatural considerations of the life of Christ, which however are not in place here.

Readings.—Ar., *Eth.*, III., vii. ; St. Thos., 2a 2æ, q. 123, art 3, in corp. ; Ar., *Eth.*, III., viii. ; St. Thos., 2a 2æ, q. 123, art. 1, ad 2 ; Ar., *Eth.*, III., vi. ; St. Thos., 2a 2æ, q. 123, art. 4, 5. For the Magnificent and Magnanimous Man, Ar., *Eth.*, IV., ii., iii. ; St. Thos., 2a 2æ, q. 129, art. 3, ad 4, 5.

SECTION IX.—*Of Justice.*

1. Justice is a habit residing in the will, prompting that power constantly to render unto everyone his own. The fundamental notion of Justice is some sort of equality. Equality supposes two terms, physically distinct, or capable of existing separately, one from the other. Between such terms alone can equality be properly predicated. Any less distinction than this leaves room only for equality improperly so called, and therefore no room for what is properly termed Justice. When therefore Plato, going about to find a definition of Justice, which is a main object in his *Republic,* acquiesces in this position, that Justice consists in every part of the soul, rational, irascible, and concupiscible, fulfilling its own proper function, and not taking up the function of another, he fails for this reason, that all Justice is relative to another, but the different parts of one soul are not properly *other* and *other,* since all go to make up one man : therefore, however much Justice may be identical with doing your own business, and leaving your neighbour free to do his, yet this relation obtaining among the various parts of the soul cannot properly be called Justice. What Plato defines is the beauty, good order, and moral

comeliness of the soul, but not Justice in any sense, inasmuch as it is not referred to any being human or divine, collective or individual, outside of the man himself.

2. Going upon the principle that all Justice is of the nature of *equality*, and is therefore relative *to another*, we arrive at the definition of *general justice*, which is all virtue whatsoever, inasmuch as it bears upon another person than him who practises it. This Justice is perfect social virtue, the crown and perfection of all virtue from a statesman's point of view ; and in that aspect, as Aristotle says, "neither morning star nor evening star is so beautiful." Whoever has this virtue behaves well, not by himself merely, but towards others—a great addition. Many a one who has done well enough as an individual, has done badly in a public capacity : whence the proverb, that office shows the man. This Justice may well be called *another man's good : * though not in the sense of the sophists of old, and the altruists of our time, that virtue is a very good thing for everyone else than its possessor. Virtue, like health, may be beneficial to neighbours, but the first benefit of it flows in upon the soul to whom it belongs : for virtue is the health of the soul.

3. Another elementary notion of Justice connects it with Law, taking Justice to be conformity to Law. This notion exhibits *legal justice*, which is the same thing, under another aspect, as the *general justice* mentioned above, inasmuch as *general justice* includes the exercise of all virtues in so far as they bear upon the good of others : and the law, to which

legal justice conforms a man, enjoins acts of all virtues for the common good. It must be observed, however, that though there is no natural virtue of which the law of man may not prescribe some exercise, still no human law enjoins all acts of all virtues, not even all obligatory acts. A man may fail in his duty though he has kept all the laws of man. In order then that *legal justice* may include the whole duty of man, it must be referred to that natural and eternal law of God, revealed or unrevealed, of which we shall speak hereafter. By being conformed to this divine law a man is a *just man*, a *righteous man*. It is this sense of Justice that appears in the theological term, *justification*. In this sense, Zachary and Elizabeth " were both just before God, walking in all the commandments of the Lord without blame." (St. Luke i. 6.)

4. *General*, or *legal, justice* is not the cardinal virtue so called, but is in one point of view identical with all virtue. Distinguished from the other three cardinal virtues is *particular justice*, which is divided into *distributive* and *commutative justice*. *Distributive justice* is exercised by the community through its head towards its individual members, so that there be a fair distribution of the common goods, in varying amount and manner, according to the various merits and deserts of the several recipients. The matters distributed are public emoluments and honours, public burdens, rewards, and also punishments. *Distributive justice* is the virtue of the king and of the statesman, of the commander-in-chief, of the judge, and of the public functionary gener-

ally. It is violated by favouritism, partiality, and jobbery. *Distributive justice* is the Justice that we adore in the great Governor of the Universe, saying that He is "just in all His works," even though we understand them not. When it takes the form of punishing, it is called *vindictive justice*. This is what the multitudes clamoured for, that filled the precincts of the Palace of Whitehall in the days of Charles I. with cries of Justice, Justice, for the head of Strafford.

5. Neither legal nor distributive justice fully answers to the definition of that virtue. Justice disposes us to give *to another his own*. The party towards whom Justice is practised must be wholly other and different from him who practises it. But it is clear that the member of a civil community is not wholly other and different from the State : he is partially identified with the civil community to which he belongs. Therefore neither the tribute of *legal justice* paid by the individual to the State, nor the grant of *distributive justice* from the State to the individual, is an exercise of Justice in the strictest sense. Again, what the individual pays to the State because he is legally bound to pay it, does not become the *State's own* until after payment. If he withhold it, though he do wrong, yet he is not said to be keeping any portion of the public property in his private hands : he only fails to make some of his private property public, which the law bids him abdicate and make over. If this be true of money and goods, it is still more evidently true of honour and services. In like manner, in the matter of *dis-*

tributive justice, the emoluments which a subject
has a claim to, the rewards which he has merited of
the State, does not become *his* till he actually gets
them into his hands.   It may be unfair and immoral
that they are withheld from him, and in that case,
so long as the circumstances remain the same, the
obligation rest with and presses upon the State,
and those who represent it, to satisfy his claim : still
the State is not keeping the individual from that
which is as yet his own.   In the language of the
Roman lawyers, he has at best a *jus ad rem*, a right
that the thing be made his, but not a *jus in re ;* that
is, the thing is not properly his before he actually
gets it.

6. *Commutative justice* alone is Justice strictly so
called : for therein alone the parties to the act are
perfectly other and other, and the matter that
passes between them, if withheld by one of the
parties, would make a case of keeping the other out
of that which he could still properly call by right his
own.   *Commutative justice* runs between two individuals, or two independent States, or between the
State and an individual inasmuch as the latter is an
independent person, having rights of his own against
the former.   This justice is called *commutative*, from
being concerned with *exchanges*, or contracts, *voluntary* and *involuntary*.   The idea of voluntary contract, like that between buyer and seller, is familiar
enough.   But the notion of an *involuntary contract* is
technical, and requires explanation.   Whoever, then,
wrongfully takes that which belongs to another,
enters into an involuntary contract, or makes an

involuntary exchange, with the party. This he may
do by taking away his property, honour, reputation,
liberty, or bodily ease and comfort. This is an
involuntary transaction, against the will of the party
that suffers. It is a contract, because the party that
does the damage takes upon himself, whether he will
or no, by the very act of doing it, the obligation of
making the damage good, and of restoring what he
has taken away. This is the obligation of *restitution*,
which attaches to breaches of *commutative justice*,
and, strictly speaking, to them alone. Thus, if a
minister has not promoted a deserving officer in
face of a clear obligation of *distributive justice*, the
obligation indeed remains as that of a duty unfulfilled, so long as he remains minister with the
patronage in his hands: but the promotion, if he
finally makes it, is not an act of restitution: it is
giving to the officer that which was not his before.
And if the opportunity has passed, he owes the
officer nothing in compensation. But if he has
insulted the officer, he owes him an apology for all
time to come : he must give back that honour which
belonged to the officer, and of which he has robbed
him. This is restitution. In a thousand practical
cases it is important, and often a very nice question
to decide, whether a particular offence, such as
failure to pay taxes, be a sin against *commutative
justice* or only against some more general form of
the virtue. If the former, restitution is due : if the
latter, repentance only and purpose of better things
in future, but not reparation of the past.

7. The old notion, that Justice is minding your

own business, and leaving your neighbour to mind
his, furnishes a good rough statement of the obligations of *commutative justice*. They are mainly
negative, to leave your neighbour alone in his right
of life and limb, of liberty and property, of honour
and reputation.   But in two ways your neighbour's
business may become yours in justice.   The first
way is, if you have any contract with him, whether
a formal contract, as that between a railway company and its passengers, or a virtual contract, by
reason of some office that you bear, as the office
of a bishop and pastor in relation to the souls of
his flock.   The second way in which *commutative
justice* binds you to positive action, is when undue
damage is likely to occur to another from some
activity of yours, If, passing by, I see my neighbour's house on fire, not having contracted to watch
it for him, and not having caused the fire myself, I
am not bound in strict justice to warn him of his
danger.   I am bound indeed by charity, but that is
not the point here.   But if the fire has broken out
from my careless use of fire, *commutative justice*
binds me to raise the alarm.

8. The most notable potential parts of Justice—
Religion, Obedience, Truthfulness—enter into the
treatise of Natural Law.

Reading.—Ar., *Eth.*, V., i.; Plato, *Rep.*, 433 A;
ib., 443 C, D, E; St. Thos., 2a 2æ, q. 58, art. 2, in corp;
ib., q. 58, art. 5 ; *ib.*, q. 58, art. 6, in corp; *ib.*, q. 58,
art. 7 ; *ib.*, q. 58, art 9, in corp. ; *ib.*, q. 61, art. 1, in
corp.; *ib.*, q. 61, art. 3, in corp.; Ar., *Eth.*, V., ii., 12,
13 ; St. Thos., 2a 2æ, q. 62, art. 1, in corp., ad 2.

CHAPTER VI.

OF THE ORIGIN OF MORAL OBLIGATION.

SECTION I.—*Of the natural difference between Good and Evil.*

1. A GRANITE boulder lying on an upland moor stands indifferently the August sun and the January frost, flood and drought. It neither blooms in spring, nor fades in autumn. It is all one to the boulder whether it remain in the picturesque solitude where the glacier dropped it, or be laid in the gutter of a busy street. It has no growth nor development: it is not a subject of evolution: there is no goal of perfection to which it is tending by dint of inward germinal capacity seconded by favourable environment. Therefore it does not matter what you do with it: all things come alike to that lump of rock.

2. But in a cranny or cleft of the same there is a little flower growing. You cannot do what you will with that flower. It has its exigencies and requirements. Had it a voice, it could say, what the stone never could: ' I must have this or that: I must have light, I must have moisture, a certain heat, some soil to grow in.' There is a course to be run by this flower and the plant that bears it, a development to be wrought out, a perfection to

be achieved. For this end certain conditions are necessary, or helpful: certain others prejudicial, or altogether intolerable. In fact, that plant has a *progressive nature*, and therewith is a subject of good and evil. Good for that plant is what favours its natural progress, and evil is all that impedes it.

3. All organic natures are progressive: that is, each individual of them is apt to make a certain progress, under certain conditions, from birth to maturity. But man alone has his progress in any degree in his own hands, to make or to mar. Man alone, in the graphic phrase of Appius Claudius, is *faber fortunæ suæ,* "the shaper of his own destiny." Any other plant or animal, other than man, however miserable a specimen of its kind it finally prove to be, has always done the best for itself under the circumstances: it has attained the limit fixed for it by its primitive germinal capacity, as modified by the events of its subsequent environment. The miserable animal that howls under your window at night, is the finest dog that could possibly have come of his blood and breeding, nurture and education. But there is no man now on earth that has done all for himself that he might have done. We all fall short in many things of the perfection that is within our reach. Man therefore needs to stir himself, and to be energetic with a free, self-determined energy to come up to the standard of humanity. It is only his free acts that are considered by the moralist. Such is the definition of Moral Science, that it deals with *human acts ;* acts, that is, whereof man is master to do or not to do. (c. i., nn. 1, 2.)

4. We have it, then, that a morally good act is an act that makes towards the progress of human nature in him who does it, and which is freely done. Similarly, a morally evil act is a bar to progress, or a diversion of it from the right line, being also a free act. Now, that act only can make for the progress of human nature, which befits and suits human nature, and suits it in its best and most distinctive characteristic. What is best in man, what characterises and makes man, what the old schoolmen called the *form* of man, is his reason. To be up to reason is to be up to the standard of humanity. Human progress is progress on the lines of reason. To make for that progress, and thereby to be morally good, an act must be done, not blindly, brutishly, sottishly, or on any impulse of passion, however beneficial in its effects, but deliberately, and in conscious accordance with the reasonable nature of the doer.

5. Whatever be man's end and highest good, he must go about to compass it reasonably. He must plan, and be systematic, and act on principle. For instance, if the public health be the highest good, the laws which govern it must be investigated, and their requirements carried out, without regard to senti-ment. If pleasure be the good, we must be artists of pleasure. If, however, as has been seen (c. ii.) the highest good of man is the highest play of reason herself in a life of contemplation, to be prepared for, though it cannot be adequately and worthily lived, in this world, then it is through following reason, through subjecting appetite to reason by

temperance, and the will to reason by justice, and
reason herself by a "reasonable service" to God,
that this end and consummation must be wrought
out.   Thus, in Plato's phrase (*Rep.*, 589 B), the
moral man acts so that "the inner man within him,
the rational part of his nature, shall be strongest;
while he watches with a husbandman's care over the
many-headed beast of appetite, rearing and training
the creature's tame heads, and not letting the wild
ones grow; for this purpose making an ally of the
lion, the irascible part of his nature, and caring for
all the parts in common, making them friends to one
another and to himself."   In this way he will meet
the true exigency of his nature *as a whole*, with due
regard to the proper order and subordination of the
parts.   He who lives otherwise, acts in contradiction
to his rational self. (c. v., s. iii., n. 3, p. 74).

6. The result of the above reasoning, if result it
has, should be to explain and justify the Stoic rule,
naturæ convenienter vivere, to live according to nature.
But some one will say: 'That is the very ideal of
wickedness: all good in man comes of overcoming
nature, and doing violence to natural cravings:
live according to nature, and you will go straight
to the devil.'   I answer: 'Live *according to a part of
your nature*, and that the baser and lower, though
also the more impetuous and clamorous part, and
you will certainly go where you say: but live *up
to the whole of your nature*, as explained in the last
paragraph, and you will be a man indeed, and will
reach the goal of human happiness.'   But again it
may be objected, that our very reason, to which the

rest of our nature is naturally subordinate, frequently prompts us to do amiss. The objection is a just one, in so far as it goes upon a repudiation of the old Platonic position, that all moral evil comes of the body, wherein the soul is imprisoned, and of the desires which the body fastens upon the soul. Were that so, all sins would be sins of sensuality. But there are spiritual sins, not prompted by any lust or weakness of the body, as pride and mutiny, self-opiniatedness, rejection of Divine revelation. The objection turns on sins such as these. The answer is, that spiritual sins do not arise from any exigency of reason, but from a deficiency of reason; not from that faculty calling upon us, as we are reasonable men, to take a certain course, in accordance with a just and full view of the facts of the case, but from reason failing to look facts fully in the face, and considering only some of them to the neglect of others, the consideration of which would alter the decision. Thus a certain proud creature mentioned in Scripture thought of the magnificence of the throne above the stars of God, on the mountain of the covenant, on the sides of the north : he did not think how such a pre-eminence would become him as a creature. He had in view a rational good certainly, but not a rational good for him. Partial reason, like a little knowledge, is a dangerous thing.

7. As it is not in the power of God to bring it about, that the angles of a triangle taken together shall amount to anything else than two right angles, so it is not within the compass of Divine omnipo-tence to create a man for whom it shall be a good

I

and proper thing, and befitting his nature, to blaspheme, to perjure himself, to abandon himself recklessly to lust, or anger, or any other passion. God need not have created man at all, but He could not have created him with other than human exigencies. The reason is, because God can only create upon the pattern of His own essence, which is imitable, outside of God, in certain definite lines of possibility. These possibilities, founded upon the Divine essence and discerned by the Divine intelligence, are the Archetype Ideas, among which the Divine will has to choose, when it proceeds to create. The denial of this doctrine in the Nominalist and Cartesian Schools, and their reference to the arbitrary will of God of the eternal, immutable, and absolutely necessary relations of possible things, is the subversion of all science and philosophy.

8. Still less are moral distinctions between good and evil to be set down to the law of the State, or the fashion of society. Human convention can no more constitute moral good than it can physical good, or mathematical or logical truth. It is only in cases where two or more courses are tolerable, and one of them needs to be chosen and adhered to for the sake of social order, that human authority steps in to elect and prescribe one of those ways of action, and brand the others as illegitimate, which would otherwise be lawful. This is called the making of a *positive law.*

Readings.—St. Thos., ia 2æ, q. 18, art. 5, in corp.; ia 2æ, q. 71, art. 2; Plato, *Rep.*, 588 B to end of bk. ix.; Ar., *Eth.*, IX., iv., nn. 4—10; Suarez,

De Legibus, II., vi., nn. 4, 11 ; Cicero, *De Legibus*, i., cc. 15—17.

Section II.—*How Good becomes bounden Duty, and Evil is advanced to Sin.*

1. The great problem of Ethics is the explanation of the idea, *I ought*. (c. i., n. 6.) We are now come close up to the solution of that problem. The word *ought* denotes the necessary bearing of means upon end. To every *ought* there is a pendent *if*. The means *ought* to be taken, *if* the end is to be secured. Thus we say : ' You *ought* to start betimes, *if* you are to catch your train.' ' You *ought* to study harder, *if* you are to pass your examination.' The person spoken to might reply : ' But what if I do miss my train, and fail in my examination ? ' He might be met with another *ought* : ' You *ought* not to miss the one, *if* you are to keep your appointment : or to fail in the other, *if* you are to get into a profession.' Thus the train of *oughts* and *ifs* extends, until we come finally to a concatenation like the following : ' You *ought* not to break your word, or to give needless pain to your parents, *if* you don't want to do violence to that nature which is yours as a reasonable being,' or ' to thwart your own moral development,'—and so on in a variety of phrases descriptive of the argument of the last section. Here it seems the chain is made fast to a staple in the wall. If a person goes on to ask, ' Well, what if I do contradict my rational self ? '—we can only tell him that he is a fool for his question. The *oughts*, such as those wherewith our illustration

commenced, Kant calls the *hypothetical imperative*, the form being, 'You must, unless:' but the *ought* wherein it terminated, he calls the *categorical imperative*, the alternative being such as no rational man can accept, and therefore no alternative at all.

2. This doctrine of the Categorical Imperative is correct and valuable so far as it goes. But then it does not go far enough. The full notion of what a man *ought*, is what he *must do under pain of sin*. Sin is more than folly, more than a breach of reason. It is mild reproach to a great criminal to tell him that he is a very foolish person, a walking unreasonableness. If he chooses to contradict his rational self, is not that his own affair? Is he not his own master, and may he not play the fool if he likes? The answer is, 'No, he is not his own master; he is under law, and his folly and self-abuse becomes criminal and sinful, by being in contravention of the law that forbids him to throw himself away thus wantonly.'

3. Kant readily takes up this idea, shaping it after his own fashion. He contends,—and herein his doctrine is not merely deficient, but positively in error,—that the Categorical Imperative, uttered by a man's own reason, has the force of a law, made by that same reason; so that the legislative authority is within the breast of the doer, who owes it obedience. This he calls the *autonomy of reason*. It is also called Independent Morality, inasmuch as it establishes right and wrong without regard to external authority, or to the consequences of actions, or to rewards and punishments. The doctrine is

erroneous, inasmuch as it undertakes to settle the matter of right and wrong without reference to external authority; and inasmuch as it makes the reason within a man, not the promulgator of the law to him, but his own legislator. For a law is a precept, a command: now no one issues precepts, or gives commands, to himself. To command is an act of jurisdiction; and jurisdiction, like justice (see c. v., s. ix., n. 1, p. 102) requires a distinction of persons, one ruler, and another subject. But the reason in a man is not a distinct subject from the will, appetites, or other faculties within him, to which reason dictates: they are all one nature, one person, one man; consequently, no one of them can strictly be said to command the rest; and the dictate of reason, as emanating from within oneself, is not a law. But without a law, there is no strict obligation. Therefore the whole theory of obligation is not locked up in the Categorical Imperative, as Kant formulated it.

4. The above argumentation evinces that God is not under any law; for there is no other God above Him to command Him. As for the ideas of what is meet and just in the Divine intelligence, though the Divine will, being a perfect will, is not liable to act against them, yet are those ideas improperly called a law to the Divine will, because intellect and will are identified in one God. Kant's doctrine makes us all gods. It is a deification of the human intellect, and identification of that intellect with the supreme and universal Reason; and at the same time a release of the human will from all authority

extraneous to the individual. This amounts to a putting off of all authority properly so called, and makes each man as sovereign and unaccountable as his Maker. " Thy heart is lifted up, and thou hast said : I am God, and sit in the chair of God : and hast set thy heart as if it were the heart of God : whereas thou art a man and not God." (Ezech. xxviii. 2.) Kant is thus the father of the pantheistic school of Fichte, Schelling, and Hegel.

5. But it has been contended that this phrase about a man who does wrong *breaking a law*, is only a metaphor and figure of speech, unless it be used with reference to the enactment of some civil community. Thus John Austin says that a *natural law* is a law which is not, but which he who uses the expression thinks ought to be made. At this rate *sin* is not a transgression of any law, except so far as it happens to be, in the lawyer's sense of the word, a *crime*, or something punishable in a human court of justice. There will then be no law but man's law. How then am I *obliged* to obey man's law ? Dr. Bain answers : " Because, if you disobey, you will be *punished*." But that punishment will be either just or unjust : if unjust, it originates no obligation : if just, it presupposes an obligation, as it presupposes a crime and sin, that is, an obligation violated. There seems to be nothing left for John Austin but to fall back upon Kant and his Categorical Imperative, and say that whoever rebels against the duly constituted authority of the State in which he lives, is a rebel against the reason that dwells within his own breast, and which requires

him to behave like a citizen. So that ultimately it is not the State, but his own reason that he has offended; and the State has no authority over him except what his own reason gives.

6. If this were true, there would be no sin anywhere except what is called *philosophical sin*, that is, a breach of the dignity of man's rational nature; and the hardest thing that could be said in reprobation of a wrongdoer, would be that he had gone against himself, and against his fellow-men, by outraging reason, the common attribute of the race.

7. Far worse than that has the sinner done. He has offended against his own reason, and thereby against a higher Reason, substantially distinct from his, standing to it in the relation of Archetype to type, a Living Reason, ἔμψυχος λόγος (cf. Ar., *Eth.*, V., iv., 7), purely and supremely rational. The Archetype is outraged by the violation of the type. Moreover, as the two are substantially distinct, the one being God, the other a faculty of man, there is room for a command, for law. A man may transgress and sin, in more than the *philosophical* sense of the word: he may be properly a *law-breaker*, by offending against this supreme Reason, higher and other than his own.

8. Here we must pause and meditate a parable. —There was a certain monastery where the monks lived in continual violation of monastic observance. Their Abbot was a holy man, a model of what a monk ought to be. But though perfectly cognisant of the delinquencies of his community, he was content to display to his subjects the edifying example

of his own life, and to let it appear that he was aware
of their doings and pained at them. He would croon
softly as he went about the house old Heli's words :
" Not so, my sons, not so : why do ye these kind of
things, very wicked things ? "   But the monks took
no notice of him. It happened in course of time
that the Abbot went away for about ten days. What
he did in that time, never transpired : though there
was some whisper of certain " spiritual exercises,"
which he was said to have been engaged in. Certain
it is, that he returned to his monastery, as he left
it, a monk devout and regular : the monk was the
same, but the Abbot was mightily altered. The
morning after his arrival, a Chapter was held ; the
Abbot had the Rule read from cover to cover, and
announced his intention of enforcing the same.
And he was as good as his word. Transgressions
of course abounded : but the monks discovered
that to transgress was quite a different thing now
from what it had been. Seeing the law proclaimed,
and the Abbot in earnest to enforce it, they too
reformed themselves : the few who would not reform
had to leave. The subsequent holy lives of those
monks do not enter into this history.

9. Now, we might fancy God our Lord like the
Abbot of that monastery in the early years of his
rule. We might fancy the Supreme Reason, dis-
pleased indeed, as Reason must be, at the excesses
and follies of mankind, but not otherwise commanding men to avoid those evil courses. Were
God to be thus quiescent, what we have called (n. 6)
philosophical sin, would indeed carry this additional

malice, beyond what was there set down, of being
an offence against God, but it would not be a
grievous offence: for it would not be a sin in the
proper sense of the term, not being a transgression
of the law of God, inasmuch as God, by the supposition, would have given no law. But the supposition
itself is absurd. God could not so withhold His
command. He is free indeed not to command, but
that only by not creating. If He wills to have
creatures, He must likewise will to bind them to
certain lines of action: which will to bind in God is
a law to the creature.

10. This assertion, that *God cannot but will to bind
His creatures to certain lines of action,* must be proved,
though in the ascent we have to mount to high
regions, and breathe those subtle airs that are
wafted round the throne of the Eternal. As God
is the one source of all reality and of all power,
not only can there be no being which He has not
created and does not still preserve, but no action
either can take place without His concurrence. God
must go with His every creature in its every act:
otherwise, on the creature's part, nothing could be
done. Now, God cannot be indifferent what manner
of act He shall concur unto. A servant or a subject
may be indifferent what command he receives: he
may will simply to obey,—to go here or there, as he
is bid, or to be left without orders where he is.
That is because he leaves the entire direction and
management of the household to his master. But
for God to be thus indifferent what action He should
lend His concurrence to, would be to forego all

design and purpose of His own as to the use and destiny of the creatures which He has made and continually preserves. This God cannot do, for He cannot act aimlessly. It would be renouncing the direction of His own work, and making the creature His superior. God is incapable of such renunciation and subservience. He must, then, will the cooperation which He lends, and the concurrent action of the creature, to take a certain course, regulated and prescribed by Himself: which is our proposition, that God cannot but will to bind His creatures to certain lines of action. If His free creatures choose to stray from these lines, God indeed still cooperates, and to His cooperation is to be ascribed the *physical goodness* of the action, not its *moral inordinateness and inopportuneness*. Still, as the action is morally inordinate, God may be said to cooperate, in a manner, where He would not: whence we gather some conception of the enormity of sin. (See c. vii., nn. 5, 6, pp. 130, 131.)

11. The lines of action laid down and prescribed by God are not arbitrary and irrespective of the subject of the command. They are determined in each case by the nature of the subject. The Author of Nature is not apt to subvert that order which proceeds from Himself. He bids every creature act up to that nature wherein He has created it. His commands follow the line of natural exigency. What this natural exigency amounts to in man in regard to his human acts, we have already seen. (c. vi., s. i., p. 109.)

12. The difference between a necessary and a free

agent is, that the former is determined by its nature to act in a certain way, and cannot act otherwise: the latter may act in more ways than one. Still, as we have seen, the nature even of a free agent is not indifferent to all manner of action. It requires, though it does not constrain, the agent to act in certain definite ways, the ways of moral goodness. Acting otherwise, as he may do, the free agent gainsays his own nature, taken as a whole, a thing that a necessary agent can nowise do. God therefore who, as we have shown, wills and commands all creatures whatsoever to act on the lines of their nature, has especial reason to give this command to His rational creatures, with whom alone rests the momentous freedom to disobey.

13. We are now abreast of the question, of such burning interest in these days, as to the connection of Ethics with Theology, or of Morality with Religion. I will not enquire whether the dogmatic atheist is logically consistent in maintaining any distinction between right and wrong: happily, dogmatic atheists do not abound. But there are many who hold that, whether there be a God or no, the fact ought not to be imported into Moral Science: that a Professor of Ethics, as such, has no business with the name of the Almighty on his lips, any more than a lecturer on Chemistry or Fortification. This statement must be at once qualified by an important proviso. If we have any duties of worship and praise towards our Maker: if there is such a virtue as religion, and such a sin as blasphemy: surely a Professor of Morals must point that out. He cannot in that case

suppress all reference to God, for the same reason that he cannot help going into the duties of a man to his wife, or of an individual to the State, if marriage and civil government are natural institutions. If there is a God to be worshipped, any book on Moral Science is incomplete without a chapter on Religion. But the question remains, whether the name of God should enter into the other chapters, and His being and authority into the very foundations of the science. I do not mean the metaphysical foundations; for Metaphysics are like a two-edged sword, that cleaves down to the very marrow of things, and must therefore reveal and discover God. But Morality, like Mathematics, takes certain metaphysical foundations for granted, without enquiring into them. On these foundations we rear the walls, so to speak, of the science of Ethics without reference to God, but we cannot put the roof and crown upon the erection, unless we speak of Him and of His law. Moral distinctions, as we saw (c. vi., s. i. n. 7, p. 113), are antecedent to the Divine command to observe them : and though they rest ultimately on the Divine nature, that ultimate ground belongs to Metaphysics, not to Ethics. Ethics begin with human nature, pointing out that there are certain human acts that do become a man, and others that do not. (c. vi., s. i., p. 109.) To see this, it is not necessary to look up above man. Thus we shall prove lying, suicide, and murder to be wrong, and good fellowship a duty, without needing to mention the Divine Being, though by considering Him the proof gains in cogency. Or rather, apart from God

we shall prove certain acts wrong, and other acts
obligatory as duties, *philosophically* speaking, with an
initial and fundamental wrongness and obligation.
In the present section we have proved once for all,
that what is wrong philosophically, or is philosophically a duty, is the same also *theologically*.
Thus the initial and fundamental obligation is
transformed into an obligation formal and complete.
Therefore, hereafter we shall be content to have
established the philosophical obligation, knowing
that the theological side is invariably conjoined
therewith. As St. Thomas says (1a 2æ, q. 71,
art. 6, ad 5): "By theologians sin is considered
principally as it is an offence against God: but by
the moral philosopher, inasmuch as it is contrary to
reason." But what is contrary to reason offends
God, and is forbidden by Divine law, and thus
becomes a *sin*. No God, no sin. Away from God,
there is *indecency* and *impropriety*, *unreasonableness*,
abomination, and *brutality*, all this in view of outraged
humanity: there is likewise *crime* against the State:
but the formal element of *sin* is wanting. With sin,
of course, disappears also the punishment of sin as
such. Thus to leave God wholly out of Ethics and
Natural Law, is to rob moral evil of half its terrors,
and of that very half which is more easily "under-
standed of the people." A consideration for school-
managers.

Readings.—St. Thos., 1a, q. 22, art. 2, in corp.
(against Lucretius, ii. 646—651); Suarez, *De Legibus*,
II., vi., nn. 3, 5—9, 13, 14, 17, 20—24.

CHAPTER VII.

OF THE ETERNAL LAW.

1. A LAW is defined to be : A precept just and abiding, given for promulgation to a perfect community. A law is primarily a rule of action. The first attribute of a law is that it be *just :* just to the subject on whom it is imposed, as being no harmful abridgment of his rights : just also to other men, as not moving him to injustice against them. An unjust law is no law at all, for it is not a rule of action. Still, we may sometimes be bound, when only our own rights are infringed, to submit to such an imposition, not as a law, for it is none, but on the score of prudence, to escape direr evils. A law is no fleeting, occasional rule of conduct, suited to meet some passing emergency or superficial disturbance. The reason of a law lies deep down, lasting and widespread in the nature of the governed. A law, then, has these two further attributes of permanence in duration and amplitude in area. Every law is made for all time, and lives on with the life of the community for whom it is enacted, for ever, unless it be either expressly or implicitly repealed. A law in a community is like a habit in an individual, an accretion to nature, which abides as part of the natural being, and guides

henceforth the course of natural action. **This**
analogy holds especially of those laws, which are not
enacted all of a sudden—and such are rarely the
best laws—but grow upon the people with gradual
growth unmarked, like a habit by the repetition of
acts, in the way of immemorial custom. I have said
that a law is for a community, that it requires amplitude and large area. A law is not laid down for an
individual, except so far as his action is of importance
to the community. The private concerns of one
man do not afford scope and room enough for a law.
Neither do the domestic affairs of one family. A
father is not a legislator. A law aims at a deep,
far-reaching, primary good. But the private good
of an individual, and the domestic good of a family,
are not primary goods, inasmuch as the individual
and the family are not primary but subordinate
beings : not complete and independent, but dependent and partial ; not wholes but parts. The individual is part of the family, and the family is part of
a higher community. It is only when we are come
to some community which is not part of any higher,
that we have found the being, the good of which is
primary good, the aim of law. Such a community,
not being part of any higher community in the same
order, is in its own order a perfect community.
Thus, in the temporal order, the individual is part of
the State. The State is a perfect community ; and
the good of the State is of more consequence than
the temporal well-being of any individual citizen.
The temporal good of the individual, then, is matter
of law, in so far as it is subservient to the good of

the State. We have, then, to hold that a law is
given to the members of a perfect community for the
good of the whole. Not every precept, therefore, is
a law: nor every superior a lawgiver: for it is not
every superior that has charge of the good of a
perfect community. Many a precept is given to an
individual, either for his private good, as when a
father commands his child, or for the private good
of him that issues the precept, as when a master
commands a servant. But every law is a precept:
for a law is an imperative rule of action, in view of
a good that is necessary, at least with the necessity
of convenience. To every law there are counsels
attached. A law may be said to be a *nucleus* of precept, having an *envelope* of counsel. Every law has
also a pendent called punishment for those who
break it: this is called the *sanction* of the law. A law
is also for *promulgation*, as a birch rod for *application*.
The promulgation, or application, brings the law
home to the subject, but is not part of the law itself.
So much for the definition of Law.

2. We have to learn to look upon the whole
created universe, and the fulness thereof, angels,
men, earth, sun, planets, fixed stars, all things visible
and invisible, as one great and perfect community,
whose King and Lawgiver is God. He is King,
because He is Creator and Lord. But lordship and
kingship are different things, even in God. It is one
thing to be lord and master, owner and proprietor of
a chattel, property and domain: it is another thing
to be king and governor, lawgiver and judge of
political subjects. The former is called *power of*

dominion, or right of ownership, the latter is *power of jurisdiction.* Power of dominion is for the good of him who wields it: but power of jurisdiction is for the good of the governed. As God is Lord of the universe, He directs all its operations to His own glory. As He is King, He governs as a king should govern, for the good of His subjects. In intellectual creatures, whose will is not set in opposition to God, the subject's good and the glory of the Lord finally coincide. God's power of dominion is the concern of theologians: the moralist is taken up with His power of jurisdiction, from whence emanates the moral law.

3. In the last chapter (s. ii., nn. 9, 10, pp. 120,121), we stated the moral law in these terms, that *God wills to bind His creatures to certain lines of action,* not arbitrary lines, as we saw, but the natural lines of each creature's being. The law thus stated takes in manifestly a wider field than that of moral action. There is in fact no action of created things that is not comprehended under this statement. It comprises the laws of physical nature and the action of physical causes, no less than the moral law and human acts. It is the one primeval law of the universe, antecedent to all actual creation, and co-eternal with God. And yet not necessary as God: for had God not decreed from all eternity to create —and He need not have decreed it—neither would He have passed in His own Divine Mind this second decree, necessarily consequent as it is upon the decree of creation, namely, that every creature should act in the mode of action proper of its kind

J

This decree, supervening from eternity upon the
creative decree, is called the Eternal Law.

4. This law does not govern the acts of God
Himself. God ever does what is wise and good, not
because He binds Himself by the decree of His own
will so to act, but because of His all-perfect nature.
His own decrees have not for Him the force of a
precept: that is impossible in any case: yet He
cannot act against them, as His nature allows not of
irresolution, change of mind, and inconsistency.

5. Emanating from the will of God, and resting
upon the nature of the creature, it would seem that
the Eternal Law must be irresistible. "Who re-
sisteth His will?" asks the Apostle. (Rom. ix. 19.)
"The streams of sacred rivers are flowing upwards,
and justice and the universal order is wrenched
back." (Euripides, *Medea*, 499.) It is only the perversion spoken of by the poet, that can anywise
supply the instance asked for by the Apostle. The
thing is impossible in the physical order. The
rivers cannot flow upwards, under the conditions
under which rivers usually flow: but justice and
purity, truth and religion may be wrenched back, in
violation of nature and of the law eternal. The one
thing that breaks this law is sin. Sin alone is properly unnatural. The world is full of physical evils,
pain, famine, blindness, disease, decay and death.
But herein is nothing against nature: the several
agents act up to their nature, so far as it goes: it is
the defect of nature that makes the evil. But sin is
no mere shortcoming: it is a turning round and
going against nature, as though the July sun should

freeze a man, or the summer air suffocate him. Physical evil comes by the defect of nature, and by permission of the Eternal Law. But the moral evil of sin is a breach of that law.

6. A great point with modern thinkers is the inviolability of the laws of physical nature, *e.g.*, of gravitation or of electrical induction. If these laws are represented, as J. S. Mill said they should be, as *tendencies* only, they are truly inviolable. The law of gravitation is equally fulfilled in a falling body, in a body suspended by a string, and in a body borne up by the ministry of an angel. There is no law of nature to the effect that a supernatural force shall never intervene. Even if, as may be done perhaps in the greatest miracles, God suspends His concurrence, so that the creature acts not at all, even that would be no violation of the physical law of the creature's action: for all that such a law provides is, that the creature, if it acts at all, shall act in a certain way, not that God shall always give the concurrence which is the necessary condition of its acting at all. The laws of physical nature then are, strictly speaking, never violated, although the *course* of nature is occasionally altered by supernatural interference, and continually by free human volition. But the laws of physical nature, in the highest generality, are identified with the moral law. The one Eternal Law embraces all the laws of creation. It has a physical and a moral side. On the former it *effects*, on the latter it *obliges*, but on both sides it is imperative; and though in moral matters it be temporarily defeated by sin, still the

moral behest must in the end be fulfilled as surely as
the physical behest. The defeat of the law must
be made good, the sin must be punished. Of the
Eternal Law working itself out in the form of punishment, we shall speak presently.

7. It is important to hold this conception of the
Eternal Law as embracing physical nature along
with rational agents. To confine the law, as modern
writers do, to rational agents alone, is sadly to
abridge the view of its binding force. The rigid
application of physical laws is brought home to us
daily by science and by experience: it is a point
gained, to come to understand that the moral
law, being ultimately one with those physical laws,
is no less absolute and indefeasible, though in a
different manner, than they.

It is hard for us to conceive of laws being given to
senseless things. We cannot ourselves prescribe to
iron or to sulphur the manner of its action. As
Bacon says (*Novum Organum*, i., Aphorism 4): " Man
can only put natural bodies together or asunder:
nature does the rest within." That is, man cannot
make the laws of nature: he can only arrange collo-
cations of materials so as to avail himself of those
laws. But God makes the law, issuing His command, the warrant without which no creature could
do anything, that every creature, rational and
irrational, shall act each according to its kind or
nature. Such is the Eternal Law.

Readings.—Suarez, *De Legibus*, I., xii.; St. Thos.,
1a 2æ, q. 90, art. 2—4; *ib.*, q. 91, art. 1, in corp., ad 1;
ib., q. 93, art. 1, in corp.; *ib.*, q. 93, art. 4, in corp.;

ib.. q. 93, art. 5, in corp.; *ib.,* q. 93, art. 6, in corp.; Suarez, *De Legibus*, II., vi.; Cicero, *De Legibus*, II., iv.; *id., De Republica*, iii. 22.

CHAPTER VIII.

OF THE NATURAL LAW OF CONSCIENCE.

SECTION I.—*Of the Origin of Primary Moral Judgments.*

1. IT is an axiom of the schools, that whatever is received, is received according to the manner of the recipient. We have spoken of the law that governs the world, as that law has existed from eternity in the mind of God. We have now to consider that law as it is received in creatures, and becomes the inward determinant of their action. Action is either necessary or free. The great multitude of creatures are wholly necessary agents. Even in free agents, most of what is in them, and much that proceeds from them, is of necessity, and beyond the control of their will. Of necessary action, whether material or mental, we shall have nothing further to say. It is governed by the Eternal Law, but it is not matter of moral philosophy. Henceforth we have to do with that law, only as it is received in free agents, as such, to be the rule of their conduct. The agents being free, the law must be received in a manner consonant with their freedom. It is proper to a free and rational being to guide itself, not to be dragged or pushed, but to

go its own way, yet not arbitrarily, but according to law. The law for such a creature must be, not a physical determinant of its action, but a law operating in the manner of a motive to the will, obliging and binding, yet not constraining it: a law written in the intellect after the manner of knowledge: a law within the mind and consciousness of the creature, whereby it shall measure and regulate its own behaviour. This is *the natural law of conscience.* It is the Eternal Law, as made known to the rational creature, whereby to measure its own free acts. The Eternal Law is in the Mind of God: the Natural Law in the minds of men and angels. The Eternal Law adjusts all the operations of creatures: the Natural Law, only the free acts of intellectual creatures. And yet, for binding force, the Natural Law is one with the Eternal Law. On a summer evening one observes the sunset on the west coast; the heavens are all aglow with the sun shining there, and the waters are aglow too, reflecting the sun's rays. The Eternal Law is as the sun there in the heavens, the Natural Law is like the reflection in the sea. But it is one light.

2. It is called the *Natural Law,* first, because it is found, more or less perfectly expressed, in all rational beings: now whatever is found in all the individuals of a kind, is taken to belong to the *specific nature,* or type of that kind. Again it is called the *Natural Law,* because it is a thing which any rational nature must necessarily compass and contain within itself in order to arrive at its own proper perfection and maturity. Thus this inner law is natural, in

the sense in which walking, speech, civilization are natural to man. A man who has it not, is below the standard of his species. It will be seen that dancing, singing—at least to a pitch of professional excellence —and a knowledge of Greek, are not, in this sense, *natural*. The Natural Law is not *natural*, in the sense of " coming natural," as provincial people say, or coming to be in man quite irrespectively of training and education, as comes the power of breathing. It was absurd of Paley (*Mor. Phil.*, bk. i., c. v.) to look to the wild boy of Hanover, who had grown up in the woods by himself, to display in his person either the Natural Law or any other attribute proper to a rational creature.

3. We call this *the natural law of conscience*, because every individual's conscience applies this law, as he understands it, to his own particular human acts, and judges of their morality accordingly. What then is conscience ? It is not a faculty, not a habit, it is an act. It is a practical judgment of the understanding. It is virtually the conclusion of a syllogism, the major premiss of which would be some general principle of command or counsel in moral matters; the minor, a statement of fact bringing some particular case of your own conduct under that law; and the conclusion, which is conscience, a decision of the case for yourself according to that principle : *e.g.*, ' There is no obligation of going to church on (what Catholics call) a *day of devotion* : this day I am now living is only a day of devotion; therefore I am not bound to go to church to-day.' Such is the train of thought, not always so explicitly

and formally developed, that passes through the
mind, when conscience works. It is important to
remember that conscience is an act of intellect, a
judgment, not on a matter of general principle, not
about other people's conduct, but about *my own
action* in some particular case, and the amount of
moral praise or blame that I deserve, or should
deserve, for it. As regards action already done,
or not done, conscience *testifies, accusing* or *excusing*.
As regards action contemplated, conscience *restrains*
or *prompts*, in the way of either obligation or counsel.

4. Conscience is not infallible: it may err, like
any other human judgment. A man may be blind,
if not exactly to his own action, at least to the
motives and circumstances of his action. He may
have got hold of a wrong general principle of conduct. He may be in error as to the application of
his principle to the actual facts. In all these ways,
what we may call the *conscientious syllogism* may be
at fault, like any other syllogism. It may be a bad
syllogism, either in logical form, or in the matter of
fact asserted in the premisses. This is an *erroneous
conscience.* But, for action contemplated, even an
erroneous conscience is an authoritative decision.
If it points to an obligation, however mistakenly,
we are bound either to act upon the judgment or get
it reversed. We must not contradict our own reason:
such contradiction is moral evil. (c. v., s. iii., n. 3, p. 74.)
If conscience by mistake sets us free of what is
objectively our bounden duty, we are not there and
then bound to that duty: but we may be bound at
once to get that verdict of conscience overhauled and

reconsidered. Conscience in this case has proceeded in ignorance, which ignorance will be either *vincible* or *invincible*, and must be treated according to the rules provided in the matter of *ignorance*. (c. iii., s. i., nn. 3—5, p. 27.) An obligation, neglected in invincible ignorance, makes a merely *material sin.* (c. iii., s. ii., n. 7, p. 33.)

5. There is another element of mind, often confounded under one name with conscience, but distinct from it, as a habit from an act, and as principles from their application. This element the schoolmen called *synderesis.**

Synderesis is an habitual hold upon primary moral judgments, as, that we must do good, avoid evil, requite benefactors, honour superiors, punish evildoers. There is a hot controversy as to how these primary moral judgments arise in the mind. The coals of dispute are kindled by the assumption, that these moral judgments must needs have a totally other origin and birth in the mind than speculative first principles, as, that the whole is greater than the part, that two and two are four, that things which are equal to the same thing are equal to one another. The assumption is specious, but unfounded. It looks plausible because of this difference, that moral judgments have emotions to wait upon them, speculative judgments have not. Speculative judgments pass like the philosophers that write them down, unheeded in the quiet of their studies. But moral judgments

* On the derivation of this word, whether from συντήρησις or συντήρησις, see *Athenæum*, 1877, vol. i., pp. 738, 798; vol. iii.' pp. 16, 48.

are rulers of the commonwealth : they are risen to as they go by, with majesty preceding and cares coming after. Their presence awakens in us certain emotions, conflicts of passion, as we think of the good that we should do, but have not done, or of the evil that goes unremedied and unatoned for. Commonly a man cannot contemplate his duty, a difficult or an unfulfilled duty especially, without a certain emotion, very otherwise than as he views the axioms of mathematics. There is a great difference emotionally, but intellectually the two sets of principles, speculative and moral, are held alike as necessary truths, truths that not only are, but must be, and cannot be otherwise : truths in which the *predicate* of the proposition that states them is contained under the *subject*. Such are called *self-evident propositions;* and the truths that they express, *necessary truths*. The enquiry into the origin of our primary moral judgments is thus merged in the question, how we attain to necessary truth.

6. The question belongs to Psychology, not to Ethics : but we will treat it briefly for ethical purposes. And first for a clear notion of the kind of judgments that we are investigating.

"The primary precepts of the law of nature stand to the practical reason as the first principles of scientific demonstration do to the speculative reason : for both sets of principles are self-evident. A thing is said to be self-evident in two ways, either *in itself,* or *in reference to us. In itself* every proposition, the predicate of which can be got from consideration of the subject is said to be self-evident. But

it happens that to one who is ignorant of the definition of the subject, such a proposition will not be
self-evident: as this proposition, *Man is a rational
being*, is self-evident in its own nature, because to
name man is to name something rational; and yet,
to one ignorant what man is, this proposition is not
self-evident. And hence it is that, as Boethius
says: 'there are some axioms self-evident to all
alike.' Of this nature are all those propositions
whose terms are known to all, as, *Every whole is
greater than its part;* and, *Things which are equal to
the same thing are equal to one another.* Some propositions again are self-evident only to the wise, who
understand the meaning of the terms: as, to one
who understands that an angel is not a body, it is
self-evident that an angel is not in a place by way of
circumscription;* which is not manifest to others,
who do not understand the term." (St. Thos., 1a 2æ
q. 94, art. 2, in corp.)

One more extract. "From the very nature of
an intellectual soul it is proper to man that, as soon
as he knows what a whole is, and what a part is, he
knows that every whole is greater than its part; and
so of the rest. But what is a whole, and what a
part, that he cannot know except through sensory
impressions. And therefore Aristotle shows that
the knowledge of principles comes to us through the
senses." (St. Thos., 1a 2æ, q. 51, art. 1, in corp.)

7. Thus the propositions that *right is to be done,
benefactors to be requited*, are self-evident, necessary

* *Circumscriptive*, which word is explained by St Thos., 1a
q. 52. art. 1.

truths, to any child who has learned by experience
the meaning of *right*, of *kindness*, and of a *return of
kindness*. ' Yes, but '—some one will say—' how
ever does he get to know what *right* and *wrong* are ?
Surely sensory experience cannot teach him that.'
We answer, man's thoughts begin in sense, and are
perfected by reflection. Let us take the idea of
wrong, the key to all other elementary moral ideas.
The steps by which a child comes to the fulness of
the idea of *wrong* may be these. First, the thing is
forbidden : then one gets *punished* for it. Punishment
and prohibition enter in by eye and ear and other
senses besides. Then the thing is *offensive* to those
we love and revere. Then it is *bad for us*. Then it
is *shameful, shabby, unfair, unkind, selfish, hateful to God*.
All these points of the idea of wrong are grasped by
the intellect, beginning with sensory presentations of
what is seen and felt and heard said. Again with
the idea of *ought*. This idea is sometimes said to
defy analysis. But we have gone about (c. vi.) to
analyse it into two elements, *nature requiring, nature's
King commanding*. The idea of *wrong* we analysed
into a breach of this natural requirement, and this
Divine command or law. Primary moral ideas, then,
yield to intellectual analysis. They are of this style :
*to be done, as I wish to be rational and please God : not
to be done, unless I wish to spoil myself and disobey
my Maker*. But primary moral ideas, compared
together, make primary moral judgments. Primary
moral judgments, therefore, arise in the intellect,
by the same process as other beliefs arise there
in matters of necessary truth.

8. Thus, applying the principle known as *Occham's razor*, that ".entities are not to be multiplied without reason," we refuse to acknowledge any Moral Sense, distinct from Intellect. We know of no peculiar faculty, specially made to receive "ideas, pleasures and pains in the moral order." (Mackintosh, *Ethics*, p. 206.) Most of all, we emphatically protest against any blind power being accredited as the organ of morality. We cannot accept for our theory of morals, that everything is right which warms the breast with a glow of enthusiasm, and all those actions wrong, at which emotional people are prone to cry out, *dreadful, shocking*. We cannot accept emotions for arbitrators, where it most concerns reasonable beings to have what the Apostle calls "enlightened eyes of the heart" (Ephes. i. 18), that we may "know to refuse the evil and to choose the good." (Isaias vii. 15.) A judge may have his emotions, but his charge to the jury must be dictated, not by his heart, but by his knowledge of the law. And the voice of conscience, whatever feelings it may stir, must be an intellectual utterance, and, to be worth anything in a case of difficulty, a reasoned conclusion, based on observation of facts, and application of principles, and consultation with moral theologians and casuists. A subjective and emotional standard of right and wrong is as treacherous and untrustworthy as the emotional justification of those good people, who come of a sudden to "feel converted."

9. It would be unnecessary, except for the wrong-headedness of philosophers, to observe that con-

science requires educating. As moral virtue is a habit of appetite, rational or irrational, a formation resulting from frequent acts; and as the child needs to be aided and assisted from without towards the performance of such acts, in order to overcome the frequent resistance of appetite to reason (c. v., s. ii., n. 4, p. 71): so the springs of conscience are certain intellectual habits, whereby the subject is cognisant of the principles of natural law, and of their bearing on his own conduct, habits which, like the habits of moral virtue, require to be formed by acts from within and succour from without, since merely the rudiments of the habit are supplied by nature. Even the first principles of morality want formulating and pointing out to children, like the axioms of geometry. The mother tells her little one: 'Ernest, or Frank, be a good boy:' while the schoolmaster explains to Master Ernest that two straight lines cannot possibly enclose a space. There is something in the boy's mind that goes along with and bears out both the teaching of his master and his mother's exhortation: something that says within him: 'To be sure, those lines can't enclose a space:' 'Certainly, I ought to be good.' It is not merely on authority that he accepts these propositions. His own understanding welcomes and approves them: so much so, that once he has understood them, he would not believe the contrary for being told it. You would not persuade a child that it was right to pull mother's hair; or that half an orange was literally, as Hesiod says, "more than the whole." He would answer that it could not be, that he knew better.

10. On one ground there is greater need of education for the conscience than for any other intellectual formation: that is because of the power of evil to fascinate and blind on practical issues of duty. Cicero well puts it:

"We are amazed and perplexed by variety of opinions and strife of authorities; and because there is not the same divergence upon matters of sense, we fancy that the senses afford natural certainty, while, for moral matters, because some men take one view, some another, and the same men different views at different times, we consider that any settlement that can be arrived at is merely conventional, which is a huge mistake. The fact is, there is no parent, nor nurse, nor schoolmaster, nor poet, nor stage play, to corrupt the judgments of sense, nor consent of the multitude to wrench them away from the truth. It is for minds and consciences that all the snares are set, as well by the agency of those whom I have just mentioned, who take us in our tender and inexperienced age, and ingrain and fashion us as they will, as also by that counterfeit presentment of good, which lurks in the folds of every sense, the mother of all evil, pleasure, under whose seductive blandishments men fail to recognise the moral good that nature offers, because it is unaccompanied by this itching desire and satisfaction." (Cicero, *De Legibus*, i., 17.)

Readings.—St. Thos., 1a, q. 79, art. 11—13; Plato, *Protagoras*, 325, 326; John Grote, *Examination of Utilitarian Philosophy*, pp. 169, 207, 208; Cardinal Newman, *Grammar of Assent*, pp. 102—112.

SECTION II.—*Of the invariability of Primary Moral Judgments.*

1. The following narrative is taken from Grote's History of Greece, c. 81.:

"It was a proud day for the Carthaginian general* when he stood as master on the ground of Himera; enabled to fulfil the duty, and satisfy the exigencies, of revenge for his slain grandfather. Tragical indeed was the consummation of this long-cherished purpose. . . . All the male captives, 3,000 in number, were conveyed to the precise spot where Hamilkar had been slain, and there put to death with indignity, as an expiatory satisfaction to his lost honour. No man can read the account of this wholesale massacre without horror and repugnance. Yet we cannot doubt, that among all the acts of Hannibal's life, this was the one in which he most gloried; that it realized in the most complete and emphatic manner, his concurrent *aspirations of filial sentiment, religious obligation, and honour as a patriot;*† that to show mercy would have been regarded as a mean dereliction of these esteemed impulses. . . . Doubtless, the feelings of Hannibal were cordially shared, and the plenitude of his revenge envied, by the army around him. So different, sometimes so totally contrary, is the tone and direction of the moral sentiments, among different ages and nations."

* Hannibal, B.C. 409, therefore not the victor of Cannae.
† Italics mine.

We may supplement this story by another from Herodotus (iii., 38):

"Darius, after he had got the kingdom, called into his presence certain Greeks who were at hand, and asked, 'What he should pay them to eat the bodies of their fathers when they died.' To which they answered, that there was no sum that would tempt them to do such a thing. He then sent for certain Indians, of the race called Callatians, men who eat their fathers, and asked them, while the Greeks were standing by, and knew by the aid of an interpreter all that was said—'What he should give them to burn the bodies of their fathers, at their decease?' The Indians exclaimed aloud, and bade him forbear such language. Such is the way of men; and Pindar was right in my judgment, when he said, 'Convention is king over all.'"

2. If any one held that the natural law of conscience was natural in the same way as the sense of temperature: if one held to the existence of a Moral Sense in all men, settling questions of right and wrong, as surely as all men know sweet things from bitter by tasting them: these stories, and they could be multiplied by hundreds, abundantly suffice to confute the error. There is no authentic copy of the moral law, printed, framed, and hung up by the hand of Nature, in the inner sanctuary of every human heart. Man has to learn his duties as he learns the principles of health, the laws of mechanics, the construction and navigation of vessels, the theorems of geometry, or any other art or science. And he is just as likely to go wrong, and has gone

K

wrong as grievously, in his judgments on moral
matters as on any other subject of human knowledge. The knowledge of duties is *natural* (as
explained in the previous section, n. 2), not because
it comes spontaneously, but because it is necessary
to our nature for the development and perfection of
the same. Thus a man *ought*, so far as he can, to
learn his duties: but we cannot say of a man, as
such, that he *ought* to learn geometry or navigation.
If a man does not know his duties, he is excused
by ignorance, according to the rules under which
ignorance excuses. (c. iii., s. i., nn. 3—5, p. 27.) If
a man does not know navigation, there is no question of *excuse* for what he was not bound to learn,
but he may suffer *loss* by his want of knowledge.

3. It was furthermore observed above (l.c.), that
the *natural* law was so called as being found expressed
more or less perfectly in the minds of all men, and
therefore being a proper element of human nature.
It remains to see how much this universal natural
expression amounts to. That is at once apparent
from our previous explanation of *synderesis*. (s. i., nn. 5,
seq., p. 139.) Not a complete and accurate knowledge of the natural law is found in all minds, far
from it; but *synderesis* is found in all. This is
apparent from Mr. Grote's own phrases, " aspirations of filial sentiment," " religious obligation,"
" honour as a patriot," *Parents are to be honoured,
we must do our duty to God and to our country*: there
Hannibal was at one with the most approved
teachers of morality. Callatian and Greek agreed
in the recognition of the commandment, *Honour thy*

father and thy mother. That was the major premiss of
them both, in the moral syllogism (s. i., n. 3, p. 135),
which ruled their respective consciences. Their
difference was upon the *applying minor*, as it is
called; the Greek regarding the dissolution of the
body into its elements by fire, and so saving it from
corruption, as the best means of honouring the dead:
the Callatians preferring to raise their parents as it
were to life again, by making them the food of their
living children. Hannibal, again, had before his
mind the grand principle of retribution, that wrong-
doing must be expiated by suffering. But he
had not heard the words "Vengeance is Mine;"
and mistakenly supposed it to rest with himself to
appoint and carry out his own measure of revenge.
Whether he was quite so invincibly ignorant on this
point, as Grote represents, is open to doubt. At
any rate he was correct in the primary moral
judgment on which he proceeded.

Reading.—St. Thos., 1a 2æ, q. 94, art. 6.

SECTION III.—*Of the immutability of the Natural Law.*

1. Besides printing, many methods are now in
vogue for multiplying copies of a document. Commonly the document is written out with special ink
on special paper: the copy thus used is called a
stencil; and from it other copies are struck off. We
will suppose the stencil to be that page of the Eternal
Law written in the Mind of God, which regulates
human acts, technically so called. The copies struck
off from that stencil will be the Natural Law in the
mind of this man and of that. Now, as all who are

familiar with copying processes know too well, it happens at times that a copy comes out very faint, and in parts not at all. These faint and partial copies represent the Natural Law as it is imperfectly developed in the minds of many men. In this sense, and as we may say *subjectively*, the Natural Law is mutable, very mutable indeed. Still, as no one would say that the document had been altered, because some copies of it were bad, so it is not strictly correct to say that the Natural Law varies with these subjective varieties. Appeal would be made to a full and perfectly printed impression of the document, one that rendered the stencil exactly. The Natural Law must be viewed in like manner, as it would exist in a mind perfectly enlightened concerning the whole duty of man, and exactly reproducing in itself that portion of the Eternal Law which ordains such duty. Were such a mind to discern a natural obligation to lie differently at two different times, all the relevant circumstances being alike in both cases, and the moral solution different, then only could the Natural Law be held to have changed.

2. But this is clearly impossible. The conclusion of a geometrical theorem is a truth for all time. There is no difference here between a complicated theorem, having many conditions, and a simpler theorem with fewer. It is indeed easier for a few than for many conditions to be all present together: but the enunciation of the conclusion supposes *all* the conditions, whatever their number. The same in a practical manner, as in the stability of a bridge. The bridge that would stand in England, would

stand in Ceylon. If it would not, there must have occurred some change in the conditions, as the heat of the tropical sun upon the girders. A point of casuistry also, however knotty, once determined, is determined for ever and aye, for the circumstances under which it was determined. The Natural Law in this sense is absolutely immutable, no less in each particular application than in the most general principles. We must uniformly pass the same judgment on the same case. What is once right and reasonable, is always right and reasonable, in the same matter. Where to-day there is only one right course, there cannot to-morrow be two, unless circumstances have altered. The Natural Law is thus far immutable, every jot and tittle.

3. No power in heaven above nor on earth beneath can dispense from any portion of the Natural Law. For the matter of the negative precepts of that law is, as we have seen, something bad in itself and repugnant to human nature, and accordingly forbidden by God: while the matter of the positive precepts is something good and necessary to man, commanded by God. If God were to take off His command, or prohibition, the intrinsic exigency, or intolerableness, of the thing to man would still remain, being as inseparable from humanity as certain mathematical properties from a triangle. Pride is not made for man, nor fornication, nor lying, nor polygamy:* human

---

* There is a theological difficulty about the polygamy of the patriarchs, which will be touched on in *Natural Law*, c. vi., s. ii., n. 4, p. 272.

nature would cry out against them, even were the
Almighty in a particular instance to withdraw His
prohibition. What would be the use, then, of any
such withdrawal? It would not make the evil thing
good. An evil thing it would still remain, unnatural,
irrational, and as such, displeasing to God, the
Supreme Reason. The man would not be free to
do the thing, even though God did not forbid it. It
appears, therefore, that the Divine prohibition, and
similarly the Divine command, which we have proved
(c. vi., s. ii., nn. 10, 11, p. 121) to be necessarily imposed in matters of natural evil and of naturally
imperative good, is imposed as a hard and fast line,
so long as the intrinsic good or evil remains the same.

4. There is, therefore, no room for Evolution in
Ethics and Natural Law any more than in Geometry.
One variety of geometrical construction, or of moral
action, may succeed another; but the truths of the
science, by which those varieties are judged, change
not. There is indeed this peculiarity about morality,
distinguishing it from art, that if a man errs invincibly, the evil that he takes for good is not
formally evil, or evil as he wills it, and the good that
he takes for evil is *formally* evil to him. (c. iii., s. ii.,
n. 7, p. 33.) So there is variation and possible Evolution in bare *formal* good and bare *formal* evil, as
ignorance gradually changes into knowledge; and
likewise Reversion, as knowledge declines into
ignorance. Even this Evolution and Reversion have
their limits: they cannot occur in the primary principles of morality, as we saw in the last section. But
morality *material* and objective,—complete morality,

where the formal and material elements agree, where real wrong is seen to be wrong, and real right is known for right—in this morality there is no Evolution. If Hannibal offered human sacrifices to his grandfather because he knew no better, and could not have known better, than to think himself bound so to do, he is to be excused, and even praised for his piety: still it was a mistaken piety; and the act, apart from the light in which the doer viewed it, was a hideous crime. An incorrupt teacher of morals would have taught the Carthaginian, not that he was doing something perfectly right for his age and country, which, however, would be wrong in Germany some centuries later, but that he was doing an act there and then evil and forbidden of God, from which he was bound, upon admonition, instantly to desist.*

5. There are Evolution and Reversion in architecture, but not in the laws of stability of structure, nor in the principles of beauty as realized in building. A combination, ugly now, was not beautiful in the days of Darius. Tastes differ, but not right tastes; and moral notions, but not right moral notions. It is true that questions of right and wrong occur in one state of society, that had no relevance in an earlier state, the conditions of the case not having arisen. But so it is in architecture; there are no arches in the Parthenon. The principle of the arch, however, held in the age of Pericles, though not applied.

---

* The author has seen reason somewhat to modify this view, as appears by the Appendix. (Note to Third Edition.)

6. The progress of Moral Science is the more and more perfect development of the Natural Law in the heart of man, a psychological, not an onto-.ogical development. And Moral Science does progress. No man can be a diligent student of morality for years, without coming to the under-standing of many things, for which one would look in vain in Aristotle's *Ethics* and *Politics*, or in Cicero, *De Officiis*, or even in the *Summa* of St. Thomas, or perhaps in any book ever written. New moral questions come for discussion as civilization ad-vances. The commercial system of modern times would furnish a theme for another De Lugo. And still on this path of ethical discovery, to quote the text that Bacon loved, "Many shall pass over, and knowledge shall be multiplied." (Daniel xii. 4.)

Readings.—St. Thos., Supplement, q. 65, art. 1, in corp.; *ib.*, q. 65, art. 2, in corp., and ad 1; Hughes, *Supernatural Morals*, pp. 67, 68, reviewed in *The Month* for August, 1891, pp. 542, 543.

SECTION IV.—*Of Probabilism.*

1. Sometimes conscience returns a clear, positive answer as to the morality of an act contemplated. True or false the answer may be, but the ring of it has no uncertain sound. At other times conscience is perplexed, and her answer is, *perhaps*, and *perhaps not.* When the woman hid Achimaas and Jonathan in the well, and said to Absalom's servants, "They passed on in haste" (2 Kings xvii. 17—21), did she do right in speaking thus to save their lives? A point that has perplexed consciences for centuries. A man's hesitation is sometimes subjective and peculiar to himself. It turns on a matter of fact, which others know full well, though he doubts; or on a point of law, dark to him, but clearly ruled by the consent of the learned. In such cases it is his duty to seek information from people about him, taking so much trouble to procure it as the importance of the matter warrants, not consulting ten doctors as to the ownership of one hen. But it may be that all due enquiries fail. The fact remains obscure; or about the law, doctors differ, and arguments conflict indecisively. What is the man to do? Take the *safe* course: suppose there is an obligation, and act accordingly? This principle, put as a command, would make human life intolerable. It is, moreover, false, when so put, as we shall presently prove. Take the *easy* course, and leave the obligation out of count? This principle is more nearly correct than the other: but it needs interpretation, else it may prove dangerously lax.

2. To return to Achimaas and Jonathan and their hostess. Some such reckoning as this may have passed through her mind: 'Lying lips are an abomination to the Lord: but is it a lie to put murderers off the scent of blood?' To that question finding no answer, she may have made up her mind in this way: 'Well, I don't know, but I'll risk it.' If that were her procedure, she did not walk by the scientific lines of Probabilism. The probabilist runs no risk, enters upon no uncertainty, and yet he by no means always follows what is

technically termed the *safe* course, that is, the course which supposes the obligation, *e.g.*, in the case in point, to have said simply where the men were. How then does the probabilist contrive to extract certainty out of a case of insoluble doubt? By aid of what is called a *reflex* principle. A *reflex* is opposed to a *direct* principle. A direct principle lays down an obligation, as it would bind one who had a perfect discernment of the law and of the facts of the case, and of the application of the one to the other, and who was perfectly able to keep the law. By a *reflex* principle, a man judges of his own act, taking account of the imperfection of his knowledge and the limitations of his power. Probabilism steps in, only where a case is practically insoluble to an agent upon direct principles. The probabilist thereupon leaves the direct speculative doubt unsolved. He relinquishes the attempt of determining what a man should do in the case in question, who had a thorough insight into the lie of the law. He leaves that aside, and considers what is his duty, or not his duty, in the deficiency of his knowledge. Then he strikes upon the principle, which is the root of Probabilism, that *a doubtful law has no binding power*. It will be observed that this is a *reflex* principle. For objectively nothing is doubtful, but everything is or is not in point of fact. To a mind that had a full grasp of the objective order of things, there would be no doubtful law: such a mind would discern the law in every case as holding or not holding. But no human mind is so perfect. Every man has to take account of his own limitations of vision in judging of his duty. The question for me is, not the law absolutely, but the law as far as I can make it out. Our proposition, then, states that when an individual, using such moral diligence of enquiry as the gravity of the matter calls for, still remains in a state of honest doubt as to whether the law binds, in that mental condition it does not bind *him*.

3. What the law does not forbid, it leaves open. Aristotle indeed (*Eth.*, V., xi., 1) says the contrary, that what the law does not command (he instances suicide), it forbids. All that he seems to mean is, that if there be an act which at times might appear advantageous, and yet is never commanded, there is a presumption of the legislator being averse to that act. Again, there are special occasions, in view of which the legislator undertakes to regulate the whole outward conduct of a man by positive enactment, as with a soldier on parade : what is not there commanded, is forbidden. But these instances do not derogate from our general proposition, which is proved in this way. The office of law is not to loose, but to bind. It declares, not what the subject may do, but what he must or must not. It does not bring liberty, but restriction. Therefore, if any one wishes to assert a restriction, he must go to a law to prove it. If he can find none, liberty remains. The law is laid on liberty. Liberty is not the outcome of law, but prior to it. Liberty is in possession. The burden of proof rests with those who would abridge liberty and impose an obligation. It is an axiom of law itself, a natural, not an arbitrary axiom, that *better is the condition of*

the possessor : which amounts in this matter to another statement, also axiomatic, that *a law binds not till it is promulgated.* But a law of which I have serious outstanding doubts whether it exists at all, or, if existent, whether it reaches my case, is for this occasion a law not duly promulgated to me. Therefore it binds me not, and my liberty remains.

4. It remains to consider what constitutes a *serious outstanding doubt.* The word *outstanding* has been already explained. It means that we have sought for certain information, and cannot procure it. Now what is a *serious* doubt? It is a doubt founded on a *positive* opinion against the existence of the law, or its applicability to the case in point, an opinion fraught with probability, *solid, comparative, practical probability.* The doubt must not be mere negative doubt, or ignorance that cannot tell why it doubts; not a vague suspicion, or sentimental impression that defies all intellectual analysis; not a mere subjective inability to make up one's mind, but some counter-reason that admits of positive statement, as we say, *in black and white.* It is true that many minds cannot define their grounds of doubt, even when these are real. Such minds are unfit to apply the doctrine of Probabilism to themselves, but must seek its application from others. The opinion against the law, when explicitly drawn out, must be found to possess a *solid* probability. It may be either an intrinsic argument from reason and the nature of the case, or an extrinsic argument from the word of some authority : but the reason or

the authority must be grave. The opinion is thus
said to be *intrinsically* or *extrinsically* probable. The
probability must also be *comparative*. There is many
an argument, in itself a very good one, that perishes
when we come to consider the crushing weight of
evidence on the other side. An opinion is *compara-
tively* probable, when after hearing all the reasons
and all the authorities on the other side, the said
opinion still remains *not unlikely*, which is all that
we mean to say of an opinion here, when we call it
probable. In ordinary English, the word *probable*
means *more likely than otherwise*, which is not the
signification of the Latin *opinio probabilis*. Lastly,
the probability must be *practical*: it must take
account of all the circumstances of the case.
Practical probability is opposed to *speculative*, which
leaves out of count certain circumstances, which are
pretty sure to be present, and to make all the
difference in the issue. Thus it is speculatively
probable that a Catholic might without sin remain
years without confession, never having any grievous
sins to confess, grievous sin alone being necessary
matter for that sacrament. There is no downright
cogent reason why a man might not do so. And
yet, if he neglected such ordinary means of grace as
confession of venial sin, having it within reach,
month after month, no one, considering " the sin
which surrounds us," would expect that man to go
without grievous scathe. In mechanics, there are
many machines that work prettily enough in speculation and on paper, where the inventors do not
consider the difficulties of imperfect material, careless

handling, climate, and other influences, that render the invention of no practical avail.

5. The safest use of Probabilism is in the field of property transactions and of positive law. There is greatest risk of using it amiss in remaining in a false religion. All turns upon the varying amount of trouble involved in *moral diligence* of enquiry, according as the matter at issue is a point of mere observance or of vital interest.

6. The point on which the probability turns must be the lawfulness or unlawfulness of the action, not any other issue, as that of the physical consequences. Before rolling boulder-stones down a hill to amuse myself, it is not enough to have formed a probable opinion that there is no one coming up. That would be Probabilism misapplied. The correct enquiry is: Does any intrinsic reason or extrinsic authority make the opinion probable, that it is lawful for mere amusement to roll down rocks with any belief short of certainty that no one will be crushed thereby? The probability, thus turned on to the lawfulness of the action, breaks down altogether. This explanation, borne in mind, will save much misapprehension.

CHAPTER IX.

OF THE SANCTION OF THE NATURAL LAW.

SECTION I.—*Of a Twofold Sanction, Natural and Divine.*

1. THE sanction of a law is the punishment for breaking it. The punishment for final, persistent breach of the natural law is failure to attain the perfect state and last end of the human soul, which is happiness. If existence be prolonged under this failure, it must be in the contrary state of misery. This failure and misery is at once a *natural result* and a *divine infliction.* It is the natural result of repeated flagrant acts of moral evil, whereby a man has made his nature hideous, corrupted and over-thrown it. (c. vi., s. i., nn. 4, 5, p. III.) For an end is gained by taking the means, and lost by neglect of the means thereto. Now, as we have seen, happiness is an intellectual act, the perfection of an intellectual or rational nature (c. ii., s. ii., p. 6); and the means to it are living rationally : for a reasonable being, to do well and fare well, must live by that reason, which is the *form* of his being. (c. vi., s. i., n. 4, p. III.) Who-ever therefore goes about contradicting the reason that is within him (c. v., s. iii., n. 3, p. 74) is not in the way to attain to happiness. Happiness the end of man, the creature of all others the most complex, is not to be stumbled upon by chance. You may make two stones lean upright one against the other by chance, but otherwise than by a methodical application of means to the end you could not support the spire of Salisbury Cathedral.

2. Man's is a progressive nature (c. vi., s. i., nn. 2, 3, p. 109), himself being the director of his own progress. Other progressive natures may be spoilt by their requirements being denied, and contrary things done to them. Man has his requirements. It depends mainly on himself whether he acts up to them or against them. If he acts against them, he so far spoils himself; and once he is thoroughly spoilt by his own doing, the final perfection of humanity is gone from him for ever. It is the natural result.

3. I have spoken (n. 1) of *repeated flagrant acts:* not that I would ignore the evil *set* of the will that results from one gross and deliberate evil deed (see c. ix., s. ii., n. 6, p. 168): but because the case is clearer where the acts have been multiplied. However we must not omit to observe, that it is not any *vice*, or evil habit, that formally unfits a man for his final happiness, but an actual evil *set* of the will, coming of actual sin unrepented of, which *set* is more decided, when that uncancelled sin is the last of many such, and the outcome of a habit. But supposing an habitual sinner to have repented, and his repentance to have been ratified by God, and that he dies, not actually in sin, but before the habit of sin has been eradicated (c. v., s. ii., n. 1, p. 69),—we

may say of him, that his "foot is set in the right way," that is, his will is actually right, and the obstacle to happiness is removed. The evil habit in him is not an actual adhesion of his will to evil, but a proneness to relapse into that state. It is only remotely and potentially evil. It is a seed of evil, which however will not germinate in the good and blissful surroundings to which the soul has been transplanted, but remain for ever sterile, or rather, will speedily decay.

4. If we leave God out of morality, and take account only of the *philosophical* aspect of sin (c. vi., s. ii., n. 6, p. 119), we have nothing further to say of the sanction than this, which has been said: 'Act against nature, and you will end by ruining your nature, and fail of your final perfection and happiness.' But now God comes in, the giver of the law of nature; and the failure, already a natural result, must henceforth be viewed also as a Divine chastisement. There is no law without a sanction. There is no law, the giver of which can allow it to be broken with impunity. A legislator who dispensed with all sanction, would rightly be taken by young and old not to be in earnest in his command. If then God must give a law to man whom He has created (c. vi., s. ii., n. 9, p. 120), He must attach a sanction to that law; and if the law is according to the exigency of human nature (c. vi., s. ii. n. 11, p. 122), so will the sanction also be the natural outcome of that exigency set at naught and that law broken.

5. Our position gains by the consideration, that the object, in the contemplation of which man's soul

L

is to be finally and perfectly blessed in the natural order, is the Creator seen through the veils of His works. (c. ii., s. iv., p. 21.) This mediate vision of God, albeit it is to be the work of a future existence, needs practice and preparation in this life. God will not be discerned by the man who has not been accustomed to look for Him. He will not be seen by the swine, who with head to earth has eaten his fill of sensual pleasures, and has cared for nothing better. He will not be seen by the covetous man and the oppressor, who never identified His image hidden away under the labour-stained dress of the poor. He will not be seen by the man, who never looked up into His face in prayer here below. He will not be seen by the earth-laden spirit, that cared nothing at all for God, that hated the mention of His name, that proclaimed Him, or at least wished Him, not to be at all.

6. It will be said that this argumentation supposes the habits of vice, contracted on earth, to remain in the soul after departure : but there is no proof of that : nay of some vices—those that have more to do with the body, as drunkenness—the habits cannot possibly remain, seeing that the appetite wherein they were resident has perished with the body. First, as regards the instance cited, I reply that we may consider drunkenness in two ways, on the one hand as a turning to the creature, on the other as a turning away from reason and the Creator. The craving for liquor cannot remain in the soul after death exactly as it was before, though it probably continues in some analogous form, as

a thirst for wild and irregular excitement : but the loathing and horror of the ways of reason and of God, engendered by frequent voluntary intoxication, still continues in the soul. And from this observation we draw the general answer, that whereas in every sin, whether sensual or spiritual, the most important part is played by the will, and the will is a spiritual, not an organic faculty, a faculty which is a main element of the soul whether in or out of the body,—therefore the evil bent and inclination of the will, which sin involves, must remain even in the departed spirit. Lastly, we may ask : To what purpose is our free-will given us, if all souls, good and bad alike, users and abusers of the liberty they had on earth, enter into their long home all of one uniform and spotless hue ?

7. Thus then it comes to be, by order of nature and good consequence, that the man who has abandoned God, goes without God ; and he who has shunned his last end and final good, arrives not unto it ; and he who would not go, when invited, to the feast, eats not of the same : and whoso has withdrawn from God, from him God withdraws. "A curse he loved, and it shall come upon him ; and he would not have a blessing, and it shall be far from him. He put on the curse like a garment, and it has gone in like water into his entrails, and like oil into his bones,—like a garment which covereth him, and like a girdle wherewith he is girded continually." (Psalm cviii. 18, 19.)

8. Conversely, we might argue the final happiness which attaches to the observance of the law of nature. (c. ii., s. v., p. 26.)

Readings.—St. Thos., *Cont. Gent.*, iii., cc. 140, 141, 143, 145.

SECTION. II.—*Of the Finality of the aforesaid Sanction.*

1. By a *final*, as distinguished from an *eternal* state, is here meant the last state of existence in a creature, whether that state go on for ever, in which case it is *final* and *eternal*, or whether it terminate in the cessation of that creature's being, which is a case of a state *final*, but not *eternal*. Whether the unhappy souls of men, who have incurred the last sentence of the natural law, shall exist for eternity, is not a question for philosophy to decide with certainty. The philosopher rules everything *a priori*, showing what must be, if something else is. Of the action of God in the world, he can only foretell that amount which is thus hypothetically necessary. Some divine action there is, of which the *congruity* only, not the *necessity*, is apparent to human eyes: there the philosopher can tell with *probability*, but not with *certainty*, what God will do. Other actions of God are wholly beyond our estimate of the reasons of them: we call them simply and entirely free. In that sphere philosophy has no information to render of her own; she must wait to hear from revelation what God has done, or means to do. Philosophers have given *reasons of congruence*, as they call them, for the reprobate sinner not being annihilated, and therefore for his *final* punishment being *eternal*. Those reasons go to evince the probability of eternal punishment, a probability which is deepened into certainty by

revelation. We shall not enter into them here, but shall be content to argue that a term is set to the career of the transgressor, arrived at which he must leave hope behind of ever winning his way to happiness, or ever leading any other existence than one of misery.

2. The previous question has shown that some punishment must attend upon violation of the natural law. Suppose a trangressor has suffered accordingly for a certain time after death, what shall be done with him in the end? If he does not continue to suffer as long as he continues to be, then one of three things: he must either pass into happiness, or into a new state of probation, or his very punishment must be a probation, wherein if he behaves well, he shall be rewarded with happiness at last, or if ill, he shall continue in misery until he amend. All this speculation, be it understood, lies apart from revelation. If then the sufferer passed out of this world, substantially and in the main a good man, it is not unreasonable that, after a period of expiatory suffering for minor delinquencies, he should reach that happiness which is the just reward of his substantial righteousness. But what of him who closed his career in wickedness exceeding great? Mere suffering will never make of him a good man, or a fit subject for happiness. But the suffering may be probationary, and he may amend himself under the trial. Against that hypothesis, philosophers have brought *a priori* arguments to show that the period of probation must end with the separation of the soul from the body. But waiving all such

arguments, let us suppose that there might be probation after probation even in the world to come. But
some human souls would continue obstinately and
unrepentingly set in wickedness, age after age, and
probation after probation : for the possible malice
of the will is vastly great. What is to become of
such obstinate characters? It seems against the
idea of probation, that periods of trial should
succeed one another in an endless series. It would
be a reasonable rule in a university, that an under-
graduate who had been plucked twenty-five times,
should become ineligible for his degree. Coming
after so many failures, neither would the degree be
any ornament to him, nor he to the university. A
soul cannot look for seasons without end of possible
grace and pardon to shine upon it. The series of
probations must end somewhere. And then? We
are come round to where we began. When all the
probation is over, the soul is found either in conformity with the natural law, which means ultimate
happiness, or at variance with the law, and becomes
miserable with a misery that shall never terminate,
unless the soul itself ceases to be.

3. It may be asked, how much conformity to the
natural law is requisite and sufficient, to exempt a
person at the end of his trial from a final doom of
misery, or to ensure his lasting happiness? The
question resolves itself into three :—how do sins
differ in point of gravity? is grave sin ever for
given? is the final award to be given upon the
person's whole life, a balance being struck between
his good and evil deeds, or is it to be simply upon

his moral state at the last moment of his career of trial?

4. It was a paradox of the Stoics, that all offences are equal, the treading down of your neighbour's cabbage as heinous a crime as sacrilege. (Horace, *Satires*, i., 3, 115—119.) But it is obvious that there is a vast difference, as well *objectively* in the matter of the offence, *e.g.*, in the instance just quoted from Horace, as also *subjectively* in the degree of knowledge, advertence, and will, wherewith the offender threw himself into the sin. Thus offences come to be distinguished as *grave* and *light*: the latter being such as with a human master would involve a reprimand, the former, instant dismissal. Final misery is not incurred except by grave offending.

5. The second question, whether grave sin is ever forgiven, cannot be answered by philosophy. Of course the sinner may see by the light of reason his folly and his error, and thereby conceive some sort of sorrow for it, and retract, and to some extent withdraw his will from it on natural grounds. This amendment of sin on its moral and philosophical side may deserve and earn pardon at human hands. But the offence against God remains to be reckoned for with God. Now God is not bound to forgive without receiving satisfaction; and He never can receive due satisfaction from man for the contempt that a deliberate, grave, and flagrant violation of the moral law puts upon the Infinite Majesty of the Lawgiver. The first thing that revelation has to teach us is whether, and

on what terms, God is ready to pardon grievous sin.

6. The balance between deeds good and evil is not struck merely at the instant of death. It is being struck continually; and man's final destiny turns on how that balance stands at the close of his time of probation. So long as he keeps the substance of the moral law, the balance is in his favour. But one downright wilful and grievous transgression outweighs with God all his former good deeds. It is a defiance of the Deity, a greater insult than all his previous life was a service and homage. It is as though a loyal regiment had mutinied, or a hitherto decent and orderly citizen were taken red-handed in murder. If however God deigns to draw the offender to repentance, and to pardon him, the balance is restored. Thus everything finally depends on man being free from guilt of grievous transgression at the instant of death, or at the end of his period of probation, whenever and wherever that end may come.

Reading.—Lessius, *De perfectionibus divinis*, l. xiii., c. xxvi., nn. 183, seq.

SECTION III.—*Of Punishment Retrospective and Retributive.*

1. The doctrine of the last section might stand even in the mind of one who held that all punishment is probational, and destined for the amendment of him who undergoes it, to humble him, to awaken his sense of guilt, and to make him fear to transgress again. On this theory of punishment, the man who in his last probational suffering refuses

to amend, must be let drop out of existence as incorrigible, and so clearly his final state is one of misery. The theory is not inconsistent with *final* punishment, but with *eternal* punishment, unless indeed we can suppose a creature for all eternity to refuse, and that under stress of torment, a standing invitation to repentance. It is however a peculiar theory, and opposite to the common tradition of mankind, which has ever been to put gross offenders to death, not as incorrigible, not simply as refuse to be got rid of, but that their fate may be a *deterrent* to others. Punishment, in this view, is *medicinal* to the individual, and *deterrent* to the community. Eternal punishment has been defended on the score of its *deterrent* force. Both these functions of punishment, the *medicinal* and the *deterrent* function, are prospective. But there is asserted a third function, which is retrospective: punishment is said to be *retributive.* It is on this ground that the justification of eternal punishment mainly rests. We are however here concerned, not with that eternity, but in an endeavour to give a full and adequate view of punishment in all its functions.

2. If punishment is never *retributive*, the human race in all countries and ages has been the sport of a strange illusion. Everyone knows what *vengeance* means. It is a desire to punish some one, or to see him punished, not prospectively and with an eye to the future, for his improvement, or as a warning to others, but retrospectively and looking to the past, that he may suffer for what he has done. Is then the idea of vengeance nothing but an unclean

phantom? Is there no such thing as vengeance to a right-minded man? Then is there an evil element, an element *essentially* and *positively* evil, in human nature. No one will deny that the idea, and to some extent the desire, of vengeance, of retaliation, of retrospective infliction of suffering in retribution for evil done, of what we learn to call in the nursery *tit for tat*, is natural to mankind. It is found in all men. We all respond to the sentiment:

> Mighty Fates, by Heaven's decree accomplish,
> According as right passes from this side to that.
> For hateful speech let speech of hate be paid back:
> Justice exacting her due cries this aloud:
> For murderous blow dealt let the murderer pay
> By stroke of murder felt.
> Do and it shall be done unto thee:
> Old is this saying and old and old again.[1]

Nor must we be led away by Mill (*Utilitarianism,* c. v.) into confounding retaliation, or vengeance, with self-defence. Self-defence is a natural idea also, but not the same as retaliation. We defend ourselves against a mad dog, we do not retaliate on him. Hence we must not argue that, because self-defence is prospective, therefore so is vengeance.

3. A thing is *essentially* evil, when there is no possible use of it which is not an abuse. Not far different is the conception of a thing *positively* evil, evil, that is, not by reason of any deficiency, or by what it is not, but evil by what it is in itself. Such an

---

[1] Æschylus, *Choophori,* 316, ooq. These lines embody the idea on which the dramas of the Shakespeare of Greece are principally founded. But when was a work of the highest art based upon an idea unsound, irrational and vicious?

essential, positive evil in human nature would vengeance be, a natural thing for which there was no natural
use, unless punishment may in some measure be
retributive. We cannot admit such a flaw in nature.
All healthy philosophy goes on the principle, that
what is natural is so far forth good. Otherwise
we lapse into Manicheism, pessimism, scepticism,
abysses beyond the reach of argument. Vengeance
undoubtedly prompts to many crimes, but so does
the passion of love. Both are natural impulses.
It would scarcely be an exaggeration to set down
one third of human transgressions to love, and
another third to revenge: yet it is the abuse in each
case, not the use, that leads to sin. If the matrimonial union were wicked and detestable, as the
Manicheans taught, then would the passion of love
be an abomination connatural to man. Such another
enormity would be the affection of vengeance, if
punishment could never rightly be retributive.

4. Aristotle, *Rhetoric*, I., x., 17, distinguishes two
functions of punishment thus : " Chastisement is
for the benefit of him that suffers it, but vengeance
is for him that wreaks it, that he may have satisfaction." Add to this the warning given to the commonwealth by the example that is made of the
offender, and we have the three functions of punishment, *medicinal*, *deterrent*, and *retributive*. As it is
medicinal, it serves the *offender* : as it is *deterrent*, it
serves the *commonwealth* : as it is *retributive*, it serves
the *offended party*, being a reparation offered to him.
Now, who is the offended party in any evil deed ?
So far as it is a sin against justice, an infringement

of any man's right, he is the offended party. He is offended, however, not simply and precisely by your violation of the moral law, but by your having, in violation of that law, taken away something that belonged to him. Consequently, when you make restitution and give him back what you took away, with compensation for the temporal deprival of it, he is satisfied, and the offence against him is repaired. If you have maliciously burnt his house down, you bring him the price of the house and furniture, together with further payment for the fright and for the inconvenience of being, for the present, houseless. You may do all that, and yet the moral guilt of the conflagration may remain upon your soul. But that is no affair of his: he is not the custodian of the moral law : he is not offended by your sin, formally viewed as sin: nor has he any function of punishing you, taking vengeance upon you, or exacting from you retribution for that. But what if his wife and children have perished, and you meant them so to perish, in the fire ? Your debt of restitution still lies in the matter which you took away. Of course it is a debt that cannot be paid. You cannot give back his "pretty chickens and their dam" whole and alive again. Still your inability to pay one debt does not make you liable to that creditor for another debt, which is part of a wholly different account. He is not offended by, nor are you answerable to him for, your *sin* in this case any more than in the former.

5. We may do an *injury* to an individual, commit a *crime* against the State, and *sin* against God. The

injury to the individual is repaired by restitution,
not by punishment, and therefore not by vengeance,
which is a function of punishment. There is no
such thing as vengeance for a private wrong, and
therefore we have the precept to forgive our enemies,
and not to avenge ourselves, in which phrase the
emphasis falls on the word *ourselves*. The clear
idea and strong desire of vengeance, which nature
affords, shows that there is such a thing as vengeance to be taken by some one : it does not warrant
every form of vengeance, or allow it to be taken by
each man for himself. It consecrates the principle
of retribution, not every application of the principle.
It is a point of *synderesis*, not of particular conduct.
The reader should recall what was said of the vengeance of Hannibal at Himera. (c. viii., s. ii., p. 144.)

6. It belongs to the State to punish *political sin*,
or crime, and to God to punish *theological sin*, which
is sin properly so called, a breach of the Eternal
Law. The man who has burnt his neighbour's
house down, though he has compensated the individual owner, may yet be punished by the State.
The owner, acting in his capacity as citizen, even
when he has been compensated as an individual,
may still hand him over to the State for punishment.
The arson was a violation, not only of *commutative*,
but of *legal* justice (c. v., s. ix., nn. 3, 6, pp. 103, 106), a
disturbance of the public peace and social order, an
outrage upon the majesty of the law. For this he may
be punished by the State, which is the guardian of all
these things, and which has jurisdiction over him
to make laws for him, and to enforce their sanction

against him. Civil punishment, besides being deterrent, is retributive for the breach of social order. It
is the vengeance of the commonwealth upon the
disturber of the public peace. Whether the State can
punish on pure grounds of retribution, away from all
hope or need of deterring possible imitators of the
crime, is a question irrelevant to our present enquiry.
Probably a negative answer should be returned.

7. We come now to the punishment of sin by
God, the Living Reasonableness, the Head of the
Commonwealth of Creation, the Legislator of the
Eternal Law, the Fountain of all Jurisdiction, Him
in whose hands rests the plenitude of the power to
punish. An evil deed may be no wrong to any individual man, no crime against the State, but it must
ever be an offence against God. It is a departure
from the order of man's progress as a reasonable
being (c. v., s. iii., n. 3, p. 74: c. vi., s. i., nn. 1—5,
p. 109), which is founded on the nature of God
Himself (c. vi., s. i., n. 7, p. 113), of which order
God is the official guardian (c. vi., s. ii., nn. 8—10,
p. 119), and which is enjoined by God's Eternal
Law. (c. vii., n. 3, p. 129.) This law extends to all
creation, rational and irrational, animate and inanimate. It bids every creature work according to his
or its own nature and circumstances. Given to irrational beings, the law is simply irresistible and
unfailing: such are the physical laws of nature, so
many various emanations of the one Eternal Law.
Given to rational creatures, the law may be resisted
and broken: sin is the one thing in the universe that
does break it. (c. vii., nn. 5—7, p. 130.) A man may act

in disregard of the Eternal Law on one or other of
its physical sides, and so much the worse for him,
though he has not broken the law, but merely ignored
its operation, as when one eats what is unwholesome.
Much more shall he suffer for having broken the
law, in the only possible way that it can be
broken, by sin. This peculiar violation draws after
it a peculiar consequence of suffering, penal and
retributive. If a man gets typhoid fever in his house,
we sometimes say it is a *punishment* on him for
neglecting his drains, even when the neglect was a
mere piece of ignorance or inadvertence. It is an
evil consequence certainly, the law, which he
thought not of, working itself out in the form of
disease. But it is not properly punishment: no
natural law has been really broken: there has been
no guilt, and the suffering is not retributive and
compensatory. It does not go to restore the balance
of the neglect. It is a lamentable consequence, not
a repayment. As, when man wrongs his fellow-man,
he makes with him an *involuntary contract* (c. v., s. ix.,
n. 6, p. 106), to restore what he takes away: so in
sinning against God, man makes another involuntary
contract, to pay back in suffering against his will
what he unduly takes in doing his own will against
the will of the Legislator. As St. Augustine says of
Judas (Serm. 125, n. 5): "He did what he liked,
but he suffered what he liked not. In his doing
what he liked, his sin is found: in his suffering
what he liked not, God's ordinance is praised."
Thus it is impossible for the Eternal Law, which

bears down all so irresistibly in irrational nature, finally to fail of its effect even upon the most headstrong and contumacious of rational creatures; but, as St. Thomas says (1a 2æ, q. 93, art. 6, in corp.), "The defect of doing is made up by suffering, inasmuch as they suffer what the Eternal Law prescribes for them to the extent to which they fail to do what accords with the Eternal Law." And St. Anselm (*Cur Deus homo*, nn. 14, 15) : " God cannot possibly lose His honour: for either the sinner spontaneously pays what he owes, or God exacts it of him against his will. Thus if a man chooses to fly from under the will of God commanding, he falls under the same will punishing." Punishment is called by Hegel, "the other half of sin." Lastly, they are God's own spoken words (Deut. xxxii. 35) : "Vengeance is Mine, I will repay."

Readings.—St. Thos., *Cont. Gent.*, iii. 140, n. 5, Amplius; *ib.*, iii., 144, nn. 8, Per hoc, and 9, Est autem.

For Plato's views on punishment see *Protag.* 324 A, B; *Gorgias*, 525; *Rep.* 380 B, 615; *Phaedo*, 113 E; *Laws*, 854 D; 862 D, E; 934 A; 957 E. Plato recognizes only the *medicinal* and the *deterrent* functions of punishment, and ignores the *retributive*. This is not to be wondered at in one who wrote: "No one is wicked voluntarily; but it is an evil habit of body and a faulty education that is the cause of every case of wickedness" (*Timaeus*, 86 E; cf. *Laws*, 731 C, D), which error receives a masterly confutation in Aristotle, *Ethics*, III. v.

CHAPTER X.

OF UTILITARIANISM.

1. THOUGH the name *utilitarian* is an English growth of this century, the philosophy so called probably takes its origin from the days when man first began to speculate on moral matters. Bentham and the two Mills, Austin, and George Grote, have repeated in England the substance of what Protagoras and Epicurus taught in Greece, two thousand years before. It is the system of Ethics to which all must incline, who ignore the spiritual side of man's nature and his hopes of a better world. **It is a** morality of the earth, earthy.

2. Utilitarianism has not been formulated like the Athanasian Creed. It is impossible to state it and combat it in a form to which all Utilitarians will subscribe. Indeed, it is an amiable weakness of theirs, when confronted with the grosser consequences that flow from their theories, to run off to some explanation, true enough, but quite out of keeping with the primary tenets of their school. We will take what may be called a "mean reading" of the indications which various Utilitarian thinkers afford of their mind and philosophy. These authorities, then, teach two main heads of doctrine :—

M

(1) That the last end and final good of man lies in this world, and consists in the greatest happiness of the greatest number of mankind, happiness being taken to mean pleasure as well of the senses as of the understanding, such pleasure as can be had in this world, along with immunity from pain. (Mill's *Utilitarianism*, 2nd Ed., pp. 9, seq.)

(2) That human acts are *right* or *wrong*, according as they are *useful* or *hurtful*, that is, according as their consequences make for or against the above-mentioned end of social happiness.

3. Consequences, as Utilitarians very properly point out, are either *general* or *particular*. They add that, in pronouncing an action to be good or evil according to its consequences, they mean the general and not the particular consequences. In other words, they bid us consider, not the immediate results of *this action*, but what would be the result to society, if *this sort of action* were generally allowed. This point is well put by Paley (*Moral Philosophy*, bk. ii., c. vii.: all three chapters, vi., vii., viii., should be read, as the best explanation of the Principle of General Consequences):

"You cannot permit one action and forbid another, without showing a difference between them. Consequently the same sort of actions must be generally permitted or generally forbidden. Where, therefore, the general permission of them would be pernicious, it becomes necessary to lay down and support the rule which generally forbids them. . . . The assassin knocked the rich villain on the head, because he thought him better out of the way than in it. If you allow this excuse in the present instance, you must allow it to all who act in the same manner, and from the same motive; that is, you must allow every man to kill any one he meets, whom he thinks noxious or useless: . . . a disposition of affairs which would soon fill the world with misery and confusion, and ere long put an end to human society."

My contention is, not with the Principle of General Consequences, which has a certain value in Ethics, and is used by many writers other than Utilitarian, but with the two stated above, n. 2, which are called the Greatest Happiness Principle and the Principle of Utility.

4. Against the Greatest Happiness Principle I have these complaints:

(1) Utilitarians from Paley to John Stuart Mill aver that their teaching is no bar to any man hoping for and striving after the happiness of the world to come. They say that such happiness cannot be better attained than by making it your principal aim to improve all temporal goods and dissipate all temporal evil. Their maxim in fact is: 'Take care of the things of earth, and the things of heaven will take care of themselves.' Whereas it was the very contrary teaching of Him, whom moderns, who see in Him no higher character, still love to call the greatest of moral teachers: "That which fell among thorns are they who have heard, and going their way, are choked with the cares and riches and pleasures of this life, and yield no fruit." (St. Luke viii. 14.)

(2) It will be said that these thorns grow of selfishness, and that these cares are the cares of individual interest, whereas the Utilitarian's delight and glory is to live, not for himself, but for the commonwealth. But how can a man, who takes pleasure to be his highest good and happiness, live otherwise than for himself? Here we come upon the unobserved fault and flaw, which entirely vitiates the Utilitarian structure. It is an union of two opposite and incompatible elements. An old poet has said:

> Vinegar and oil in one same vessel pour,
> They stand apart, unfriendly, all the more.
> (Æschylus, *Agam.*, 330, 331.)

Utilitarianism consists of a still more unfriendly and unwholesome mixture of two elements, both of them bad, and unable to stand together, Hedonism and Altruism. Hedonism is the doctrine that the main object and end of life is pleasure: which is the position laid down in so many words by Mill (l. c.), that "actions are right in proportion as they tend to promote happiness; and "by happiness is intended pleasure and the absence of pain." If Hedonism were sound doctrine, the Pleasant and the Good would be identical, and the most pleasant pleasure would ever be the best pleasure. That would take away all distinction of *kind* or *quality* among pleasures, and differentiate them only by intensity and duration. This was Paley's doctrine, a fundamental point of Hedonism, and therefore also of the Utilitarian philosophy. John Mill, very honourably to himself, but very fatally to the system that he was writing to defend, parted company with Paley.

We have argued against Paley (c. iv., s. iii., nn. 3—5, p. 55), that there is a *better* and a *worse* in pleasures, quite distinct from the *more* or *less* pleasurable, even if that *more* be taken *in the long run* in this world.

Again it may be considered that pleasure, even the best and highest, is a sort of efflorescence from activity, and is for activity, not activity for it; and better is the activity, whatever it be, than the pleasure which comes thereof; wherefore no pleasure, as pleasure, can be the highest good and happiness of man.

Hedonism then is an error. But errors may be opposed to one another as well as to the truth. Hedonism is opposed to Altruism in this way. A man may take pleasure in seeing other people enjoy themselves. Nothing is more common, except the pleasure taken in enjoying one's own self. But if a man only feeds the hungry that he may have the satisfaction of seeing them eat, is it the hungry or himself that he finally seeks to gratify? Clearly, himself. That is the behaviour of the Hedonist, he acts for his own pleasure even in his benevolence. The Altruist, on the contrary, professes never to act for self, but for society. So that society flourish, he is ready to be crushed and ruined, not in the matter of his pleasure only, but even in that of his own good. Selfishness, by which he means all manner of regard to self, is, upon his conscience, the unforgiven sin. But Hedonism is selfishness in the grossest form, being the mere pursuit in all things of pleasurable feeling—feeling being always particular and limited to self, in contradistinction to good, which is universal and diffuses itself all round. The Hedonist seeks his own pleasure, where the Altruist forbids him to take thought, let alone for his gratification, but even for his good. Thus an Hedonist cannot be Altruist to boot; and, trying to combine the two characters, the Utilitarian is committed to a self-contradiction.

If he relinquishes Hedonism, and holds to Altruism, pure and simple, his position is not much improved. Altruism overlooks the fact, that man, as compared with other men, is a *person*, the centre of his own acts, not a *thing*, to be entirely referred to others. He is in relation with others, as child, father, husband, master, citizen; but these relations do not take up the whole man. There is a residue within,— an inner being and life, which is not referable to any creature outside himself, but only to the Creator. For this inner being, man is responsible to God alone. The good of this, the " inner man of the heart," is each individual's proper and primary care. Altruism, and Utilitarianism with it, ignore the interior life of the soul, and substitute human society, that is, ultimately, the democratic State, in place of God.

(3) Another confusion that the Greatest Happiness Principle involves, is the mistaking the political for the ethical end of life. The political end, which it is the statesman's business to aim at, and the citizen's duty to subserve, is " the natural happiness of the commonwealth, and of individuals as members of the commonwealth, that they may live in it in peace and justice, and with a sufficiency of goods for the preservation and comfort of bodily life, and with

that amount of moral rectitude which is necessary for this outward peace and preservation of the commonwealth, and the perpetuity of the human race." (Suarez, *De Legibus*, III., xi., 7.) This is all the good that the Utilitarian contemplates. He is satisfied to make a good *citizen*, a good *husband*, a good *father*, for the transactions of this life. He has no concern to make a good *man* up to the ethical standard, which supposes the observance of the whole natural law, duties to God, and duties within himself, as well as duties to human society, and by this observance the compassing of the everlasting happiness of the man's own individual soul.

Against the Principle of Utility I find these charges:

(1) It takes the sign and indication of moral evil for the evil itself, as if the physician should take the symptom for the disease. It places the wickedness of an act in the physical misery and suffering that are its consequences. This is, I say, a taking of the indication for the thing indicated. An act is bad in itself and by itself, as being a violation of the rational nature of the doer (c. vi., s. i.), and being bad, it breeds bad consequences. But the badness of the act is moral; the badness of the consequences, physical. There is an evident intrinsic irrationality, and thereby moral evil, in such sins as intemperance, peevishness, and vanity. But let us take an instance of an act, apparently harmless in itself, and evil solely because of the consequences. Supposing one insists upon playing the piano for his own amusement, to the disturbance of an invalid who is lying

in a critical state in the next room.   Do the mere
consequences make this otherwise innocent amusement evil?   Yes, if you consider the amusement in
the abstract : but if you take it as *this human act*, the
act is inordinate and evil in itself, or as it is elicited
in the mind of the agent.   The volition amounts to
this : 'I prefer my amusement to my neighbour's
recovery,' which is an act unseemly and unreasonable
in the mind of a social being.   Utilitarians fall into
the capital error of ignoring the intrinsic value of
an act, and estimating it wholly by extrinsic results,
because they commonly follow the phenomenalist
philosophy, which breaks away from all such ideas
as *substance* and *nature*, and regards nothing but
sequences and coexistences of phenomena.   To a
phenomenalist the precept, *Live up to thy nature*, can
have no meaning.

(2) Aristotle (*Ethics*, II., iv., 3) draws this distinction between virtue and art, that "the products of
art have their excellence in themselves : it suffices
therefore that they are of this or that quality : but
acts of virtue are not done virtuously according to
the quality of the thing done, but according to the
state of mind of the doer ; first, according to his
knowledge of what he was about ; then, according
to his volition, as that was guided or not guided
by the proper motives of the virtue ; thirdly, according to the steadiness and fixedness of his will ;
whereas all these considerations are of no account
in a work of art, except the single one of the artist
being aware of what he was about."   Elsewhere
(*Ethics*, VI., iv., 2), he says that virtue is distinguished

from art as being *action*, not *production*. The Principle of Utility confounds virtue with art, or perhaps
I should say, with manufactures. It judges conduct,
as one would shoemaking, by trial of the product,
or net result. So far from being solicitous, with
Aristotle, that volition should be "guided by the
proper motives of the virtue" which there is question
of practising (c. v., s. viii., n. 4, p. 96 : Ar. *Eth.*, III.,
viii.), Mill (*Utilitarianism*, p. 26) tells us that "utilitarian moralists have gone beyond almost all others
in affirming that the motive has nothing to do with
the morality of the action." By *motive* he understands what we have called *the end in view*. (c. iii.,
s. ii., n. 2, p. 31.) So that, if one man waits on the
sick for the love of God, and another in hope of a
legacy, the morality of these two acts is the same,
just as it makes no difference to the usefulness of a
pair of boots, what motive it was that set the shoemaker to work. True, Mill admits that the motive
has "much to do with the worth of the agent : "
but that, he hastens to explain, is inasmuch as "it
indicates . . . a bent of character from which useful,
or from which hurtful actions are likely to arise."
Even so,—the shoemaker who works to earn money
for a carousal, is not likely to go on producing
useful articles so long as another, who labours to
support his family. Such is the moral difference
that Mill places between the two men ; one instrument of production is longer available than the
other.

(3) Another well established distinction is that
between *harm* and *injury*, injury being wilful and

unjust harm. The housemaid, who in arranging the
room has burned your manuscript of "sugared
sonnets," has done you no injury, for she meant
none, but how vast the *harm* to the author and to
mankind! Harm is visible in the effects: but injury
only upon examination of the mind of the agent.
Not so, however, the Utilitarian thinks: harm being
equal, he can make no difference between a tyrant
and a man-eating tiger. Thus George Grote says of
a certain murderous usurper of the kingdom of
Macedon: " You discover nothing while your eye
is fixed on Archelaus himself. . . . But when you
turn to the persons whom he has killed, banished,
or ruined—to the mass of suffering that he has
inflicted—and to the widespread insecurity which
such acts of iniquity spread through all societies
where they become known—there is no lack of argument which prompts a reflecting spectator to brand
him as [a most dangerous and destructive animal,
no] a disgraceful man." (Grote's *Plato*, ii., p. 108.)
Why Archelaus is described in terms of the tiger,
and then branded as a disgraceful man, we are at a
loss to conceive, except in this way, that the writer's
philosophy forsook him at the end of the sentence,
and he reverted to the common sense of mankind.
But he should have either ended the sentence as
suggested in the parenthesis, or have been willing to
call the man-eater of the Indian jungle, who has
"learned to make widows, and to lay waste their
cities," *a disgraceful tiger;* or lastly, he should have
looked back, where he declared it was vain to
look, upon Archelaus himself, and discerned in him

that moral deformity, and contradiction of reason, whereof a brute beast is incapable, but which is a disgrace and a stain upon humanity.

A later writer, who presses Utilitarianism into the service of Socialism, is plainer-spoken than Grote, and says bluntly: "To be honestly mistaken avails nothing. Thus Herbert Spencer—who is under the delusion that we have come into this world each for the sake of himself, and who opposes, as far as he can, the evolution of society—is verily an immoral man. . . . Right is every conduct which tends to the welfare of society; wrong, what obstructs that welfare." (Gronlund, *Co-operative Commonwealth*, pp. 226, 227.) Thus is overlaid the difference between harm and injury, between physical and moral evil: thus is the meaning of a *human act* ignored: in this abyss of chaos and confusion, which Utilitarianism has opened out, Moral Philosophy finds her grave.

(4) The Principle of Utility sees in virtue a habit of self-sacrifice, useful to the community, but not naturally pleasant, and therefore not naturally good and desirable, to him that practises it, but made pleasurable and good and desirable to him by practice. (Mill, pp. 53—57.) In this way virtue becomes naturally a very good thing for every one else but its possessor, but to him it is a natural evil, inasmuch as it deprives him of pleasure, which natural evil by habit is gradually converted into a factitious and artificial good, the man becoming accustomed to it, as the proverb says, "like eels to skinning." This theory is the resuscitation of one

current among the Sophists at Athens, and described by Plato thus.—The natural good of man is to afford himself every indulgence, even at the expense of his neighbours. He follows his natural good accordingly: so do his neighbours follow theirs, and try to gratify themselves at his expense. Fights ensue, till mankind, worried and wearied with fighting, make a compact, each to give up so much of his natural good as interferes with that of his neighbour. Human society, formed on this understanding, enforces the compact in the interest of society. Thus the interest of society is opposed to the interest of the individual, in this that it keeps him out of his best natural good, which is to do as his appetite of pleasure bids him in all things, though it compensates him with a second-class good, by preventing his neighbours from pleasure-hunting at his expense. If then his neighbours could be restrained, and he left free to gratify himself, that would be perfect bliss. But only a despot here or there has attained to it. The ordinary man must pay his tax of virtue to the community, a loss to him, but a gain to all the rest: while he is compensated by the losses which their virtue entails upon them.

Such was the old Athenian theory, which John Mill, the Principle of Utility in his hand, completes by saying that by-and-bye, and little by little (as the prisoner of Chillon came to love his dungeon), the hampered individual comes to love, and to find an artificial happiness in, those restrictions of his liberty, which are called Virtue.

It was against this theory that Plato wrote his

Republic, and, to compare a little thing to a great, the whole account of moral good being in consonance with nature, and of moral obligation rising out of the nature of the individual man, as has been set forth in this brief Text-book, may serve for a refutation of the perverse doctrine of Utilitarianism.

Readings.—Plato, *Republic,* pp. 338 E, 339 A, 343 C, D, E, 344 A, B, C, 358 E, 359 A, B, 580 B, C.

ETHICS AND NATURAL LAW.

PART II.   NATURAL LAW.

WE assume in Natural Law the preceding treatise on Ethics, and also the principal truths of Natural Theology.

CHAPTER I.

OF DUTIES OF GOD.

SECTION I.—*Of the Worship of God.*

1. *Worship* is divided into *prayer* and *praise*. To pray, and present our petitions to the Most High, is a privilege; a privilege, however, which we are bound to use at times, as the necessary means for over-coming temptations and inclinations to evil. We praise and adore God for His sovereign excellence, which excellence, nevertheless, would found in us no positive duty if we stood free of all dependence upon God. In such an hypothesis we should lie simply under the negative duty of not thinking of God, speaking of Him, or acting towards Him otherwise

than with all reverence.   So we should behave to
the Great Stranger, with civility, with admiration
even and awe, but not with cordiality, not with
loyalty, not with homage, not with love.   Very
different are our relations and our duties to God
our Lord, "in whom we live, move, and have our
being." There is nothing in us or about us, no positive
perfection of ours whatsoever, that is not His gift,
and a gift that He is not giving continually, else it
would be lost to us.   We are therefore bound in
His regard, not merely to abstention but to act.
And first, for inward acts, we must habitually feel,
and at notable intervals we must actually elicit,
sentiments of adoration and praise, of thanksgiving,
of submission, of loyalty and love, as creatures to
their Creator, and as vassals to their very good
Lord, for He is our Creator and Lord in the
natural order, not to say anything here of the
supernatural filiation, by which, as the Church says,
"we dare" to call God "Our Father."

2. We must also express these sentiments by
outward act.   All the signs of reverence, which man
pays to his human superior, must be paid to God
"with advantages": bowing passes into prostration, uncovering the head into kneeling, kissing the
hand into offering of incense: not that these particular developments are necessary, but some such
development must take place.   We shall not be
content to think reverential thoughts, but we shall
say, or even sing, great things of God's greatness
and our indebtedness and duty: such a vocal
exercise is psalmody.   We shall represent in

symbolic action our dependence on the Lord of
life and death, and also our sinfulness, for which
He might justly strike us dead : such a representation is sacrifice.

3. All this we must do, first, for the sake of our
own souls, minds and hearts, to quicken the inward
sentiment of adoration and praise. " Worship,
mostly of the silent sort," worship, that finds no
expression in word or gesture,—worship away from
pealing organs and chants of praise, or the simpler
music of the human voice, where no hands are
uplifted, nor tongues loosened, nor posture of
reverence assumed, becomes with most mortals a
vague, aimless reverie, a course of distraction,
dreaminess, and vacancy of mind, no more worth
than the meditations of the Lancashire stone-
breaker, who was asked what he thought of during
his work,—" Mostly nowt."

4. Again, what the body is to the soul, that is
exterior devotion to interior. From the soul interior
devotion springs, and through the body it manifests
itself. Exterior devotion, without the inward spirit
that quickens it, is worship unprofitable and dead :
it tends at once to corruption, like the body when
the soul has left it. Interior devotion, on the other
hand, can exist, though not with its full complement,
without the exterior. So that it is only in the union
of the two together that perfect worship is given to
God by men as men. Upon which St. Thomas has
this naïve remark, that "they who blame bodily
observance being paid to God, evidently fail to
remember that they themselves are men."

N

Thus we pay tithe to God for soul and body, by acts of religion interior and exterior. But man is, under God, the lord of this earth and of the fulness thereof. He must pay tithe for that too by devoting some portion of it to the direct service of God, to whom it all primarily belongs. For " mine is the gold and mine the silver." (Aggeus ii. 9.) Such are the words that God spoke through His prophet to incite His people to restore his sanctuary.

6. It is therefore not true to say that the sole reason of outward worship is to move the worshipper to interior devotion. It is not true that St. Peter's at Rome, and Cologne Cathedral, and the Duomo of Milan, with all their wealth and elaborate ceremonial, exist and are kept up solely because, things of earth as we are, we cannot be depended upon to praise God lovingly within the white-washed walls of a conventicle, or according to the simple ritual of the Society of Friends. We would not, even if we could, pray habitually among such surroundings, where we could afford to better them. We have before us the principle of St. Thomas (1a 2æ, q. 24, art. 3, in corp.) :

"Since man's good consists in reason as in its root, the more actions proper to man are performed under the direction of reason, the more perfect will man's good be. Hence no one doubts that it belongs to the perfection of moral good, that the actions of our bodily members should be directed by the law of reason, . . . as also that the passions of the soul should be regulated by reason."

This means, not merely that if the bodily members

or the passions stir at all, it is a good and desirable thing for them to be ruled by reason ; but further that it is a positive addition to human perfection that they should stir and be active, provided reason guide them. (*Ethics*, c. iv., s. i., n. 6, p. 45.)

It certainly is an action proper to man to express in gesture, in voice, in concert and company with his fellow-men, and by employment of whatever is best and fairest and brightest under his command in the material creation, his inward affections of loyalty, of homage and devotion, of awe and reverence, of gratitude and love to his Creator.

Good as these affections are in the heart of the worshipper, they receive an external complement of goodness and perfection by being blazoned forth in vocal utterance, singing, bending of knees,—by the erection and embellishment of temples, and offerings of gold, silver, precious stones, and incense,—and by men thronging those temples in multitudes for social worship,—provided always that the inward devotion of the heart be there, to put a soul into these outward demonstrations and offerings.

7. Concerning these religious observances interior and exterior, it is as idle to pretend that they are *useful* to Almighty God as it is irrelevant to object that they are *useless* to Him. Of course they are useless to Him. All creation is useless to God. A Being who can never receive any profit, increment, or gain, dwells not within the region of utilities. Theologians indeed distinguish between intrinsic and extrinsic glory, that is, between the glory which God gives Himself by His own contemplation of

His own essence, and the glory which His creatures give Him. They say that God is thus capable of extrinsic increment, to which increment the praise and worship of His creatures is useful. But, after all, they are fain to avow that the whole of this extrinsic increment and glory is no real gain to God, giving Him nothing but what He had before in an infinitely more excellent mode and manner from and of Himself. Thus it appears that the extrinsic glory of God, to which the worship paid Him by man contributes, is valued, not because it is properly *useful to Him*, but because He is most properly and highly *worthy of it*. " Thou art worthy, O Lord our God, to receive glory and honour and power: because thou hast created all things, and for thy will they were, and have been created." (Apoc. iv. 11.) And being worthy of this glory, He wills to have it, and does most strictly exact it, for which reason He is called in the Scripture *a jealous God*. So those who reflect some sparkle of God's Majesty, and under some aspect represent His person upon the earth, as do princes, lay and ecclesiastical, have many observances of honour and respect paid to them, which are not *useful* as supplying a *need*—for who needs a salute of twenty-one guns ? nevertheless their dignity is *worthy* of them, and they require them accordingly.

8. What man feels strongly, he expresses in word and action. What all men feel strongly, they express by meeting together for the purpose. So that, if strong religious feeling is an element in every good and reasonable man's character, it is

bound to find expression, and that a social expression. Men must worship together according to some external form and ritual. God may reveal what He wills that ritual to be. In fact He did give such a revelation and prescription to the Jews. To Christians He has spoken in His Son, and still speaks in His Church. Any other than the one sacrifice that He has instituted, or any other public religious ritual than is approved by the religious authority which He has established, is to Him of itself, and apart from the invincibly erroneous devotion of them that pay it, an abomination: for He has "not chosen it." Still we cannot say that, in every possible state of things, God is bound to reveal the ritual that He desires, or is bound Himself to designate the authority that shall fix the ritual which alone He will accept and allow of. If the will of God is not thus expressed, a ritual must still be drawn up. In a matter that excites the mind, as religion does, and where a large field is open for hallucination and eccentricity, it will not do to have individuals parading methods of worship of their own invention. Here the Greek maxim comes in, τίμα τὸ δαιμόνιον κατὰ τὰ πάτρια, "honour the Deity after the fashion of thy country." Religious authorities must be set up, in the same way that the civil power is set up. These authorities will determine, not the object, but the outward manner of worship. Every great nation, or important member of the human family, would come probably to have its own characteristic rite; and within each rite there would be local varieties.

Readings.—St. Thos., *Contra Gentiles*, iii., 119 ;
2a 2æ, q. 81, art. 4, in corp.; *ib.*, q. 81, art. 7
ib., q. 84, art. 2 : *ib.*, q. 85, art. 1, in corp., ad 1, 3 ;
ib., q. 91.

Section II.—*Of Superstitious Practices.*

1. Superstition is the abuse of religion. It is
superstition, either to worship false gods, or to
worship the true God with unauthorized rites, or
to have dealings with wicked spirits, whether those
spirits have once animated human bodies or not.
Of the first head, the only avowed instance within
our civilization is the Positivist worship of the
Great Being, that is, of the collective Worthies of
Humanity, if indeed it amounts to worship. The
second head might have been meditated by Archbishop Cranmer with advantage, when he was
drawing up the Edwardine Ordinal. Under the
third head comes Spiritualism, which we shall
here not discuss in detail, but merely indicate certain
principles upon which it must be judged.

2. "There is nothing superstitious or unlawful
in simply applying natural agencies to the production of certain effects, of which they are supposed
to be naturally capable. . . . We must consider
whether there is a fair appearance of the cause
being able to produce the effect naturally. If there
is, the experiment will not be unlawful : for it is
lawful to use natural causes in order to their proper
effects." (2a 2æ, q. 96, art. 2, in corp., ad 1.) But
this we must understand under two provisos. First,
that the "fair appearance" spoken of be not opposed

by a considerable force of evidence, whether of authority or of reason, tending the other way: for in this matter, which is not a mere matter of legality, it is not permissible to run risks of becoming familiar with God's enemies. Secondly, that the cause, though natural, be not morally prejudicial. Not even a natural cause, brandy for instance, may be used to all its effects. Thus for the mesmeric sleep, though that should be proved to be purely natural, yet the weakening of the will thence ensuing, and the almost irresistible dominion acquired by the operator over his patient, render it imperative that such a remedy should not be applied without grave necessity, and under an operator of assured moral character.

3. St. Thomas continues in the place last quoted: "Wherefore, if there is no fair appearance of the causes employed being able to produce such effects, it needs must be that they are not employed to the causation of these effects as causes, but only as signs, and thus they come under the category of preconcerted signals arranged with evil spirits."

The modern Spiritualist is only too forward to avow his understanding with the unseen powers; but he will have it that the spirits that he deals with are good and harmless. We must prove the spirits by the general effects of their communications—whether they be in accordance with the known laws of morality, and the assured teachings of religion, natural and revealed. Also we must consider, from what we know from approved

sources concerning God, and His holy angels, and
the spirits of the just, either already made perfect,
or still suffering for a time, whether they are likely
to respond to such signs as Spiritualists commonly
employ.   Also we must not ignore, what revelation
tells us, of an "enemy," a "father of lies," who
"changes himself into an angel of light," and who
is ever ready, so far as it is permitted him, to eke
out curiosity, folly, and credulity, such as he found
in Eve.

   Readings.—St. Thos., 2a 2æ, q. 93; *ib.*, q. 95,
art. 4, in corp.

SECTION III.—*Of the duty of knowing God.*

   1. Religious worship is bound to its object, and
cannot possibly be fixed in the hearts of men and
the institutions of society, if the object be doubtful
and fluctuating.   False religion has often been set
off with elaborate and gorgeous ceremonial, which
has been kept up even after the performers had
come to see in all that light and lustre a mere vain
and unsubstantial show.   Such were the rites of
Roman polytheism, as enacted by augurs and
pontiffs, the colleagues of Cicero and Cæsar.   But
though that worship was maintained, and even
augmented, for political purposes, without a creed,
yet never could it have arisen without some creed,
however mistaken, earnestly held of old.   A firm
interior conviction is the starting-point of all
outward worship.   But if the modern living worshipper is without creed and conviction; if he be

a scoffer at heart, or at least a doubter; what a hollow, horrid skeleton thing is his religion,—all the more horrid, the grander its dress! That is not worship, but mummery.

2. If then to worship God is a duty, as we have proved, it is a duty likewise to know God. This supposes that God is knowable, a fact which it does not lie within the province of this work to prove. To an unknown God, all the worship we could render would be to build Him an altar, without priest, prayer, or sacrifice, and so leave Him in His solitude. God is knowable by the *manifestation* of His works (Rom. i. 19); and where He is pleased to speak, by the *revelation* of His word. Apart from revelation—and, under a certain order of Providence, God might have left us without revelation—we should study our Creator as He is made manifest in the world around us, in the existence of perishable things, in the order of the universe, in the region of things eternally possible and knowable, in moral truths, in the mental life and conscience of man. Philosophy would be our guide in the search after God. Men with less leisure or ability for specula-tion would acquiesce in the pronouncements of philosophers on things divine; and, in the hypo-thesis which we are contemplating, Providence would doubtless arrange for the better agreement and harmony of philosophers among themselves. Their trumpet would not send forth so uncertain a blast, were that the instrument, in the counsels of God, whereby the whole duty of religion was to be regulated. As it is, we know better than philo-

sophy could teach us: for God hath spoken in His Son.

Readings.—*C. Gent.*, i., 4 ; 1a 2æ, q. 91, art. 4, in corp.

CHAPTER II.

OF THE DUTY OF PRESERVING LIFE.

Section I.—*Of Killing, Direct and Indirect.*

1. In a hilly country, two or three steps sometimes measure all the interval between the basins of two rivers, whose mouths are miles apart. In the crisis of an illness the merest trifle will turn the scale between death and recovery. In a nice point of law and intricate procedure, the lawyer is aware that scarcely more than the thickness of the paper on which he writes lies between the case going for his client or for the opposite party. To rail at these fine technicalities argues a lay mind, unprofessional and undiscerning. *Hair-splitting*, so far as it is a term of real reproach, means splitting the wrong hairs. The expert in any profession knows what things to divide and distinguish finely, and what things to take in the gross. Moral Science in many respects gives its demonstrations. and can give them, only "in the way of rough drawing," as Aristotle says. (παχυλῶς καὶ τύπῳ, *Ethics*, I., iii., 4.) But there are lines of division exceeding fine and nice in natural morality no less than in positive law. The student must not take scandal at the fine lines and

subtle distinctions that we shall be obliged to draw
in marking off lawful from unlawful action touching
human life.

2. *It is never lawful directly to kill an innocent man.*
Understand *innocent* in the social and political sense,
of a man who has not, by any *human act* (*Ethics*, c. i.,
n. 2, p. 1) of his own, done any harm to society so
grievous as to compare with loss of life. To kill, or
work any other effect, *directly*, is to bring about that
death, or other effect, willing the same, *either as an
end desirable in itself*, as when a man slays his enemy,
whose death of its own sheer sake is to him a satisfaction and a joy, or *as a means to an end*, as Richard
III. murdered his nephews to open his own way to
the throne. We must then in no case compass the
death of the innocent, either *intending* it as an *end*,
or *choosing* it as a *means*. The assertion is proved
by these considerations. To kill a man is to destroy
the human nature within him : for, though the soul
survives, he is man no more when he is dead. Now
to destroy a thing is to subordinate that thing entirely
to your self and your own purposes : for that individual thing can never serve any other purpose, once
it is destroyed. The man that is killed is then sub-
ordinated to the slayer, wholly given up, and as we
say, *sacrificed*, to the aims and purposes of him who
slays him. But that ought not to be, for man is a
person. Body and soul in him make one person, one
personal nature, which *human personality* is destroyed
in death. Now it is the property of a person to be
what we may call *autocentric*, referring its own operations to itself as to a centre. Every *person*—and

every intelligent nature is a person*—exists and acts primarily for himself. A *thing* is marked off from a *person* by the aptitude of being another's and for another. We may venture to designate it by the term *heterocentric*. A person therefore may destroy a thing, entirely consume and use it up for his own benefit. But he may not treat a person as a thing, and destroy that, either for any end of pleasure that he finds in destroying it, or in view of any gain or good, whereunto that destruction serves him as a means.

3. In the above argumentation account has not been taken of God, to whom for His sovereign dominion all created personalities stand in the light of *things*, and may be destroyed at His pleasure. But account has been taken of the State, to which the individual is subordinate as a citizen, but not as a man and a person. It is permitted no more to the State than to the individual ever to destroy the innocent *directly*.

4. An effect is brought about *indirectly*, when it is neither *intended* as an *end* for its own sake, nor *chosen* as a *means* making towards an end, but attaches as a circumstance concomitant either to the end intended or to the means chosen. The case of a circumstance so attaching to the means chosen is the only case that we need consider here in speaking of *indirect*, *concomitant*, or *incidental* effects. The study of these incidents is of vast importance to the moralist. Most cases of practical difficulty to decide between right and wrong, arise out of them. They

* The exception apparent in the Incarnation is not relevant here.

are best illustrated in the manner of killing. That one matter, well worked out, becomes a pattern for other matters in which they occur. (*Ethics*, c. iii., s. ii., p. 31.)

5. A man is killed *indirectly*, or *incidentally*, when he perishes in consequence of certain means employed towards a certain end, without his death being willed by the employer of those means, or in any way serving that agent to the furtherance of the end that he has in view. If a visitor to a quarry were standing on a piece of rock, which a quarryman had occasion to blast, and the man fired the train regardless of the visitor, the latter would be *incidentally* killed. Now incidental killing, even of the innocent, is not under all circumstances unlawful. Where the end in view is in the highest degree important, the means may be taken thereto, provided always that such an issue as the shedding of innocent blood be not itself the means discerned and elected as furthering the end: for no end however urgent can justify the employment of any evil means. (*Ethics*, c. iii., s. ii., nn. 3, 13, pp. 32, 36.) Suppose in the instance just given the quarryman saw that, unless that piece of rock where the visitor stood were blown up instantly, a catastrophe would happen elsewhere, which would be the death of many men, and there were no time to warn the visitor to clear off, who could blame him if he applied the explosive? The means of averting the catastrophe would be, not that visitor's death, but the blowing up of the rock. The presence or absence of the visitor, his death or escape, is all one to the end intended: it has no bearing thereon at all.

6. We must then distinguish between *means* and

circumstances. The means help to the end, the circumstances of the means do not. When the end is
of extreme urgency, circumstances may be disre-
garded : the means become morally divested of them.
So I have seen an island in a river, a nucleus of rock
with an environment of alluvial soil. While the
stream was flowing placidly in its usual course, the
island remained intact, both rock and earth. But
when the water came rushing in a flood, which was
as though the island itself had gone speeding up the
river, the loose matter at its sides was carried away,
and only the central rock remained. The ordinary
flow of the river past the island, or the gentle motion
of the island up-stream, keeping all its bulk, represents a man acting for an end to which reason
attaches no great importance. He must then take
a diligent review of all the circumstances that have
any close connection with his action, to see if there
is any that it would be wrong for him to will directly.
And if there is, he must abstain from willing it even
indirectly : that is, he must abstain from doing the
action, which cannot be done without that objectionable circumstance attending it. On the other hand,
the floating island being towed rapidly up-stream,
with its loose sides falling away, portrays the condition of one acting for a purpose of imperative
urgency : he considers the means to that end, and
if they are good, he concentrates his will upon them
and uses them, disregarding, or even deploring, but
nowise willing or being responsible for, the evil con-
comitants which go with those means, but do not
make for his end. Thus it is, that a circumstance

which in ordinary cases goes to make the adoption
of certain means reasonable or unreasonable, comes,
in a case of great urgency, to weigh for nothing in
the balance of reason, owing to the extreme and
crying reasonableness of the end in view. Nor is
this the end justifying the means, for that unhappy
circumstance is never a means to the end. (*Ethics,*
c. iii., s. ii., n. 8, p. 34.)

7. To illustrate by a diagram:

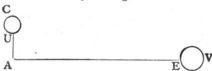

A, the *agent,* a bead on a wire, can move only on
the line A E, that alone being the line of means to
the end.

E V, *reasonableness of end in view,* attracting A.

U C, the amount of moral evil which the *untoward circumstance* would involve, if it were willed
directly. This U C repels A, tending to jam it on
the line A E, which is absolutely rigid.

A E, remoteness, difficulty, and uncertainty of
the end in view.

A U, remoteness of untoward circumstance from
means chosen, which A is just in the act of taking.
Then, for lawful action, the reasonableness required
in the end in view is represented by the variation—

$$EV \propto \frac{UC \cdot AE}{AU}$$

We observe that when AU is zero, while UC . AE
remains a finite quantity (representing an appre-
ciable evil), then EV becomes infinite: that is to

say, when the distance, difference, or distinction between the evil circumstance and the means comes down to nothing at all, and the evil thing actually is the very means taken, then an infinite urgency of end in view would be requisite to justify the using of that means: in other words, no end possible to man can ever justify an evil means.

Readings.—St. Thos., 2a 2æ, q. 64, art. 6; Cardinal de Lugo, *De Justitia et Jure*, disp. 10, n. 125.

SECTION II.—*Of Killing done Indirectly in Self-defence.*

1. On the question, whether it is lawful for one man to kill another in self-defence, St. Thomas writes (2a 2æ, q. 64, art. 7) :

" There is nothing to hinder one act having two effects, of which one only is within the intention [and election] of the doer, while the other is beside his intention [and election, that is, is neither intended as an end nor elected as a means]. . . . From the act therefore of one defending himself a twofold effect may follow, one the preservation of his own life, the other the killing of the aggressor. Now such an act, in so far as the preservation of the doer's own life is intended, has no taint of evil about it, seeing that it is natural to everything to preserve itself in being as much as it can. Nevertheless, an act coming of a good intention may be rendered unlawful, if it be not in proportion to the end in view. And therefore, if any one uses greater violence than is necessary for the defence of his life, it will be unlawful. But if he repels the violence in a moderate way, it will be a lawful defence : for according to the Civil and

Canon Laws it is allowable *to repel force by force with the moderation of a blameless defence.* Nor is it necessary to salvation for a man to omit the act of moderate defence in order to avoid the killing of another; because man is more bound to take thought for his own life than for the life of his neighbour. But because to kill a man is not allowable except by act of public authority for the common good, it is unlawful for a man to intend [that is, elect and choose as a means] to kill another man in order to defend himself, unless he be one who has public authority, who intending [electing] to kill a man in order to his own defence, refers this to the public good."

2. The right then of self-defence even to the shedding of blood involves a mere exercise of indirect killing for a proportionably grave cause. The cause in question is the defence of your own life, or your friend's, or of some other good or possession that can weigh with life, as the honour and inviolability of your person, or a large sum of money. This must be in present danger of being taken away otherwise than in due course of justice. The danger must be present, and even imminent, not prospective. The right of self-defence even to the grievous harming of the aggressor, endures only while the danger from him is imminent, not when it is past, or the evil is already done. The right supposes no moral obliquity, no formal injustice on the part of the aggressor: he may be a madman making for you with a drawn sword. Nay further, not even *material injustice*—that is, the quality of an act which would be *formally* unjust, if only the agent knew what he

o

was about—is required.   All that is requisite is that your life, or something equivalent to life, be threatened, *not in due course of law*.

3. The essential idea of self-defence is that of stopping a trespasser, one who, however innocently, is going about to trench on that good which you have a right to maintain and reserve to yourself.   It is then no act of authority that you perform, but the dealing of one private person with another.   Indeed, the party stopped is hardly regarded as a person: no account is taken of his demerits: he is regarded simply as an abridger and diminisher of what you have a right to preserve intact.   You stop a man as you stop a horse, only with more regard to *the moderation of a blameless self-defence*, not using more violence than is necessary here and now to preserve what you have to preserve.

4. The stopping, unfortunately, has often to be done in a hurry: there is no time to wait: for the next moment, unless you act promptly, it will be all too late, or all to no purpose, to act at all.   Being done in a hurry, it has to be done in a rough-and-ready way, with such instruments as are to hand: you cannot afford to be nice about the means, carefully purifying them, and shaking off the dust of objectionable circumstances.   Now to stop a man in mid career all on a sudden, to render him powerless where he was about to strike, motionless in the direction whither he was about to go, and that in an instant, is of common necessity a rude treatment, very dangerous to him who experiences it, and under some conceivable circumstances hopelessly fatal.

Still the fatality—in plain words, the death of the aggressor—is not *directly willed*. It is neither *intended* as an *end*, nor *chosen* as a *means to an end*. It is not welcomed as an end and desirable consummation : on the contrary, it is put up with most reluctantly as coming from your act : for you, a private individual, have no right to will and effect the death of any man, however guilty, as will be proved hereafter. It is not chosen as a means : for, formally as his death, it is no means to your end, which was the averting of all present danger to your right. For that it was enough to *stop* the trespasser ; and you chose the means as a *stopping* means, not as a *killing* means. True, in stopping him you killed him, but you did not kill him to stop him. You struck him to stop him : that your blow was a mortal blow, was a circumstance which you did not choose and could not help. All killing then in self-defence is indirect.

5. By this explanation, resting on St. Thomas—in opposition to Cardinal de Lugo (*De Just. et Jure*. 10, 149) and others, who allow killing in self-defence to be the actual means chosen, and therefore directly willed —we save four grand positions in Moral Science :

(*a*) The axiom, that *it is never lawful directly to take the life of an innocent man*. For the person who perishes by occasion of your defending yourself, may be innocent *formally*, and even *materially* also.

(*b*) Likewise the axiom, that *it is never lawful for a private individual to kill any one whatever*. We say, from a technical standpoint, that he does not *kill* but *arrests the onset of* the aggressor.

(c) We are in hearty accord with the positive law of all civilized countries, which views with extreme suspicion all deaths said to be done in self-defence, the law being jealous of the blood of its citizens, and reserving the shedding thereof to itself. We teach that only by process of law can a man ever be directly slain, his death made a means of, and the person, who strikes him, really willing and seeking, exactly speaking, to kill him.

(d) The initial error is revealed of a theory that we shall have to combat at length hereafter, the theory of Hobbes and Locke, that the power of the State is the mere agglomeration of the powers of the individuals who compose it. It appears by our explanation that the individual has no power strictly to take life in any case, or ever to kill directly, as the State does when it executes a criminal.

As a fifth point gained, we may mention the efficacious argument afforded, as will presently be shown, against the acceptance of a duel under any conceivable circumstances, a thesis otherwise not easy to establish by reason.

6. In view of the question of the origin of civil government, we must carefully collect the differences between self-defence and punishment. Death occasioned in self-defence is *indirect*: death inflicted as punishment is *direct*. Punishment is an act of *authority*, of *distributive justice*, which lies from ruler to subject (*Ethics*, c. v., s. ix., n. 4, p.104): self-defence is of equal against equal. Punishment is *medicinal* to him who suffers it, or *deterrent* on behalf of the com

munity, or *retributive* in the way of vengeance. (*Ethics*, c. ix., s. iii., n. 4.) Self-defence is not on behalf of the community, still less for the good of the aggressor, but for the good of him who practises it and for the preservation of his right : neither is it retributive and retrospective, as vengeance is, but simply prospective and preventive of a harm immediately imminent. Finally, the right to punish abides day and night : but the right of self-defence holds only while instant aggression is threatened.

7. These two diverse ideas of *self-defence* and *vengeance* were confounded by the Greeks under the one verb ἀμύνεσθαι. They are confounded by Mill, *On Utility*, in the fifth chapter where he speaks (p. 77) of the "instinct of self-defence," which nine lines below he converts into "the natural feeling of retaliation or vengeance." It is a common but a grave mistake, and the parent of much bad philosophy.

Readings.—St. Thos., 2a 2æ, q. 64, art. **7.**

Section III.—*Of Suicide.*

1. By suicide we shall here understand the *direct compassing of one's own death*, which is an act never lawful. There is no difficulty in seeing the unlawfulness of suicide for ordinary cases. The world could not go on, if men were to kill themselves upon every slight disappointment. But neither are they likely so to do. It is the hard cases, where men are apt to lay violent hands on themselves, that put the moralist on his mettle to restrain them by reasons. Why should not the solitary invalid destroy himself, he whose life has become a hopeless torture, and

whose death none would mourn? Why should not
a voluntary death be sought as an escape from temptation and from imminent sin? Why should not the
first victims of a dire contagion acquiesce in being
slaughtered like cattle? Or if it be deemed perilous
to commit the departure from life to each one's
private whim and fancy, why not have the thing
licensed under certificate of three clergymen and
four doctors, who could testify that it is done on
good grounds?

2. To all these questions there is one good answer
returned by Paley on the principle of General Consequences. (*Ethics*, c. x., n. 3, p. 178.)

"The true question of this argument is no other
than this: May every man who chooses to destroy
his life, innocently do so? Limit and distinguish
the subject as you can, it will come at last to this
question. For, shall we say that we are then at
liberty to commit suicide, when we find our continuance in life becomes useless to mankind? Any
one who pleases, may make himself useless; and
melancholy minds are prone to think themselves
useless when they really are not so. . . . In like
manner, whatever other rule you assign, it will ultimately bring us to an indiscriminate toleration of
suicide, in all cases in which there is danger of its
being committed. It remains, therefore, to enquire
what would be the effect of such a toleration: evidently, the loss of many lives to the community, of
which some might be useful or important; the affliction of many families, and the consternation of all:
for mankind must live in continual alarm for the fate

of their friends, when every disgust which is powerful enough to tempt men to suicide, shall be deemed
sufficient to justify it." (*Moral Philosophy*, bk. iv.,
c. iii.)

A word in confirmation of Paley on the plan of
the medico-clerical certificate. There would be
doctors, and I fear clergymen too, who would get a
name for giving these certificates easily : under their
hand many a patient might be smothered by his
attendants with or without his own consent. Many
another wretch would consider, that if the learned
and reverend gentlemen empowered to license his
departure from life only felt what he had to endure,
there would be no difficulty about the certificate : so
he would depart on presumed leave. The whole
effect would be to make men less tender of their
own lives, and by consequence of those of others, to
the vast unsettling of society.

3. An argument from general consequences, however, does not go down into the depths of things.
There is always something morally crooked and inordinate in an action itself, the general consequences
whereof are bad. It remains to point out the moral
crookedness, inordination, and unreasonableness,
that is intrinsic to the act of suicide, apart from its
consequences. We find the inordination in this,
that suicide is an act falling upon undue matter,
being an act destructive of that which the agent has
power over only to preserve. It is natural to every
being, animate and inanimate, to the full extent of its
entity and power, to maintain itself, and to resist
destruction as long as it can. This is the struggle

for existence, one of the primary laws of nature. Man has intelligence and power over himself, that he may conduct his own struggle well and wisely. He may struggle more or less, as he sees expedient, looking to higher goods even than self-preservation in this mortal life: but he may not take that power of managing himself, which nature invests him with for his preservation, and use it to his own destruction. Should he do so, he perverts the natural order of his own being, and thereby sins. (*Ethics*, c. vi., s. i., nn. 1—5, p. 109.)

4. It may be objected, that man is only bound to self-preservation so long as life is a blessing; that, when the scale of death far outweighs that of life in desirableness, it is cruelty to himself to preserve his life any longer, and a kindness to himself to destroy it; that in such a plight, accordingly, it is not unnatural for a man to put himself, not so much out of life as out of misery. To this argument it is sometimes answered that, whereas death is the greatest of evils, it is foolish and wicked to resort to dying as a refuge against any other calamity. But this answer proves too much. It would show that it is never lawful even to wish for death: whereas under many conditions, such as those now under consideration, death is a consummation devoutly to be wished, and may be most piously desired, as a gain and by comparison a good: as Ecclesiasticus says (xxx. 17): "Better is death than a bitter life, and everlasting rest than continual sickness." The truth seems to be, that there are many things highly good and desirable in themselves, which become evil

when compassed in a particular way. The death of a great tyrant or persecutor may be a blessing to the universe, but his death by the hand of an assassin is an intolerable evil. So is death, as the schoolmen say, *in facto esse,* and everlasting rest, better than a bitter life, but not death *in fieri,* when that means dying by your own hand. There the unnaturalness comes in and the irrationality. A mother, watching the death agony of her son, may piously wish it over : but it were an unmotherly act to lay her own hand on his mouth and smother him. To lay violent hands on oneself is abidingly cruel and unnatural, more so than if the suicide's own mother slew him.

5. But though a man may not use actual violence against his own person, may he not perhaps cease to preserve himself, abstain from food, as the Roman noble did, in the tortures of the gout, and by abstaining end them ? I answer, a man's taking food periodically is as much part of his life as the coursing of the blood in his veins. It is doing himself no less violence to refuse food ready to hand, when he is starving, on purpose that he may starve, than to open a vein on purpose to bleed to death. This, when the food is readily accessible : the case is otherwise when it is not procurable except by extraordinary means.

6. Another consideration. To destroy a thing is the exclusive right of the owner and master of the same. If therefore man is his own master, in the sense that no one else can claim dominion over him, may he not accordingly destroy himself ? The metaphysician will point out that *master* denotes a

relation, that every relation has two terms, that consequently a man cannot be his own master any more than he can be his own father; and that, not owning himself, he may not destroy himself. But, leaving this metaphysical argument for what it is worth, we observe that man has a Master, Owner, Proprietor, and Sovereign Lord, God Almighty. To take your own life is to usurp the dominion of God. It is wronging the Lord of life and death. But none is wronged against his will: God is willing that murderers should be hung, may He not also be willing that men in misery should hang themselves? To this query suffice it for the present to reply, that God governs us for our good; and that capital punishment makes for the good of the community, but never suicide. (c. viii., s. viii., n. 7, p. 349.)

7. It was the doctrine of Aristotle and the Greeks, that the citizen belongs to the State, and that therefore suicide was robbing the State and doing it a formal injury. But no modern State takes this view of its subjects. No modern mind would place suicide in the same category of crime with robbing the Exchequer.

8. The great deterrent against suicide, in cases where misery meets with recklessness, is the thought,

In that sleep of death what dreams may come!—

above all, the fear of being confronted with an angry God. Away from belief in God's judgments and a future state, our arguments against suicide may be good logic, but they make poor rhetoric for those

who need them most. Men are wonderfully imita-
tive in killing themselves. Once the practice is
come in vogue, it becomes a rage, an epidemic.
Atheism and Materialism form the best *nidus* for
the contagion of suicide. It is a shrewd remark
of Madame de Stael: "Though there are crimes of
a darker hue than suicide, yet there is none other
by which man seems so entirely to renounce the
protection of God."

Readings.—Ar., *Eth.*, III., vii., 13; *ib.*, V., xi.,
nn. 1—3; St. Thos., 2a 2æ, q. 64, art. 5; St. Aug.,
De Civitate Dei, i., cc. 26, 27; Paley, *Mor. Phil.*,
bk. iv., c. iii.

Section IV.—*Of Duelling.*

1. A duel may be defined: A meeting of two
parties by private agreement to fight with weapons
in themselves deadly. The meeting must be *by
agreement:* a chance meeting of Montagues and
Capulets, where the parties improvise a fight on the
spot is not a duel. The agreement must be *private :*
anything arranged by public authority, as the encounter of David with Goliath, that in the legend
of the Horatii and Curiatii, or the *wager of battle*
in the Middle Ages is not a duel. It is enough that
the weapons be *in themselves deadly*, as swords or
pistols, though there be an express stipulation not
to kill: but a pre-arranged encounter with fists, with
foils with buttons on, or even perhaps with crab-
sticks, is not a duel.

2. The hard case in duelling is the case of him
who receives the challenge. Let us make the

case as hard as possible. In a certain army,
every challenge sent to an officer is reported to
a Court of Honour. If the Court decide that it
ought to be accepted, accept the officer must, or
lose his commission and all hope of military distinction. In this army, say, there is an officer of
high promise who is believed to object to duels
on conscientious grounds. An enemy pretends to
have been insulted, and challenges him, on purpose
to see him refuse and have to go down into the
ranks, his career spoilt. The Court of Honour
rules that the duel must come off. Of this very
case, Reiffenstuel, a canonist of repute, about the
year 1700, writes:

"The answer is, . . . that they who in such cases
are so necessitated and constrained to offer, or
accept, a duel, as that unless they offered, or accepted
it, they would be held cowardly, craven, mean, and
unfit to bear office in the army, and consequently
would be deprived of the office that they actually
enjoy, and support themselves and their family by,
or would for ever forfeit all hope of promotion,
otherwise their due and desert,—these I say in
such a case are free from all fault and penalty,
whether they offer or accept a duel." (In lib. v.
decret., tit. 14, nn. 30, 31.)

The author protests in his Preface that he
wishes his opinions "all and each to be subject to
the judgment, censure, and correction of the Holy
Catholic Church." The opinion above quoted was
condemned, word for word as it was uttered, by
Pope Benedict XIV. in 1752.

Now for Reiffenstuel's reason. "The reason," he says, "is, because in such a case as is supposed the acceptance and offering of a duel is an absolutely necessary, and thereby a just and lawful, defence of your reputation, or goods of fortune, and, by equivalence, even of your life, against an unjust aggressor, who we suppose does you an injury, and thereby gives you no choice but to call him out, or calls you out, and accordingly assails you in words, &c. Hence, as for the needful defence of reputation, or of goods of fortune of great consequence, it is lawful, with the moderation of a blameless defence, to kill an unjust aggressor, so it will be also lawful to offer and accept a duel, and therein slay the other party." Reiffenstuel here evidently supposes that killing done in self-defence is *direct*. Those who agree with him on that point, proceed to draw differences between self-defence and accepting a challenge. Of course the two are not the same. The true difficulty for them lies in making out how the reasons which justify self-defence in their view of it, do not also justify the acceptance of a duel : how, if I may make another man's death a *means* to the preservation of my vital right, I may not as well make another man's risk of death and my own, which is all that a duel amounts to, also a *means*, none other being at hand, to the preserving of my no less vital right. This grave objection does not touch us. We have denied that killing in self-defence is direct. On the lines of that denial we meet Reiffenstuel's argument simply as follows.

3. In self-defence, the aggressor is slain *indirectly*

In a duel, not indeed the death itself, or mutual slaughter of the combatants, is *directly* willed, but the risk of mutual slaughter is directly willed. But we may not directly will the risk of that which we may not directly do. And the combatants may not directly do themselves or one another to death. Therefore they may not directly risk each his own and his antagonist's life. But this risk is of the essence of a duel. Therefore duelling is essentially unlawful.

4. Such is the clenched fist, so to speak, of our argument. Now to open it out, and prove in detail the several members. In self-defence, neither the death of the aggressor nor the risk of his death is directly willed, whereas the risk of death is directly willed in a duel, which difference entirely bars the argument from self-defence to duelling. For a duel is a means of recovering and preserving honour, which is effected by a display of fortitude, which again consists in exposing yourself to the risk of being killed, and, as part of the bargain, of killing the other man. The risk to life is of the essence of a duel: it only attains its end— of establishing a man's character for courage—by being dangerous to life. Fortitude essentially consists in braving death. (*Ethics*, c. v., s. viii., n. 1, p. 94.) Deadly weapons, chosen because they are deadly and involve a risk of life in fighting with such arms, are the apt and express means for showing readiness to brave death. If the weapons were not deadly, there would be no point in the duel. As a matter of fact, where our definition of duel is veri-

fied, and weapons in themselves deadly are used, the encounter cannot be other than dangerous, especially between foes and where the blood is up. In the French army, where the regimental fencing-master stands by, sword in hand, ready to parry any too dangerous thrust, serious results still have occurred. If any man will have it that short smooth-bore pistols at forty paces in a fog are not to be counted dangerous weapons, all we can say is that MM. Gambetta and De Fourton, the one being nearly blind, and the other having lost an eye, did not fight a duel. In a duel then the danger of being killed and of killing is *directly* willed; it is the precise *means chosen* to the end in view.

5. We have proved already that it is not lawful directly to procure one's own death, nor the death of another innocent man. If any one contends that his antagonist is not innocent, not even in a *political* sense (c. ii., s. i., n. 2, p. 203), we must here assume against him, what we shall afterwards prove, that the guilty are not to be *directly* put to death except by public authority. But what we may not directly bring about, we may not directly risk the occurrence of. As I may not throw myself down a cliff, so neither may I walk along the edge precisely for the chance of a fall. I may often walk there *with* the chance of falling, but not *because* of the chance. It will be said that the English love of fox-hunting and Alpine climbing is largely owing to the element of danger present in those amusements. But it is not the danger pure and simple, that is chosen for amusement: it is the prospect of overcoming

danger by skill.   The same may be said of Blondin
on the tight-rope : it was his skill, not his mere risk,
that was admired.   There are some risks that no
skill can obviate, as those of Alpine avalanches.
We may face a mountain slope where avalanches
occur, but we must not hang about there because of
the avalanches, making our amusement or bravado
of the chance of being killed.   That would be
willing the risk of death *directly,* as it is willed in
duelling.

Readings.—Paley, *Mor. Phil.,* bk. iii., p. 2, c. ix.;
St. Thos., 2a 2æ, q. 72, art. 3.

CHAPTER III.

OF SPEAKING THE TRUTH.

SECTION I.—*Of the Definition of a Lie.*

1. " LET none doubt," says St. Augustine, "that he
lies, who utters what is false for the purpose of
deceiving.   Wherefore the utterance of what is false
with a will to deceive is unquestionably a lie."   The
only question is, whether this definition does not
contain more than is necessary to the thing defined.
The objective falseness of what is said makes a *material* falsehood : the will to utter what is false makes
a *formal* falsehood (*Ethics,* c. iii., s. ii., n. 7, p. 33) :
the will to create a false impression regards, not the
falsehood itself, but the effect to follow from it.   If
a person says what is not true, but what he takes to

be the truth, he tells indeed a material lie, but at the same time he puts forth no *human act* (*Ethics,* c. i., n. 2, p. 1) of lying. If on the other hand he says what he believes to be false, though it turns out true, he tells a formal lie, though not a material one, and moreover, he does a *human act* of lying. But *human acts* are the subject-matter of morality. The moralist therefore is content to define the *formal lie :* the *material* aspect of the lie is irrelevant to his enquiry. A formal lie is saying what one believes not to be true, or promising what one intends not to perform : briefly, it is *speaking against one's mind.*

2. We shall show presently that to speak against one's mind is intrinsically, necessarily, and always evil. But when a thing is thus evil in itself, there is no need to bring into the definition of the act, from a moral point of view, the intention with which it is done. There is no use in prying into ends, when the means taken is an unlawful means for any end. If a person blasphemes, we do not ask why he blasphemes : the intention is not part of the blasphemy : the utterance is a sin by itself. But if a person strikes, we ask why he strikes, to heal or to slay, in self-defence or in revenge. So, if speaking against one's mind is a thing indifferent and colourless in point of morality, and all depends on the intention with which we do it, so that we may speak against our minds to put another off, but not to deceive him, then certainly the intention to deceive must be imported into the definition of lying. But if, as we shall prove presently, the act

P

of so speaking is by no means indifferent and colour-less, but is fraught with an inordinateness all its own, then the intention may be left out of the ques-tion, the act is to be characterised on its own merits, and *speech against one's mind* is the definition of a lie.

3. Then, some one will say, it would be a lie for a prisoner in solitary confinement to break the silence of his cell with the exclamation, *Queen Anne is not dead.* The answer is simple: it takes two to make a speech. A man does not properly speak to himself, nor quarrel with himself, nor deal justly by himself. Not that it would be a lie to deny the death of Queen Anne even in public: for speech is an outward affirmation, the appearance of a serious will to apply predicate to subject: but in this case there is no appearance of a serious will: on the contrary, from the manifest absurdity of the asser-tion, it is plain that you are joking and do not mean to affirm anything. This perhaps is as far as we can go in permission of what are called *lies in jest.*

Readings.—St Thos., 2a 2æ, q. 110, art. 1.

SECTION II.—*Of the Evil of Lying.*

1. Human society cannot go on, if men are to be allowed indiscriminately to lie to one another. Thucydides (iii., 83) gives as the reason of the ex-travagant length to which faction ran in Greece in his time: "For there was no power to reconcile the parties, no plighted word reliable, no oath held in awe." Even in trifles no one likes to be lied to, and we are not to do to our neighbour what we would

not have done to ourselves. The laws of good fellowship require that we should " put away lying, and speak the truth every man with his neighbour : for we are members one of another." (Ephesians iv. 25.) This at least in ordinary circumstances. The same good fellowship requires that in ordinary circumstances we should respect the lives and property of our fellow-men.

2. But it is lawful to take life in pursuance of the just judgment of authority : it is lawful to seize upon property in self-preservation. These exceptions stand very harmoniously with the well-being of society, or rather are required by it, as we shall see later on. The law against lying, so far as it is founded on the general prejudice done to society by the shock of social confidence, and on the particular annoyance of the party lied to, may seem to admit of similar exceptions. Whoever has no reasonable objection to having life and property taken from him in certain contingencies, can he reasonably complain of any hurt or inconvenience that he may suffer from a lie being told him at times ?

3. I put forward this difficulty, not as though it were without its answer in the principle of General Consequences : still it is a difficulty. Besides, if the whole harm of lying is in the unpleasant effect wrought upon the deceived hearer, and the scandal and bad consequences to society at large, it is a long way to go round to show that lying is impossible to God. He in whose dominion are all the rights and claims of man, is not to be restrained by

the mere reluctance of His creatures to be deceived, or by the general bad effects of a lie upon the edifice of human credit. As Master He might impose this annoyance upon the individual, these bad consequences upon society : or by His Providence He might prevent their occurring, whenever He willed in His utterances to swerve from the truth. The only help for the argument for the Divine veracity on these grounds, is to urge with Plato that none of the motives which lead men to lie can ever find place in the mind of God : that a lie is a subterfuge, an economy, a device resorted to under stress of circumstances, such as can never serve the turn of the Supreme Being. But though God be inaccessible to human reasons for departing from the truth, may He not have higher reasons, mysterious, and unsearchable, for such a deviation ? It is long arguing out this point. Better bring the discussion sharp round with the question : Is there not some element in the Divine Nature itself, which makes it impossible for God to speak false ?

4. Undoubtedly there is such an element, deep down, even at the root of the sanctity of God. God is holy in that, being by essence the fulness of all being and all goodness, He is ever true to Himself in every act of His understanding, of His will, and of His power. By His understanding He abidingly covers, grasps, and comprehends His whole Being. With His will He loves Himself supremely. His power is exercised entirely for His glory—entirely, but not exclusively, for God's last and best external glory is in the consummated happiness of His

creatures. Whatever God makes, He makes in His
own likeness, more or less so according to the degree
of being which He imparts to the creature. And as
whatever God does is like Him, and whatever God
makes is like Him, so whatever God says is like
Him: His spoken word answers to His inward
word and thought. It holds of God as of every
being who has a thought to think and a word to
utter:

> To thine own self be true,
> And it must follow as the night the day,
> Thou canst not then be false to any man.

5. God's sanctity is in His being true to Himself.
His veracity is part of His sanctity. He cannot in
His speech, or revelation of Himself, contradict
what He really has in His mind, without ceasing to
be holy and being no longer God. But the sanctity
of intellectual creatures must be, like their every
other pure perfection, modelled on the corresponding
perfection of their Maker. Holiness must mean
truthfulness in man, for it means truthfulness in
God. God's words cannot be at variance with His
thought, for God is essential holiness. Nor can
man speak otherwise than as he thinks without
marring the attribute of holiness in himself, that is,
without doing wrong.

6. To speak against one's mind is an act falling
upon undue matter. Words are naturally signs of
thoughts. Not that the words of any given language,
as English or German, have any natural connection
with the thoughts that they express; but it is natural
to men, natural to every intellectual being, to have

some mode of expressing his thoughts by outward signs; and once a sign is recognized as the sign of a certain thought, so long as the convention remains unrepealed, whoever uses that sign, not having in his mind at the time the thought which that sign signifies, but the contradictory to it, is doing violence to the natural bond between sign and thing signified, by putting forward the former where the latter is not behind it.   And since the due and proper matter for the sign to be put upon is the presence in the mind of the thought signified, to make that sign where the opposite thought is present, is, as St. Thomas says, an act falling upon undue matter. The peculiar spiritual and moral inviolability of the connection between word and thought, appears from the consideration which we have urged of the arche-type holiness of God.   This then is the real, in-trinsic, primary, and inseparable reason, why lying, or speech in contradiction with the thought of the speaker, is everywhere and always wrong.

7. Grotius (*De Jure Belli et Pacis*, l. iii., c. i., nn. 11, seq.) argues a lie to be wrong solely inasmuch as it is " in conflict with the existing and abiding right of the person spoken to."   If *right* here means some-thing binding in *commutative justice* (*Ethics*, c. v., s. ix., n. 6, p. 106), we deny that any such right is violated by what is called a *simple* lie, that is, an untruth not in the matter of religion, and not affecting the character, property, or personal well-being of our neighbour. For if a simple lie is a violation of commutative justice, it carries the obligation of restitution (*Ethics*, c. v., s. ix., n. 6, p. 107); that is, we are bound to tell the

truth afterwards to the person that we have lied to,
even in a matter of no practical consequence,—quite
a new burden on the consciences of men. Again, if
the bar to lying were the hearer's right, whoever
had dominion over another's right might lie to him;
the parent might lie to the child, the State to the
citizen, and God to man, a doctrine which, away
from its application to God, Grotius accepts. Lastly
since *volenti non fit injuria*, the presumed willingness
of the listener would license all manner of officious
and jocose lies, as the authority of the speaker
would sanction official fabrications. Thus, what
with official, and what with officious speeches, it
would be very hard to believe anybody.

8. By our rejection of Grotius' theory we are
enabled to answer Milton's question : " If all killing
be not murder, nor all taking from another, stealing
why must all untruths be lies ? " Because, we say,
killing and taking away of goods deal with rights
which are not absolute and unlimited, but become
in certain situations void ; whereas an untruth turns,
not on another's right, but on the exigency of the
speaker's own rational nature calling for the concord
of the word signifying with the thought signified,
and this exigency never varies. *Untruth* and *falsehood* are but polite names for a *lie*.

Readings.—St. Thos., 2a 2æ, q. 110, art. 3, in
corp., ad. 4 ; *ib.*, q. 109, art. 2, 3, in corp. ; Ar., *Eth.*,
IV., vii. ; Plato, *Rep.*, 382, 389 B, C.

SECTION III.—*Of the keeping of Secrets without Lying.*

1. There are *natural* secrets, secrets of *promise,* and secrets of *trust.* A *natural* secret is all a man's own private history, which he would not have made public, as also all that he discovers by his own observation of the similar private history of his neighbours. If a man finds out something about his neighbour, and, after he has found it out for himself, the neighbour gets him to promise not to publish it, that is a secret of *promise.* Lastly, if one man comes to another, as to a lawyer, or a surgeon, for professional advice, or simply to a friend for moral counsel, and in order thereto imparts to him some of his natural secrets, those secrets, as they are received and held by the person consulted, are called secrets of *trust.* This latter kind of secret is privileged above the other two. A natural secret, and also a secret of promise, must be delivered up on the demand of an authority competent to inquire in the department where the secret lies. But a secret of trust is to be given up to no inquirer, but to be kept against all who endeavour to come by it, except where the matter bodes mischief and wrong to a third party, or to the community, and where at the same time the owner of the secret cannot be persuaded to desist from the wrong. This proviso does not hold for the *seal of confession,* which is absolutely inviolable.

2. The main art of keeping a secret is, not to talk about it. If a man is asked an awkward question, and sees no alternative but to let out or lie, it

is usually his own fault for having introduced the subject, or encouraged the questioner up to that point. A wise man lets drop in time topics which he is unwilling to have pressed. But there are unconscionable people who will not be put off, and who, either out of malice or out of stupidity, ply you with questions against all rules of good breeding. This direct assault may sometimes be retaliated, and a rude question met by a curt answer. But such a reply is not always prudent or charitable, and would not unfrequently convey the very information required. Silence would serve no better, for silence gives consent, and is eloquent at times. There is nothing left for it in such cases but to lock your secret up, as it were, in a separate compartment of your breast, and answer according to the remainder of your information, which is not secret, private, and confidential. This looks very much like lying, but it is not lying, it is speaking the truth under a *broad mental reservation.*

3. *Mental reservation* is an act of the mind, limiting the spoken phrase so that it may not bear the full sense which at first hearing it seems to bear. The reservation, or limitation of the spoken sense, is said to be *broad* or *pure*, according as it is, or is not, indicated externally. A *pure mental reservation*, where the speaker uses words in a limited meaning, without giving any outward clue to the limitation, is in nothing different from a lie, and is wrong as a lie is always wrong. A good instance is Archbishop Cranmer's oath of fealty to the Pope, he having previously protested—of course out of hearing of

the Pope or the Pope's representative—that he meant that oath in no way to preclude him from labouring at the reformation of the Church in England, that is, doing all the evil work which Henry VIII. had marked out for him in the teeth of the Roman Bishop.* Even *broad mental reservation* is permissible only as a last resource, when no other means are available for the preservation of some secret which one has a duty to others, or grave reason of one's own, to keep.

4. The point to make out is that no lie is told. To speak under a reservation is a lie, if it is speech against the mind of the speaker. But how can it be aught else than speech against the mind, when the heart thinks *yea*, and the tongue says *nay* ? We answer that, in the case contemplated, the thought of the heart is, *secrets apart*, *nay*; and though the word on the lips is *nay* simply, yet we must not take that word as the whole locution, but as a mere text, to which the situation of the speaker and the matter spoken of form a commentary, legible to any observant eye. The word is an *annotated text; nay* in the body of the page, with *secrets apart* inscribed in the margin. The adequate utterance is the whole page, text and gloss together; that speech answers to the thought in the speaker's mind; therefore it is no lie.

5. The essential requisite is that the gloss, *secrets apart*, be not written in the speaker's private mind, but be outwardly and publicly manifest in the matter spoken of, which must be one that clearly admits of

* Strype's *Cranmer*, i., pp 27, 28; *ib.*, ii., Appendices 5, 6; ed. Oxon., 1812.

secrets, and in the circumstances of the speaker, who is driven into a corner, and obliged to answer something, and yet cannot by any prudent man be expected to answer out of the fulness of all the knowledge that he may possibly possess.

6. Nor let it be said that all confidence in the replies given to our questions is hereby destroyed. For most questions are in matters that do not admit of a secret. There the qualification, *secrets apart,* which may be said to attach to all answers, has no value and meaning: it is mathematically equal to zero ; and we may take the answer in full assurance just as it reaches our ear. Again, when a person volunteers a statement unasked, he cannot be supposed to be reserving secrets. But when delicate subjects are touched on, and inquiry is pushed to extremity by an unauthorized questioner, *secrets apart* is the handwriting on the wall.

7. But why is not this qualification spoken out with the tongue ? Sometimes it safely may be, and then it should be so added. But, as the addition is unusual, our taking the trouble to express it would often certify to the inquirer that his suspicions were correct, though we ought not to tell him so. Our aim then must be to give such an oral answer as we should return, were the suspicion quite unfounded. Our questioner, if he is a prudent man, will piece out our phrase with the addition, *secrets apart ;* and he will understand that he can get nothing out of us either way, which is exactly what we wish him to understand. His unauthorized interrogatory has been met by speech that amounts to silence, arguing

indeed our prudence, but leaving him as wise as before on the forbidden topic. If he is a thoughtless man, he is deceived, not by any intention or election of ours, but indirectly so far as we are concerned, an incidental deception which he has brought on himself.

8. This then is a convention that obtains, not of positive institution, but dictated by nature herself, that on a matter which admits of being secret, any answer elicited under stress of necessity must be so construed, as that any grave secret that may be touched, not being morally in the power of the respondent to reveal, shall be taken to remain reserved.

9. We may therefore sometimes avoid seeming to know what we know, or to be what we are. But we may never of our own proper motion step forward and court observation as being what we are not, or knowing what is against or beyond our knowledge. We may dissemble occasionally, but not simulate. The dissembler of a secret wishes for obscurity and silence: he wants to have the eyes of men turned away from him and their curiosity unroused. Whatever he says or does is to divest the idea of there being anything particularly interesting about him. But he who simulates—call him pretender, impostor, or quack—is nothing, if not taken notice of. The public gaze is his sunshine: obscurity gives him a deadly chill. His ambition is to appear out of the ordinary, being really quite within common lines: the dissembler is in some respect beyond the ordinary, but wishes

not to show himself otherwise than as an ordinary
mortal with ordinary knowledge. The pretender is
on the offensive, challenging attention : the dissembler is on his defence against notice. "Simu-
lation," says Bolingbroke, "is a stiletto, not only
an offensive but an unlawful weapon, and the use
of it may be rarely, very rarely, excused, but never
justified. Dissimulation is a shield, as secrecy is
armour : and it is no more possible to preserve
secrecy in the administration of public affairs without dissimulation than it is to succeed in it without
secrecy." (*Idea of a Patriot King.*)

Readings.—De Lugo, *De Just. et Jure*, 14, nn. 135,
141, 142 ; *The Month* for March, 1883 ; Lockhart's
Life of Scott, vi., 26.

CHAPTER IV.

OF CHARITY.

1. IT is the difference between sensible apprehension
and intellectual knowledge, that the former seizes
upon a particular object and it only, as *this sweet :*
the latter takes its object as the type of a class of
similars, *this and the like of this, this sweet as one of
the class of sweet things.* In like manner the love of
passion, which is the love of sense, regards one sole
object. Titius is in love with Bertha alone, not
with woman in general. But an intellectual love
is the love of a type of beauty or goodness, of *this*
object and of others as they approach in likeness

to it.   Whoever loves William from an intellectual appreciation of his patriotism, in loving him loves all patriots.   Every animal loves itself with a brute, sensible love, not a love to find fault with, nor yet a noble and exalted sentiment—a love purely self-regarding, quite apart from the good that is in self, but embracing self simply as self, and self alone. This is the first love of self even in man.   But over and above this animal and sensible love, which no man lacks, there is in all men worthy of the name a second self-regarding affection of an intellectual cast, whereby a man loves himself as discerning with the eye of his soul the excellence of his own nature—"how noble in reason, how infinite in faculty, in form and moving how express and admirable, in action how like an angel, in apprehension how like a god, the beauty of the world, the paragon of animals."   Intellectual self-complacence overflows from self to similars.   It is not self-love, it is love of the race, "the milk of human kindness," philanthropy.

2. But man is a disappointing creature, after all a mere "quintessence of dust," unless he can rise above himself by relation with some superhuman being, and make his final fortune in some better region than this world.   Reason requires that we love ourselves, and love our fellow-men, for and in order to the development of the highest gifts and capacities that are in us.   These are gifts and capacities divine, preparing us to find our everlasting happiness in God. (*Ethics*, c. ii., s. iv., n. 2, p. 22.) The love that we bear to ourselves and our neigh-

bour, in view of our coming from God and going to God, is called the love of *charity*. Charity differs from philanthropy in looking beyond the present life, and above creatures. A materialist and atheist may possess philanthropy, but not charity.

3. Beside the twofold love, animal and intellectual, which we bear ourselves, we may also and should love ourselves with the love of charity, seeing God's gifts in us, and desiring the perfection of those gifts in a happy eternity occupied with God. The charity which we should thus bear to ourselves is the model of that which we owe to our neighbour, whom we are to love *as ourselves*, not with the same intensity, but with the same quality of love, wishing him the good, human and divine, temporal and eternal, which we wish for ourselves, though not so earnestly as we wish it for ourselves. Our love for ourselves is stronger than for our neighbour: for, if love comes of likeness, much more does it come of identity. But by reason of the vast preponderance of the good that is rational and eternal over that which is material and temporal; and also by reason of the principle laid down by St. Thomas, that "as to the sharing together of (eternal) happiness, greater is the union of our neighbour's soul with our soul than even of our own body with our soul" (2a 2æ, q. 26, art. 5, ad 2),—we are bound to love our neighbour's eternal good better than our own temporal good, and in certain special conjunctures to sacrifice the latter to the former. We have no duty and obligation of loving his temporal good

above our own temporal good. But it is often matter of commendation and counsel to sacrifice our temporal interest to our neighbour's. This sacrifice is no breach of the order of charity, beginning at home : since what is resigned of material and perishable profit is gained in moral perfection. Especially commendable is the surrender of private good for the good of the community. Charity, or philanthropy, taking this form, bears the name of patriotism and public spirit.

4. Charity, like material forces, acts in a certain inverse ratio to the distance of the object. Other considerations being equal, the nearer, the dearer. Nay, nearness and likeness to ourselves goes further than goodness in winning our love. This is natural, and charity presupposes nature, and follows its order. As we have more charity for ourselves than for others whom we acknowledge to be better men, so likewise for our kinsmen and intimate friends. We may put the matter thus. Charity consists in wishing and seeking to procure for a person the good that leads to God. One element is the intensity and eagerness of this wish and search ; another is the greatness of the good wished. Now we wish those who are better than ourselves to be rewarded according to their deserts with a greater good than ourselves : but this wish is but lukewarm compared to the intensity of our desire that we and our friends with us may attain to all the good that we are capable of.

5. The Christian precept to love our enemies is merely the enforcement of a natural obligation. The

obligation stands almost self-evident as soon as it is cleared of misunderstanding. The love of enemies is not based on the ground of their being hostile and annoying us. It would be highly unnatural to love them on that score. Nor are we in duty bound to show to one who hates us special offices of friendship, except we find him in extreme need, *e.g.*, dying in a ditch, as the Good Samaritan found the Jew: otherwise it is enough that we be animated towards him with that common charity, which we bear to other men who are not further off from us than he is. If Lucius offend Titius, there being no other tie between them than the tie of friendship, Titius may, where the offence is very outrageous, henceforth treat Lucius as a stranger. The question of scandal has sometimes to be regarded, but that is an extrinsic circumstance to our present subject. Nor are we concerned to say what is the better thing for Titius to do, but to say all that he is bound to do. He is bound to render himself as void of wilful malice, and as full of ordinary courtesy and good feeling towards Lucius, as he is in the case of Sempronius, a man whom he never heard of till this day. But if there be some other antecedent tie between them besides the tie of friendship,—for instance, if Titius and Lucius are two monks of the same convent, two officers in the same regiment, two partners of one firm,—Titius is no longer justified in treating Lucius as a stranger. He must regard him with *ordinary* charity; now ordinary charity between two brother-officers, or two fellow-monks, is not the same as between men who have no such

Q

tie one with another. This is why we laid it down that we must be animated towards him who has offended us "with that common charity, which we bear to other men *who are not further off* from us than he is."

6. This then being the exact obligation, the same is easily established. We must love our enemies, because the reasons given for loving all mankind (nn. 1, 2) are not vitiated by this or that man having treated us shamefully. The human nature in him still remains good actually, and still more, potentially; and if good and hopeful, to that extent also lovable. Nor is this lovableness a mere separable accident. Rather, it is the offensive behaviour of the man that is the separable accident. At that we may well be disgusted and abominate it. But the underlying substance remains good, not incurably tainted with that vicious accident. We must attend to the substance, which *is*, rather than to the accident, which *happens*, and may be abolished. Let us endeavour to abolish the accident, still so that we respect and regard the substance. Let us seek for redress under the guidance of prudence according to the circumstances of the case, but not for the ruin of our enemy. Let us not render evil for evil, but even in exacting a just satisfaction, make it of the nature of that compensatory evil, which is by consequence good. Let us *be angry* with our enemy, but *sin not* by hating him. (*Ethics*, c. iv., s. iv., n. 3.) We may seek satisfaction for any *wrong* we have suffered: in grave cases we must have recourse to the State for that:

but the *sin*, if any, of our adversary is not our concern to punish or to seek vengeance for. (*Ethics*, c. ix., s. iii., n. 4.)

7. The same reasoning holds good even of *public enemies*, tyrants, persecutors, anarchists, assassins. We must include them in our prayers, wish for their conversion, and, though their case appear hopeless, we must not damn them before their time. If we found one of them dying by accident of cold or asphyxia, we should be bound by a grave obligation to use all ordinary efforts to bring him round and recover him. Still we may use our best efforts to bring them to justice, even to capital punishment, according to the procedure of public law established in the country, and not otherwise. We may also with an *inefficacious* desire, that is, a desire that finds no vent in action, desire their death under an alternative thus, that either living they may cease to do evil, or that God may call them away to where the wicked cease from troubling. But we must not desire, nor be glad of, their death by any unlawful means, for that were to sympathise with crime.

8. Real charity shows itself in action, succouring a neighbour in need, which is sometimes a counsel, sometimes a duty. It is an axiom, that *charity is not binding with grave inconvenience*. The gravity of the inconvenience in prospect must be measured against the urgency of the need to be relieved. A neighbour is technically said to be in *extreme need*, when he is in imminent peril of deadly evil to soul or body, and is unable to help himself. We are

under severe obligation of charity to succour any whom we find in this plight.

9. By charity we give of our own to another: by justice we render to another that which is his. Charity neglected calls for no restitution, when the need that required it is past away: justice violated cries for restitution, for what we have taken away from our neighbour remains still his. The obligations of justice are negative, except for the fulfilment of contracts: obligations in charity are largely positive. (*Ethics*, c. v., s. ix., n. 7, p. 108.)

Readings.—*C. Gent.*, III., 117; 2a 2æ, q. 26, art. 4; *ib.*, art. 7; *ib.*, art. 8; 2a 2æ, q. 25, art. 8; *ib.*, art. 9: *ib.*, art. 6; Ferrier, *Greek Philosophy*, Socrates, nn. 13, 26, 27, 29. (*Remains*, vol. i., pp. 227, seq.)

CHAPTER V.

OF RIGHTS.

SECTION I.—*Of the definition and division of Rights.*

1. A *right* is that in virtue of which a person calls anything his own. More elaborately, a right is a *moral power residing in a person, in virtue whereof he refers to himself as well his own actions as also other things, which stand referred to him in preference to other persons.* A right is a *moral power*, as distinguished from physical force or ability. It resides in a *person*, a being whom we call *autocentric*, as distinguished from a *thing*, which is *heterocentric*. (c. ii., s. i., n. 2, p. 203.)

A person is his own, a thing is another's. Every
intellectual nature is a person except the Humanity
of Christ, an exception which does not concern us
here. To the Creator all created personalities are
as things, but that again is not our concern in this
place, where we treat of the relations between man
and man. It will have to be noted hereafter with
great emphasis, that the *individual* man is a *person*,
not a thing and chattel, in relation to the *State*, and
consequently has rights against the State.

2. Every intellectual being has the attribute of
reflex consciousness. It may turn its regard in upon
itself, and call itself *me*, and its powers and activities
mine. It certainly has the physical ability of acting
for self, and using its powers consciously for its own
ends. Does this physical ability represent also a
moral power? Is the agent justified in exercising
it? and are his fellows under a moral obligation
of justice to leave him free to exercise it? (*Ethics,* c.
vi., s. i., nn. 5. 6, p. 111.) We have seen that morality
consists in acting up to one's own intellectual or
rational nature. Since then the calling oneself
me, and one's power *mine*, and the using those
powers for purposes which one's reason approves,
is the distinguishing feature of an intellectual, or
rational, and personal being, that being is morally
warranted so to act. He calls himself his own, and
his powers his own, and they are his own by the
very fact of his calling them so by a natural act.
And, as justice is to give to another his own, others
are bound in justice to leave him free to dispose of
himself and his powers, at least within certain

limits. But this would be for man a barren freedom, were he not empowered to lay hold of and make his own some things, nay many things, outside of himself, for man is not self-sufficient, but has many natural necessities, and many psychical cravings to boot. Therefore man's right of preference extends, not only to his own actions, but also to external things, which he may make his own to act upon.

3. Rights are either *connatural* or *acquired*. Connatural rights spring from the very being of a man, as he is a person. Such are the rights to life, to honour, to personal liberty—that is, freedom to go where you will—to civil liberty—that is, not being a slave—also the rights to marry and to acquire property. Acquired rights spring from some deed of man, annexing something to his personality. Such are the rights to property, duly entered upon, to reputation, to the political franchise, and all rights that come by contract. Acquired rights may descend to heirs.

4. Rights again are *alienable* and *inalienable*, which division does not coincide with the preceding. Those rights are inalienable, shorn of which a man cannot work out his last end. Some rights are thus permanently and universally inalienable, as the right to life : others are so occasionally and for particular persons.

5. The correlative of *right* is *duty :* so that, wherever one man has a right, his neighbours have a duty in justice to leave him free to exercise the same. But the converse is not true, that wherever

one man has a duty towards another, that other has a right to its performance, for there are duties of charity, which do not impart a corresponding right, but only a *claim.* *Duties* that correspond to *rights* are called by English moralists *perfect* duties. *Duties* answering to *claims* only they call *imperfect.*

6. Of duties, some are *positive*, which bind *always*, [a] *not for always*, as the duty of adoring God. We are always bound to adore, we are not bound to be always adoring. Other duties are negative, and bind *always, for always*, as the duties of sobriety and chastity. The former class of duties we may more easily be excused from, because they can be deferred, and it is at times morally impossible to take them up. But negative duty, as Mr. Gladstone has finely said, "rises with us in the morning, and goes to rest with us at night: it is the shadow that follows us wheresoever we go, and only leaves us when we leave the light of life."

7. Only a *person* has rights, as appears by the definition of a *right.* Again, only persons have duties, for they only have free will. No one has duties without rights, and no man has rights without duties. Infants and idiots, in whom the use of reason is impeded, having notwithstanding rights, are said to have duties also *radically.* Hence it is wrong to make an idiot commit what is in him a *material* breach of some negative duty, as of temperance. Positive duties he is excused from.

8. Some have taught that all human rights are consequences of duties; a man having first a duty

to perform, and then a right to the means necessary to its performance. But this doctrine appears more pious than probable. For, first, the type and example of sovereign right, God, has no duties. (*Ethics*, c. vi., s. ii., n. 4, p. 130.) Then again, a man may have a right conjoined with a duty—not of justice, of course, but of some other virtue, as of religion—not to use that right. But if rights were consequent upon duties, the right would cease in such a case; and to pretend to exercise it would be a sin against justice, which it is not.

SECTION II.—*Of the so-called Rights of Animals.*

1. Brute beasts, not having understanding and therefore not being persons, cannot have any rights. The conclusion is clear. They are not autocentric. They are of the number of *things*, which are another's: they are chattels, or cattle. We have no duties to them,—not of justice, as is shown; not of religion, unless we are to worship them, like the Egyptians of old; not of fidelity, for they are incapable of accepting a promise. The only question can be of charity. Have we duties of charity to the lower animals? Charity is an extension of the love of ourselves to beings like ourselves, in view of our common nature and our common destiny to happiness in God. (c. iv., nn. 1, 2, p. 239.) It is not for the present treatise to prove, but to assume, that our nature is not common to brute beasts but immeasurably above theirs, higher indeed above them than we are below the angels. Man alone speaks, man alone

hopes to contemplate for ever, if not—in the natural order—the Face of his Father in Heaven, at least the reflected brightness of that Divine Face. (*Ethics*, c. ii., s. iv., nn. 3, 4.) We have then no duties of charity, nor duties of any kind, to the lower animals, as neither to stocks and stones.

2. Still we have duties *about* stones, not to fling them through our neighbour's windows; and we have duties *about* brute beasts. We must not harm them, when they are our neighbour's property. We must not break out into paroxysms of rage and impatience in dealing with them. It is a miserable way of showing off human pre-eminence, to torture poor brutes in malevolent glee at their pain and helplessness. Such wanton cruelty is especially deplorable, because it disposes the perpetrators to be cruel also to men. As St. Thomas says (1a 2æ, q. 102, art. 6, ad 8):

" Because the passion of pity arises from the afflictions of others, and it happens even to brute animals to feel pain, the affection of pity may arise in man even about the afflictions of animals. Obviously, whoever is practised in the affection of pity towards animals, is thereby more disposed to the affection of pity towards men : whence it is said in Proverbs xii. 10 : ' The just regardeth the lives of his beasts, but the bowels of the wicked are cruel.' And therefore the Lord, seeing the Jewish people to be cruel, that He might reclaim them to pity, wished to train them to pity even towards brute beasts, forbidding certain things to be done to animals which seem to touch upon cruelty. And therefore He forbade them to seethe the kid in the mother's milk (Deut. xiv. 21), or to muzzle the treading ox (Deut. xxv. 4), or to kill the old bird with the young." (Deut. xxii. 6, 7.)

3. It is wanton cruelty to vex and annoy a brute beast *for sport*. This is unworthy of man, and disposes him to inhumanity towards his own species. Yet the converse is not to be relied on : there have been cruel men who have made pets of the brute creation. But there is no shadow of evil resting on the practice of causing pain to brutes *in sport*, where the pain is not the sport itself, but an incidental concomitant of it. Much more in all that conduces to the sustenance of man may we give pain to brutes, as also in the pursuit of science. Nor are we bound to any anxious care to make this pain as little as may be. Brutes are as *things* in our regard : so far as they are useful to us, they exist for us, not for themselves ; and we do right in using them unsparingly for our need and convenience, though not for our wantonness. If then any special case of pain to a brute creature be a fact of considerable value for observation in biological science or the medical art, no reasoned considerations of morality can stand in the way of man making the experiment, yet so that even in the quest of science he be mindful of mercy.

4. Altogether it will be found that a sedulous observance of the rights and claims of other men, a mastery over one's own passions, and a reverence for the Creator, give the best assurance of a wise and humane treatment of the lower animals. But

to preach kindness to brutes as a primary obligation, and capital point of amendment in the conversion of a sinner, is to treat the symptom and leave unchecked the inward malady.

Reading.—St. Thos., 2a 2æ, q. 25, art. 3.

SECTION III.—*Of the right to Honour and Reputation.*

1. *Honour* is the attestation of another's excellence. *Reputation* is the opinion of many touching another's life and conduct. Honour is paid to a man to his face, whereas his reputation is bruited behind his back. Honour is taken away by *insult*, reputation by *detraction*. If the detraction involve a falsehood, it is called *calumny* or *slander*. The name *backbiting*, given to detraction, points to the absence of the person spoken of. But no one meets with an insult except where he is present, either in person or by his representative.

2. Both honour and reputation are goods that a man can call his own, and has a right to, but on different titles. Honour, some honour at least, appertains to a man simply for his being a man: reputation is won by deeds. Honour is primarily a connatural right: reputation is acquired. An entire stranger has no reputation, but a certain honour is his due to start with.

3. As there is a right to honour and a right to reputation, so insult and detraction are sins, not against charity, but against commutative justice, calling for restitution. (*Ethics*, c. v., s. ix., n. 6, p. 106.) We must tender an apology for an insult, and labour

to restore the good name that our detracting tongue has taken away.

4. Calumny is a double sin, one sin against truth, and another sin, the heavier of the two, against justice. If the blackening tale be true, the first sin is absent, but the second is there. The truth of the story is no justification for our publishing it. Though it is wrong to lie, it is not always right to blurt out the truth, especially when we are not asked for it. There are unprofitable disclosures, unseasonable, harmful, and wrongful. But, it will be said, does not a man forego his right to reputation by doing the evil that belies his fair fame? No, his right remains, unless the evil that he does, either of its own proper working or by the scandal that it gives, be subversive of social order. If he has committed a crime against society, he is to be denounced to the authorities who have charge of society: they will judge him, and, finding him guilty, they will punish him and brand him with infamy. If, again, he does evil, though not immediately against society, yet in the face of society and before the sun; he shocks the public conscience and rends his own reputation. But the evil private and proper to himself that any man works in secret, is not society's care, nor affects his social standing, nor brings any rightful diminution to his good name. If all our secret and personal offences are liable to be made public by any observer, which of us shall abide it? Our character is our public character; and that is not forfeit except for some manner of public sin.

5. Suppose a veteran, long retired, has made a

name for military prowess by boasting of battles
wherein he never came into danger, is the one old
comrade who remembers him for a skulker and a
runaway, justified in showing him up? No, for that
reputation, however mendaciously got together, is
still truly a good possession: it is not a fruit of
injustice, therefore it is no matter of restitution:
nor is it any instrument of injustice, which the
holder is bound to drop: thus, as he is not bound
to forego it, now that he has got it, so his neighbour may not rightfully take it from him.

Reading.—St. Thos., 2a 2æ, q. 73, art. 1.

SECTION IV.—*Of Contracts.*

1. A *contract* is a bargain productive of an obligation of commutative justice in each of the contracting parties. A *bargain* is a consent of two wills
to the same object. Thus a promise, before it is
accepted, is not a bargain. But even after acceptance a promise is not a contract, for the promiser
may not choose to bind himself in justice, but only
in good faith, while the promisee is under no obligation whatever.

2. There are such things as *implicit contracts*,
attached to the bearing of certain offices, whereby a
man becomes his brother's keeper. The liability
contracted is limited by the nature of the office:
thus a physician is officially bound in justice as to
his patient's pulse, but not officially as to his purse.
Where there is no explicit contract, the duties which
the subjects of a person's official care have towards
him are not duties of commutative justice. Thus

these *implicit contracts* are not strictly contracts, as failing to carry a full reciprocity.

3. Contracts are either *consensual* or *real*, according as they are either complete by the mere consent of the parties, or further require that something should change hands and pass from one to the other. What contracts are consensual, and what real, depends chiefly on positive law. No natural law can tell whether buying and selling, for instance, be a consensual or a real contract. The interest of this particular case is when the goods are lost in transmission: then whichever of the two parties at the time be determined to be the owner, apart from culpable negligence or contrary agreement of the sender, he bears the loss, on the principle, *res perit domino*.

4. Contracts are otherwise divided as *onerous* and *gratuitous*. In an onerous contract either party renders some advantage in return for the advantage that he receives, as when Titius hires the horse of Caius. In a gratuitous contract all the advantage is on one side, as when Titius does not hire but borrows a horse. The Roman lawyers further distinguish contracts, somewhat humorously, into *contracts with names* and *contracts without names*, or *nominate* and *innominate*, as anatomists name a certain bone the *innominate bone*, and a certain artery the *innominate artery*. *Innominate contracts* are reckoned four: *I give on the terms of your giving,* otherwise than as buying and selling,—to some forms of this there are English names, as *exchange* and *barter: I do on the terms of your doing: I do on*

the terms of your giving: I give on the terms of your doing.

Readings.—De Lugo, *De Just. et Jure,* 22, nn. 1, 2, 5, 6, 9, 16, 17. For buying and selling and the frauds incident thereto, Paley, *Moral Philosophy,* bk. iii., p. 1, c. vii.

SECTION V.—*Of Usury.*

1. We must distinguish *use value* and *market value.* The use value of an article of property is the esteem which the owner has of it from every other point of view except as a thing to sell. Thus a man values his overcoat on a journey as a protection from cold and rain. A book is valued that was held in the dying hand of a parent. This is use value. The market value of an article is the estimate of society, fixing the rate of exchange between that and other articles, so much of one for so much of another, *e.g.,* between mahogany and cedar wood, considered as things to sell.

2. Answering to this twofold value is a twofold exchange, *private exchange,* which regards use value; and *commercial exchange,* which is founded on market value. If I part with my watch to a sailor for carrying me across an arm of the sea where there is no public ferry, that is private exchange. If I pay the ordinary fare where there is a public ferry, that is commercial exchange.

3. Private exchange begins in the need of at least one of the contracting parties. It is an act of charity in the other party to accommodate him by offering the thing needed. If the offer is made otherwise than as a gift, and is accepted, he who

avails himself of it is bound in justice to see that the afforder of the accommodation is compensated for the loss that he suffers in affording it. Thus far the recipient is bound in justice, and no further in that virtue. However wholesome or profitable the thing be to him that gets it, the supplier cannot charge for that but only for the loss that he himself suffers, or the gain that he foregoes, in handing the thing over, or the pains that he takes, or the hardship that he endures, or the risk that he runs, in rendering the service desired. If all the labour to be undergone, or damage incurred, or risk encountered, by the sailor who goes about by private bargain to be my ferryman, is fairly met by the remuneration of a thirty-shilling watch, he has no right to stipulate for any more, not though the passage that he gives me sets me on the way to a throne. The peculiar advantage that I have in prospect does not come out of him, but out of myself. He must not pretend to sell what is not his, what attaches, not to him, but to me. He can only sell his own loss, risk, pains and labour. At the same time, if I have any gentlemanly or generous feeling in me, I shall be forward to bestow extra remuneration on one who has rendered me so timely a service : but this is matter of my gratitude, not of his right and claim in justice. Gratitude must not be put into the bill. And this much of private exchange.

4. Commercial exchange is conducted according to market value. Apart from dire necessity—and one in dire necessity is not fit to enter into commercial exchanges—the rule is, that a seller may

always ask the market value of his article, however much that may be above what the thing cost him, or the use value which it bears to him. Thus, if one finds in his garden a rare Roman coin—so far as his tastes go, a paltry bit of metal—he may sell it for whatever price numismatists will offer: whereas, if there were no market for coins, but only one individual who doted on such things, the finder could make no profit out of that individual, the coin having neither market value with the community, nor use value in the eyes of the finder.

5. As there is a twofold value, and a twofold exchange, so a twofold character is impressed on the great instrument of exchange, money. Money, in one character, is an instrument of private exchange: in its other character, to mercantile men more familiar, it is an instrument of commercial exchange. In the one, it represents use value to the particular owner, more or less to him than it would be to some other owner: in the other, it represents market value, the same to all at the same time.

6. Leo X. in the Fifth Council of Lateran, 1515, ruled that—" usury is properly interpreted to be the attempt to draw profit and increment, without labour, without cost, and without risk, out of the use of a thing that does not fructify." In 1745 Benedict XIV. wrote in the same sense to the Bishops of Italy: " That kind of sin which is called usury, and which has its proper seat and place in the contract of *mutuum*, consists in turning that contract, which of its own nature requires the amount returned exactly to balance the amount

R

received, into a ground for demanding a return in excess of the amount received." *Mutuum*, be it observed, is a loan for a definite period, of some article, the use of which lies in its consumption, as matches, fuel, food, and, in one respect, money. We shall prove this to be properly a *gratuitous* contract. (s. iv., n. 4, p. 254.)

7. Usury then is no mere taking of exorbitant interest. There is no question of more or less, but it is usury to take any interest at all upon the loan of a piece of property, which

(*a*) is of no use except to be used up, spent, consumed :

(*b*) is not wanted for the lender's own consumption within the period of the loan :

(*c*) is lent upon security that obviates risk :

(*d*) is so lent that the lender foregoes no occasion of lawful gain by lending it.

8. When all these four conditions are fulfilled, and yet interest is exacted upon a loan, such interest is usurious and unjust. And why? Simply by reason of the principle that we laid down before, speaking of private exchange (n. 3), a principle that is thus stated by St. Thomas :

"If one party is much benefited by the commodity which he receives of the other, while the other, the seller, is not a loser by going without the article, no extra price must be put on. The reason is, because the benefit that accrues to one party is not from the seller, but from the condition of the buyer. Now no one ought to sell to another that which is not his, though he may sell the loss that he

suffers. He, however, who is much benefited by
the commodity he receives of another, may spontaneously bestow some extra recompense on the
seller: that is the part of one who has the feelings
of a gentleman." (2a 2æ, q. 77, art. 1, in corp.)

9. St. Thomas speaks of sales, but the principle
applies equally to loans. It is upon loans of money
that interest is commonly taken, and of money-loans
we speak. Clearly, according to the doctrine stated,
the lender can claim the compensation of interest,
if he has to pinch himself in order to lend, or lends
at a notable risk. He is selling his own loss,—or
risk, which is loss once removed. But supposing he
has other monies in hand, and the security is good,
and he has enough still left for all domestic needs,
and for all luxuries that he cares to indulge in,—
moreover he has nothing absolutely to do with his
money, in the event of his not lending it, but to
hoard it up in his strong box, and wait long months
till he has occasion to use it: in that case, if he
lends it he will be no worse off on the day that he
gets it back, no worse off in the time while it is
away, than if it had never left his coffers. Such is
the contract of *mutuum*, shorn of all accidental
attendant circumstances, a contract, which "of its
own nature," as Benedict XIV. says, that is, apart
from circumstances, "requires the amount returned
exactly to balance the amount received." Not though
the borrower has profited of the loan to gain king-
doms, is any further return in strict justice to be
exacted of him on that precise account.

10. But now an altered case. Suppose land is

purchaseable, and it is proposed to stock a farm with cattle, and rear them, and convey them to a large town where there is a brisk demand for meat— the supposition is not always verified, nor any supposition like it, but suppose it verified in some one case—then, though the lender has other monies in hand for the needs of his household, and the security is good, yet the money is not so lent as that he foregoes no occasion of lawful gain by lending it. He foregoes the purchase of land and farm stock, or at least delays it, and delay is loss where profit is perennial. On that score of gain forfeited he may exact interest on the money that he lends, which interest will be no usury. The title of interest here given is recognized by divines as *lucrum cessans*, "interruption of profit." The interest is taken, so far as it goes upon a lawful title, not upon the fact of the borrower's profit—that is irrelevant—but upon the profit that the lender might have made, had he kept the money in hand.

11. This latter case (n. 10) represents that putting of money out to interest, which is an essential feature of modern commerce. The former case (n. 9) is the aspect that money-lending commonly bore in the Middle Ages. In those days land was hard to buy, agriculture backward, roads bad, seas unnavigable, carrying-trade precarious, messages slow, raids and marauders frequent, population sparse, commerce confined to a few centres, mines unworked, manufactures mostly domestic, capital yet unformed. Men kept their money in their cellars, or deposited it for safety in religious houses: whence the stories

of treasure-trove belonging to those days. They took out the coin as they wanted it to spend on housekeeping, or on war, or feasting. It was very hard, next to impossible, to lay out money so as to make more money by it. Money was in those days really barren—a resource for housekeeping, not for trade—a medium of private, not of commercial exchange—a representative of use value, not of market value. Apart from risk of non-repayment, to take interest for money that you had no use for but to hoard, was getting "a breed of barren metal:" it was taking up what you laid not down: it was making profit out of your neighbour's need, or your neighbour's gain, where there was no corresponding need unsatisfied, or gain forfeited, on your part: it was that "attempt to draw profit and increment, without labour, without cost, and without risk, out of the use of a thing that does not fructify," which the Fifth Lateran Council defines to be usury.

12. In our time, thanks to steam and electricity, the increase of population, and continued peace, the whole world has become one trading community, representing now more, now less abundant opportunities for the investment of money, and the conversion of it into other lucrative commodities. Money consequently with us is not a mere medium of private exchange for the purposes of housekeeping: it is a medium of commercial exchange. It represents, not use value, but market value. To be a thousand pounds out of pocket for a year means an opportunity of gain irretrievably lost, gain that could have been made otherwise than by money-lending.

Where this is so, and so far as it is so, the lender
may without violation of justice point to *lucrum
cessans*, gain lost, and arrange beforehand with the
borrower for being reimbursed with interest.

13. The transition from mediæval housekeeping,
with its use values and private exchange, to the
mercantile society of modern times, was not made
in a day, nor went on everywhere at the same rate.
It was a growth of ages. In great cities commerce
rapidly ripened, and was well on towards maturity
five centuries ago. Then the conditions that render
interest lawful, and mark it off from usury, readily
came to obtain. But those centres were isolated.
Like the centres of ossification, which appear here
and there in cartilage when it is being converted
into bone, they were separated one from another by
large tracts remaining in the primitive condition.
Here you might have a great city, Hamburg or
Genoa, an early type of commercial enterprise, and,
fifty miles inland, society was in its infancy, and the
great city was as part of another world. Hence the
same transaction, as described by the letter of the
law, might mean lawful interest in the city, and
usury out in the country—the two were so discon-
nected. In such a situation the legislator has to
choose between forbidding interest here and allowing
usury there ; between restraining speculation and
licensing oppression. The mediæval legislator chose
the former alternative. Church and State together
enacted a number of laws to restrain the taking of
interest, laws that, like the clothes of infancy, are
not to be scorned as absurd restrictions, merely

because they are inapplicable now, and would not fit the modern growth of nations. At this day the State has repealed those laws, and the Church has officially signified that she no longer insists on them. Still she maintains dogmatically that there is such a sin as usury, and what it is, as defined in the Fifth Council of Lateran.

Readings.—St. Thos., 2a 2æ, q. 77, art. 1; Ar., *Pol.*, I., ix.; St. Thos., 2a 2æ, q. 77, art. 4; *The Month* for September, 1886; *The Nineteenth Century* for September, 1877, pp. 181, seq.

CHAPTER VI.

OF MARRIAGE.

Section. I—*Of the Institution of Marriags.*

1. MARRIAGE is defined by the Canonists: *the union of male and female, involving their living together in undivided intercourse.* In the present order of Providence, the marriage contract between baptized persons is a sacrament, under the superintendence of the Church, the fertile theme of canonists and theologians. As philosophers, we deal with marriage as it would be, were there no sacraments, no Church, and no Incarnation, present or to come. This is marriage in the order of pure nature.

2. It is natural to all animals to propagate their kind, natural therefore also to man; and being natural, it is so far forth also a good thing, unless

we are to say with the Manicheans, that the whole
of corporeal nature is an evil creation. Nay, so
urgent is the natural appetite here, that we must
argue the existence, not of a mere permission, but of
an exigency of nature, and consequent command of
God (*Ethics*, c. vi., s. ii., nn. 11, 12, p. 122), for the propagation of the human species. Besides, there is in
the individual the duty of self-preservation, therefore
likewise in the race. Again, the old cannot subsist
at all without the support of the young, nor lead a
cheerful existence without their company. Imagine
a world with no youth in it, a winter without a
spring!

3. There is this difference between self-preservation and the preservation of the race, that if a man
will not eat, none can eat for him; but if one man
omit the propagation of his kind, another can take
it up. There are many things necessary for the
good of mankind, which are not to be done by every
individual. Not all are to be soldiers, nor all builders,
though houses are needful, and sometimes war. Nor
is it desirable that the human race should be multiplied to its utmost capacity. It is enough here to
mention without discussing the teaching of Malthus,
how population presses on the means of subsistence,
the latter increasing in an arithmetical, the former
in a geometrical ratio. Without going the whole
way with Malthus, modern economical writers are
commonly a little Malthusian, and shrink from giving
to all and each of their species the word to " increase
and multiply."

4. But, it will be said, sickly and consumptive

subjects, and still more those who have any tendency
to madness, may well be excused from having
children; so too may they be excused whose poverty
cannot keep a family; excused too is the inveterate
drunkard, and all habitual criminals, by the principle
of heredity, lest they transmit to posterity an evil
bodily predisposition; but the healthy and the
virtuous, men sound of mind and limb, of life un-
spotted, and in circumstances easy, the flower of
the race,—none of these surely should omit to raise
up others to wear his lineaments: we want such
men multiplied. I answer, on natural grounds
alone: You may counsel, but you cannot compel,
either by positive law or ethical precept any man
or woman to seek to have children. You surely will
not breed men by selection, like cattle, as Plato
proposed. The union of the sexes, especially the
married union, is an act to be of all others the most
entirely free, spontaneous, uncommanded, and unconstrained. It should be a union of intense mutual
love. But a man may not meet with any woman
that he can love with passion; or, meeting such, he
may not be able to win her. Nor, considering the
indeterminateness of points of health, capacity, and
character, could any certain list be drawn up of
persons bound to have issue. Thus the utmost that
can be argued is a counsel in this direction, a counsel
that mankind ordinarily are ready enough to comply
with. But if any one of seeming aptitude excuses
himself on the score of finding no partner to his
liking, or of a desire to travel, or of study, or still
more, of devotion—and why should not a man, even

of natural piety, go out into solitude, like St. Antony, to hold communion with his Maker?—all these excuses must be taken. It is lawful then in the state of mere nature, upon any one of many sufficient grounds, to stand aside and relinquish to your neighbour the privilege and responsibility of giving increase to the human family.

5. But if it is no one individual's duty to propagate his kind, how is it that we have laid down that there is such a duty? For the duty is incumbent upon them that alone can do it, and it can only be done by individuals. The answer rests on a distinction between *proximate* and *remote* duty. The propagation of the race is the remote duty of every individual, but at present the proximate duty of none. A *remote* duty is a duty not now pressing but which would have to be performed in a certain contingency, which contingency happening, the duty becomes *proximate*. If there appeared a danger of our race dying out, the survivors would be beholden, especially those in power, to take steps for its continuance. Rewards might then be held out, like the *jus trium liberorum* instituted at Rome by Augustus; and if necessary, penalties inflicted on celibacy. In this one extreme case the matrimonial union might be made matter of legal constraint. But when will such constraint become necessary?

6. The continuance of the human race must be wrought out by man and woman standing in that abiding and exclusive relation to one another, which constitutes the state of marriage. Nature abhors promiscuity, or free love. It is the delight of writers

who use, perhaps abuse, Darwin's name, to picture primitive mankind as all living in this infrabestial state. But "the state supposed is suicidal, and instead of allowing the expansion of the human race, would have produced infertility, and probably disease, and at best only allowed the existing numbers to maintain, under the most favourable circumstances, a precarious existence. To suppose, therefore, that the whole human race for any considerable time were without regular marriage, is physiologically impossible. They could never have survived it.' (Devas, *Studies of Family Life*, § 101.)

7. Even if the alleged promiscuity ever did prevail—and it may have obtained to some extent in certain degraded portions of humanity—its prevalence was not its justification. The practice cannot have been befitting in any stage of the evolution of human society. As in all things we suppose our readers to have understanding, we leave it to them to think out this matter for themselves. Suffice it here to put forward two grand advantages gained and ends achieved, which are called by theologians "the goods of marriage."

8. The first good of marriage is the *offspring* that is born of it. Nature wills, not only the being, but the well-being of this offspring, and that both in the physical and in the moral order. Very important for the physical health of the child it is, that it be born of parents whose animal propensities are under some restraint ; such restraint the bond of marriage implies. Then, in the moral order, the child requires to be educated with love, a love that shall be guided

by wisdom, and supported by firmness. Love, wisdom, and firmness, they are the attributes of both parents; but love is especially looked for from the mother, wisdom and firmness from the father. And, what is important, both have an *interest* in the child such as no other human being can take. We are speaking of the normal father or mother, not of many worthless parents that actually are; for, as Aristotle often lays it down, we must not judge of a thing from its bad specimens. No doubt, the State could establish public nurseries and infant schools, and provide a staff of nurses and governesses, more scientific educators than even the normal parent; but who, that has not been most unhappy in his origin, would wish his own infancy to have been reared in such a place? What certificated stranger can supply for a mother's love?

9. The second good of marriage is the *mutual faith* of the partners. Plato never made a greater mistake than when he wrote that "the female sex differs from the male in mankind only in this, that the one bears children, while the other begets them;" and consequently that "no occupation of social life belongs to a woman because she is a woman, or to a man because he is a man, but capacities are equally distributed in both sexes, and woman naturally bears her share in all occupations, and man his share, only that in all woman is weaker than man." (*Republic*, 454 D; 455 D.) Over against this we must set Aristotle's correction: "Cohabitation among human kind is not for the mere raising of children, but also for the purposes of a partnership in life: for from the

first the offices of man and woman are distinct and different: thus they mutually supply for one another, putting their several advantages into the common stock." (Ar., *Eth.*, VIII., xii. 7.)   Elsewhere he sets forth these several offices in detail: "The nature of both partners, man and woman, has been pre-arranged by a divine dispensation in view of their partnership: for they differ by not having their faculties available all to the same effect, but some even to opposite effects, though combining to a common end: for God made the one sex stronger and the other weaker, that the one for fear may be the more careful, and the other for courage the more capable of self-defence; and that the one may forage abroad, while the other keeps house: and for work the one is made competent for sedentary employments, but too delicate for an out-door life, while the other makes a poor figure at keeping still, but is vigorous and robust in movement; and touching children, the generation is special, but the improvement of the children is the joint labour of both parents, for it belongs to the one to nurture, to the other to chastise." (Ar., *Econ.*, i. 3.)

These passages are enough to suggest more than they actually contain, of two orders of qualities arranged antithetically one over against another in man and woman, so that the one existence becomes complementary to the other, and the two conjoined form one perfect human life.   This life-communion, called by divines *fides*, or mutual faith, is then the second good fruit of marriage. Indeed it is the more characteristically human good, *offspring* being rather related to the animal side of our nature. But as animal and rational elements make one human being, so do *offspring* and *mutual faith* constitute the adequate good of that human union of the sexes, which we call marriage.

10. Whatever good there is in marriage, connections formed by either party beyond the marriage-bed, are agents of confusion to the undoing of all that good and the practical dissolution of the marriage.

Readings.—Contra Gentes, iii., 122; *ib.,* iii., 126; *ib.,* iii., 136; Devas, *Studies of Family Life,* §§ 90—101, where he disposes of the proof of primitive promiscuity, drawn from the fact that in early societies kinship is traced and property claimed only through the mother.

Section II.—*Of the Unity of Marriage.*

1. *Both man and woman are by nature incapable of a second marriage, while their former marriage endures.* No woman can have two husbands at the same time, which is *polyandry;* and no man can have two wives at the same time, which is *polygamy.* The second marriage attempted is not only *illicit,* but *invalid:* it is no contract, no marriage at all, and all cohabitation with the second partner is sheer adultery. This is a great deal more than saying that polyandry and polygamy are unlawful.

2. That is by nature no marriage, which is inconsistent with the natural ends of marriage, *offspring* and *mutual faith.* But polyandry is thus inconsistent with the good of offspring, and polygamy with mutual

faith. It is not meant that polyandry makes the
birth of children impossible. But nature is solicitous,
not for the mere birth, but for the rearing and good
estate of the child born. Now a child born fatherless is in an ill plight for its future education.
Posthumous children in lawful wedlock are born
fatherless: that is a calamity: but what shall we
think of an institution which makes that calamity to
the child sure always to occur? Such an institution
is polyandry. For in it no man can ever know his
own child, except by likeness, and likeness in a baby
face is largely as you choose to fancy it. Again, is
the polyandrous wife to be, or not to be, the head of
the family? If not, the family—for it ought to be
one family, where there is one mother—will have as
many heads as she has husbands, a pretty specimen
of a house divided against itself. If she is to be
the head, that is a perversion of the natural order
of predominance between the sexes. In any case,
polyandry is little better than promiscuity: it is fatal
to the family and fatal to the race; and children
born of it are born out of marriage.

3. Against polygamy the case in natural law is
not quite so strong as against polyandry. Still it is
a strong case enough in the interest of the wife. The
words spoken by the bride to the bridegroom in the
marriage rite of ancient Rome, *Ubi tu Caius, ego
Caia*, "Where you are master, I am mistress,"
declare the relation of *mutual faith* as it should be,
namely, a relation of equality, with some advantage,
preference, and pre-eminence allowed to the husband, yet not so great advantage as to leave *him*

free where *she* is straitly bound, and reduce her to the servile level of one in a row of minions to his passion and sharers of his divided affections. Polygamy in all ages has meant the lowering of womankind:

He will hold thee—
Something better than his dog, a little dearer than his horse.

At its strongest, the love of man for woman, where polygamy obtains, is a flame of passion, that quickly spends itself on one object, and then passes to another; not a rational, enduring, human affection. It is also a fact, that the increase of the race is not greater in polygamy than in monogamy. Thus, as a practice that runs strongly counter to one of the great purposes of marriage, and is, to say the least, no help to the other, and carries with it the humiliation of the female sex, polygamy is justly argued to be abhorrent to nature.

4. It is beside the purpose of this work to enter into the questions of morality that arise out of Holy Scripture, considered as an inspired record of the actions of the Saints. But the polygamy of the patriarchs of old so readily occurs to mind, that it is worth while to mention four conceivable explanations, if only to indicate which is and which is not reconcilable with our philosophy. The first explanation would be, that polygamy is not against the natural law, but only against the positive divine law, which was derogated from in this instance. We have made it out to be against the natural law. The second explanation would be that God gave the

patriarchs a dispensation, strictly so called, from this point of the natural law. We have maintained that God cannot, strictly speaking, dispense from one jot or tittle of natural law. (*Ethics*, c. viii., s. iii., nn. 1—3, p. 147.) A third explanation would be founded on the words of St. Paul to the Athenians (Acts xvii. 30), about "God overlooking the times of this ignorance." This would suppose that mankind, beginning in monogamy, from passion and ignorance lapsed quickly into polygamy: that the patriarchs in good faith conformed to the practice of their time; and that God, in their case as with the rest of mankind, awaited His own destined hour for the light of better knowledge to break upon the earth. A fourth explanation would be this. God by His supreme dominion can dissolve any marriage. By the same dominative power He can infringe and partially make void any marriage contract without entirely undoing it. The marriage contract, existing in its fulness and integrity, is a bar to any second similar contract, as we have proved. But what, on this theory, the Lord God did with the marriages of the patriarchs was this: He partially unravelled and undid the contract, so as to leave room for a second contract, and a third, each having the bare essentials of a marriage, but none of them the full integrity.

The explanation however most in accordance with our views (see Appendix) would be, that the prohibition of polygamy, being a secondary precept of the natural law, failed in its application in that age of lapsed humanity, when a woman was better

s

one of many wives, all protected by one husband, than exposed to promiscuous violence and lust. (Cf. Genesis xx.; Isaias iv. 1.)

Readings.—*Contra Gent.*, iii., 124; Suarez, *De Legibus*, II., xv., 28.

SECTION III.—*Of the Indissolubility of Marriage.*

1. This section is pointed not so much against a *separation*—which may take place by mutual consent, or without that, by grievous infidelity or cruelty of one party—as against a divorce *a vinculo*, which is a dissolution of a marriage in the lifetime of the parties, enabling each of them validly and lawfully to contract with some other. The unity of marriage is more essential than its indissolubility. Nature is more against polygamy than against divorce. Even Henry VIII. stuck at polygamy. In the present arrangement, a divorce *a vinculo* is obtainable in three cases. First, when of two unbaptized persons, man and wife, the one is converted, and the unconverted party refuses to live peaceably in wedlock, the convert may marry again, and thereupon also the other party. So the Church understands St. Paul, 1 Cor. vii. 13, 15. Again, the Pope can grant a divorce *a vinculo* in the marriage of baptized persons before cohabitation. Such a marriage in that stage is also dissolved by the profession of one of the parties in a religious order. Beyond these three cases, the Catholic Church allows neither the lawfulness nor the validity of any divorce *a vinculo* by whomsoever given to whatsoever parties.

2. It is ours to investigate the lie of the law of nature, having due regard to the points marked, antecedently to our search, by the definition of infallible authority. Nothing can be done in the Church against the law of nature : since therefore divorce *a vinculo* is sometimes recognized in the Church, it may be contended that marriage is not by nature absolutely indissoluble. On the other hand, it is a proposition censured by Pius IX. in the Syllabus, n. 67 : " By the law of nature the bond of marriage is not indissoluble." Thus it appears we must teach that marriage is naturally indissoluble, still not absolutely so, just as a safe is justly advertised as fire-proof, when it will resist any conflagration that is likely to occur, though it would be consumed in a blast-furnace or in a volcano. So marriage is indissoluble, if it holds good for all ordinary contingencies, for all difficulties that may be fairly reckoned with and regarded as not quite improbable, for every posture of affairs that the contracting parties before their union need at all consider. Or, if the three cases of divorce actually allowed are to be traced to the dominative power of God (*Ethics*, c. vii., n. 2, p. 129), we may teach that marriage is by nature absolutely indissoluble, and that divorce is as much against the law of nature as the killing of an innocent man, excepting in the case of God's dominion being employed to quash the contract or the right to life. But against this latter view is to be set the consideration, that God is manifestly averse to using His dominative power to overturn natural ordinances. He does not hand the innocent over to death except in the due course of physical nature: why then should He ever put forth His power against the marriage-tie, unless it be that nature herself in certain cases postulates its severance? But if such is ever nature's petition, the universal and unconditional permanence of the marriage-tie cannot be a requisition of nature, nor is divorce absolutely excluded by natural law.

3. Thomas Sanchez, than whom there is no greater authority on this subject, records his opinion that "a certain inseparability is of the nature of marriage," but that "absolute indissolubility does not attach to marriage by the law of nature." He adds: "if we consider marriage as it is an office of nature for the propagation of the race, it is hard to render a reason why for the wife's barrenness the husband should not be allowed to put her away, or marry another." (*De Matrimonio*, l. ii., d. 13, n. 7.) We proceed to prove that "a certain inseparability is of the nature of marriage," so that marriage may truly be said to be indissoluble by the law of nature. Whether this natural indissolubility is absolute, and holds for every conceivable contingency, the student must judge by the proofs.

4. If a divorce *a vinculo* were a visible object on the matrimonial horizon, the parties would be strongly encouraged thereby to form illicit connections, in the expectation of shortly having any one of them they chose ratified and sanctified by marriage. Marriage would be entered upon lightly, as a thing easily done and readily undone, a state of things not very far in advance of promiscuity.

Between married persons little wounds would fester, trifling sores would be angered into ulcers: any petty strife might lead to a fresh contract, made in haste and repented of with speed: then fond, vain regrets for the former partnership. Affinity would be a loose bond of friendship between families; and after divorce it would turn to enmity. The fair but weaker sex would suffer the more by this as by all other matrimonial perversions: for the man has not so much difficulty in lighting upon another love, but the woman—she illustrates the Greek proverb of a fallen estate:

> Mighty was Miletus in the bygone days of yore.

The divorced wife offers fewer attractions than the widow.

5. It is well to bear in mind that, at least by the positive ordinance of God in the present order of His Providence, the marriage of baptized persons, after cohabitation, is absolutely indissoluble; and no marriage can be dissolved except in the three cases specified. (n. 1.)

Readings.—Leo XIII., Encyclical on Christian Marriage, *Arcanum divinæ sapientiæ;* St. Thomas, *Contra Gent.,* iii., 123.

CHAPTER VII.

OF PROPERTY.

SECTION I.—*Of Private Property.*

1. PROPERTY was called by the Romans *res familiaris*, the stuff and substance of the family. Property may be held by the individual for himself alone: but any large accumulation of it is commonly held by the head of a family, actual or potential, for the family; and he cherishes it for the sake of his family as much as, or even more than, for his own sake. This is to be borne in mind, for many errors in theory and in practice spring from a large proprietor figuring as an individual, and not as a sort of *corporation sole* in his capacity of paterfamilias.

2. We have seen (c. v., s. i., n. 2, p. 245) how man acquires a right over external goods, as it were setting the seal of his own personality upon them. It appears upon further consideration, that this right must extend beyond the mere making things your own for immediate use and consumption; it must extend to the *storing* of things for future and perennial use. Otherwise we have Communism. Communism allows men to hold property collectively in a common stock, and allows each member of the community to take for his peculiar

own out of that stock whatever for the moment he needs; but it will not permit him to appropriate private means of subsistence against any notable time to come. Communism is very good in a family, which is an imperfect community, part of a higher community, the State. It is very good in a monastery, which is like a family: again, very good in the primitive Church at Jerusalem, which existed for the time on quasi-monastic lines: very good even in a perfect community, if such there be, of tropical savages, for whom nature supplies all things, bananas to eat and palm-leaves to wear, without any human labour of production; but very bad and quite unworkable everywhere else. St. Thomas, following Aristotle, puts it pithily and sufficiently: "Private property is necessary to human life for three reasons: first, because every one is more careful to look after what belongs to himself alone than after what is common to all or to many, since all men shun labour and leave to others what is matter of joint concern, as happens where there are too many servants: on another ground, because human affairs are more orderly handled, if on each individual there rests his own care of managing something, whereas there would be nothing but confusion, if every one without distinction were to have the disposal of any thing he chose to take in hand: thirdly, because by this means society is the rather kept at peace, every member being content with his own possession, whence we see that among those who hold any thing in common and undivided ownership strifes not unfrequently arise." (2a 2æ, q. 66, art. 2, in corp.)

3. If any revolutionist yet will have the hardihood to say with Proudhon, "Property is theft," we shall ask him, "From whom?" He will answer of course, "From the community." But that answer supposes the community to have flourished, a wealthy corporation, before private property began. Needless to say that history knows nothing of such a corporation. The saying, that *in the beginning all things were in common,* is not true in the sense that they were *positively* in common, like the goods of a corporation, which are collective property: but simply that they were *negatively* in common, that is, not property at all, neither of corporation nor of individual, but left in the middle open to all comers, for each to convert into property by his occupation, and by his labour to enhance and multiply. This must be modified by the observation, that the first occupants were frequently heads of families, or of small clans, and occupied and held for themselves and their people.

4. The saying, that *all things are in common by the law of nature,* must be received with still greater reserve. Really with as much truth it might be said that all men are unmarried, or unclad, or uneducated, by the law of nature. Nature unaided by human volition provides neither property, nor clothing, nor marriage, nor education, for man. But nature bids, urges and requires man to bestir his voluntary energies for the securing of all these things. The law of nature does not prescribe this or that

particular distribution of goods, as neither does it join this man with that woman in marriage, nor insist on plaids rather than coats, nor set all boys to learn algebra, nor fix a ritual for divine worship; but it insists in the vague upon some worship, some education, some clothing, some marriage, and some distribution of goods, leaving the determination in each case to choice, custom, and positive law, human and divine.

5. All property that can ever be immediately serviceable for saving human life, is held under this burden, that a perishing fellow-creature, who cannot otherwise help himself in a case of *extreme need* (c. iv., n. 8, p. 243), may make such use of the property of another as shall suffice to rescue him from perishing off-hand. If he draws largely on another for this purpose, he ought to make compensation afterwards, if he has the means. This has been taken for a piece of the primeval rock of Communism cropping up from underneath subsequent human formations, —quite a mistaken notion. There is no Communism whatever in the transaction. Up to the instant when the needy man seizes the article that he requires to save him from death, that article still belongs to the owner from whom he takes it, who is bound in charity to give it to the needy party, but not in justice. Extreme need does not confer ownership, nor dispossess any previous owner: but it confers the right of taking what is another's as though it belonged to no one; and in the taking, the thing passes into the ownership of the new occupant, so that for the previous owner forcibly to

resume it would be a violation of justice. English law does not recognise this right—properly enough, for with us it would be made a plea for much stealing—but refers the destitute to the parish. The law is considerately worked by the magistrates. A starving man, who took a loaf off a baker's tray, has been known to be sentenced to a few hours' imprisonment with two good meals.

6. As St. Paul says (2 Cor. xii. 14), "parents ought to lay up for their children," that they in whom their own existence is continued, may not be left unprovided for at their decease. The amount laid up necessary for this purpose, ought not to be diverted from it. Thus much at least Natural Law can tell us of the right of inheritance. And concerning testamentary right these natural considerations are forthcoming, that it adds to the desirability of property, that it secures deference to the wealthy in their old age, and that the abolition of it might be frustrated by an apparatus of confidential *donationes inter vivos*, that is to say, making the property over in trust before death. Further enlargement of the natural basis of testamentary right may be effected by the judicious reader.

Readings.—Ar., *Pol.*, II., v., nn. 1—16; De Lugo, *De just. et jure*, vi., nn. 2—6; *ib.*, xvi., nn. 143, 144; Locke, *Of Civil Government*, c.v.; *id.*, *Of Government*, nn. 88, 89.

Section II.—*Of Private Capital.*

1. Reverting to a former section (c. v., s. v., nn. 1—5, p. 255) we lay down this distinction: Goods held

for their *use value* are *consumer's wealth* : goods held
for their *market value* are *producer's wealth*, otherwise
called *capital*. Capital then is that wealth which
a man holds for the purpose of gaining further
wealth by means of commercial exchange. It is
represented by the razors that are made, not to mow
the manly beard, or youthful moustache, of the
maker, but, as the Yorkshire vendor put it, "to
sell."

2. Those economists who would allow no private
ownership of capital, but would have all capital to
be State property, are called Socialists. They stand
distinctly apart from the Communists, whom we
have been labouring to refute in the last section.
The Communist forbids all private property : the
Socialist allows private property, but in the shape
of *consumer's wealth* alone. The Communist ignores
the necessity of labour : the Socialist schemes to
make all men work. The Communist contemplates
a hand-to-mouth dispensation of all things : the
Socialist locks all things up, wages in private coffers,
capital in government stores. The Communist is a
madman : the speculations of the Socialist are sometimes deep.

3. To what are we to attribute the rise of
Socialism, and its growth and propagation so fast
and vigorous, that, its supporters say with some
colour of evidence, it is a theory destined within a
measurable space of time to pass into actual
practice, whether men will or no? The cause is
not far to seek. There has lighted a plague upon
all civilized countries, an outbreak fearful and

severe: only by the great blessing of Providence, joined to drastic remedial measures on our part, can we cope with the evil. The plague is a cancerous formation of luxury growing out of a root of pauperism. It is a disease old as the world, but the increase of commerce and intercommunication has occasioned its bursting upon our generation in a peculiarly virulent form. And what is more, ours being a talking age, the disease is made the staple of speeches infinite, and the masses are clamouring for a remedy. The remedy proposed is Socialism.

4. Socialism in its essence is an attempt to transfer to the State, governed by universal suffrage, the wealth, and with the wealth the social duties, of what have hitherto been the wealthy and governing classes. It is not enough for the multitude that they are getting the political power out of the hands of the landlord and the capitalist: they envy the one his broad acres, and the other his investments. All must be theirs, sovereignty and wealth alike. If wealth has its duties, the people collectively with cheerful acceptance will undertake those duties. 'It shall be ours, not only to be king, but to be employer, patron, landlord, educator. We will assign to the workman his wages, just and ample and perennial: we will adjust production to demand: we will be the restorers of agriculture: we will monopolise the carrying-trade: we alone will sell whatever shall be sold: we will wash the workman in public baths: his taste shall be elevated by our statues and pictures, our theatres, our music-halls, and our churches; we will gratify his curiosity with

our news-agencies, feed his thought with our popular philosophy, educate his children as our own in our primary and secondary schools. Furthermore, we will provide the long desiderated career open to talents. The stupid boy, though his father was our Prime Minister, shall be made a cabin-boy, or a scavenger's assistant, an awful example to young gentlemen who fail to pass the Government examinations: while we will pick up, not the gutter child, for there shall be no more children in gutters, but the son of the woman at the mill, and testing him and assigning his career, first by school examinations, and then by his official performances, we will make him in time Poet Laureate or President of the Board of Trade, according to the bent of his genius.' The astonished workman turns round upon the exhibitors of this fairy vision: 'And pray who are You?' 'Oh, you, we, the people, all of us together. Come put your shoulder to the wheel, and up goes our enterprise. Or rather our first motion is downwards: down with landlords and cotton-lords and lords of parliament, down with contractors and stock-jobbers and all who live on the interest of their money, and then our honourable multitude will possess and administer and govern.'

5. If angels are to hold the collective ownership of capital and the government of men in the Socialist Commonwealth; or if every citizen, retaining in his private capacity all the follies and vices that human flesh is heir to, shall still be vested in angelic attributes, whenever he sits as legislator or

judge, or acts on the executive of a Socialist commission,—then this new Commonwealth is likely to prove a blessed substitute for the rule of the higher classes, which in one way or another has hitherto obtained in civilized society.   But till angelic attributes descend on earth, we shall not find a cure for the evils of cities and countries in simply doubling the functions of government, and placing all sovereign rights, and all the most important of proprietory rights and duties, in the hands of a numerical majority.

6. Capital, as we have seen, is a collection of market or exchange values in view of further exchange.   If we call supply S and demand D, market value is a social estimate of the fraction $\frac{D}{S}$. Another definition has been given : Market value is a social estimate of the amount of socially useful labour which a given article contains. This second definition contains this much of truth in it, that directly as the demand for an article, and inversely as the supply of the same, is the amount of labour which men find it worth their while to spend upon that article for commercial purposes.   Otherwise the definition is unsatisfactory and involved, and leads to endless discussion.   Without entering into these discussions, we will remark an ambiguity in the term on which they all roll, the term *labour,* which ambiguity is at the bottom of three fourths of the sophistries of popular Socialism.

7. There were two pillars put at the entrance of Solomon's temple, one on the right hand and the other on the left : that which was on the right hand

he called, according to the Septuagint, *Direction,*
κατόρθωσις, and that on the left hand, *Strength,* ἰσχύς.
(2 Par. iii. 17.)   Further we are told that Solomon
set seventy thousand men to carry burdens on their
shoulders, and eighty thousand to hew stones in the
mountains, and three thousand six hundred to be
overseers of the work of the people. (2 Par. ii. 18.)
The history is manifest.   Strength and Direction
build the Temple: Strength, or Manual Labour,
represented by the hodmen and quarrymen, and the
rest of the " hands : " Direction, or Mental Labour,
represented by the overseers.   Yet not by them
alone : surely we must count in as doers of mental
labour the designer of the Temple, or at least of its
decorations, that " most wise and skilful man, my
father Hiram ; " and still more King Solomon himself and David, the two royal minds that originated
and perfected the idea ; and David's generals, Joab
and Banaias, who secured the peace that was necessary as a condition of the building ; and innumer-
able other men of place and power in the nation,
but for whose thought and prudence the strength of
the workman would have been thrown away like a
river poured out in the Libyan desert.   From this
example, eked out with a little thought of his own,
the reader may estimate the wisdom and credit of
those who tell factory hands that it is their labour
which produces all the wealth of their employer,
and that, in the day when every man shall receive
his due, the employer shall be made a workmen like
themselves, and his wealth shall go to the increase
of their common wages.

8. Certainly, it will be said, the employer should be paid for his mental labour, but why at so enormously higher a rate than the manual labourers? If we say, 'because his labour is more valuable,' some Socialists would join issue on the score that labour is valuable according to the time that it takes, and the employer works shorter hours than his men. But this taking account of *quantity* alone in labour is an ignoring of the distinction which we have drawn of two *qualities* or *orders* of labour, mental and manual; one more valuable than the other as being scarcer and in greater demand, so that a short time of one may be set against a long time of another, like a little gold against a heap of brass. Any man accustomed to both orders of labour must have observed, that while he can work with his hands at almost any time when he is well, the highest labour of his intellect can be done only at rare intervals, and that in one happy hour he will sometimes accomplish more than in a day. As the same man differs from himself at different times, so does one man from another in the average value of his mental efforts: this value is not measured by time.

9. Abandoning this untenable position, Socialists still ask: 'But is the difference in the value of their labour quite so vast as is the interval between the profits of the employer and the pay of his poor drudges?' Honestly we cannot say that it is. We are fain to fall back upon the consideration, that the employer contributes, not only his brains to the work, but his capital. 'Ah, that is just it,' is the

Socialists' quick reply: 'We propose to relieve him of his capital, and remunerate his brainwork only: by that means we shall be able to pay sufficiently handsome wages for management, according to the ratio of mental and manual labour, and at the same time have a sufficiently large surplus over to raise the wages of his needy comrades, those seventy thousand hodmen and eighty thousand quarrymen.' It may be remarked that, if labour is to be bought like commodities at the lowest market-price, this is promising to pay for manual labour at a far higher figure than it is commercially worth. But let that pass: it is only an *argumentum ad hominem.*

10. Two reasons may be given for turning away from this seductive proposal, and leaving capital (not *consumer's wealth* merely) in private hands,— and that not only in the hands of what we may call *mentally productive capitalists*, men who oversee their own enterprises and manage their own work- men, but even of *unproductive capitalists*, men who have shares in and reap profits out of a business which they never meddle with. The first reason is, because this position of the productive, and still more that of the unproductive capitalist, is a prize for past industry expended upon production. To understand this, we must recollect once more that men work, not as individuals, but as heads of families. Every working man, from the sailor to the shop-boy, covets for himself two things, pay and leisure. The same two things do mentally pro- ductive labourers covet. But they covet them, not for themselves alone, but for their families, and more

T

even for their families than for themselves. They weary their brains, planning and managing, that in old age they may retire on a competence, and hand down that same competence, undiminished by their having lived on it, to their children. Thus the young man works and produces, that the old man, and the child to come, may have exemption from productive labour, an abiding exemption, which cannot be unless he is allowed to live on the interest of accumulated capital. These positions of affluence and rest—sinecures they are, so far as production is concerned—are the prizes awarded to the best productive labour. What they who do that labour aim at, is not wages but exemption from toil : their wish is not so much to be wealthy and have leisure themselves as to found a family in wealth and leisure,— the one possible foundation of such a family being a store of private capital. Socialists of course will offer nobler prizes for the best productive labour,— honour, and the satisfaction of having served the community, a satisfaction which they would have men trained from childhood to relish above all other joys. Unfortunately, this taste is yet unformed, and the stimulus of these nobler prizes is still unproved by experience. Meanwhile men do work hard, to the advantage of the community, for the ignobler prize of family affluence and ease. Socialists are going to take away the good boy's cake and give him a sunflower.

11. The second reason for leaving capital in private, even unproductive hands, begins from the consideration, that the highest end of man on earth

is not production, just as it is not consumption, of the necessaries and luxuries of life. Aristotle bids us, as much as possible in this life, "to play the immortal (ἀθανατίζειν), and do our utmost to live by the best element in our nature," that is, the intellect. (*Ethics*, c. ii., s. ii., n. 7, p. 9.) There is the intellectual life of the statesman in the practical order : and in the speculative order, that of the poet, of the artist, of the scholar, of the devout contemplative—the outcome of learned and pious leisure, and freedom from vulgar cares. One man ascending into this higher and better region helps his neighbour to follow. The neighbour can follow, even though he be not free from productive cares, but the leader ought to be free, if he is to soar a high, sustained and powerful flight, and guide others aloft. These unproductive capitalist families then form what we may call, by a figure which rhetoricians call *oxymoron*, something which comes very near a bull,—we may call them an *endowed lay-clergy :* they are told off from the rest of men to lead the way in doing, and causing to be done, the highest work of humanity. The absence of the First Class of Workers would render the Socialist Utopia a very vulgar place.

12. Nature's ideal is : *To all, plenty : to some, superabundance.* The superabundance of some is not necessarily incompatible with all having plenty : nay it is a positive furtherance of that and of still higher ends, as has been shown. But it is a position of advantage that may be abused, and is abused most wantonly : hence there comes to be question of Socialism.

Readings.—*Socialism* (Catholic Truth Society); *Nineteenth Century* for June, 1885, "Royal Commission for Housing the Poor;" Devas, *Groundwork of Economics*, §§ 149, 150, 261; Ar., *Pol.*, I., v.; Ar., *Eth.*, X. viii.; "A Socialist's Dream" in *The Month* for January and February, 1891. Also Devas, *Political Economy* (Stonyhurst Series), bk. iii., cc. vi. xi.

Section III.—*Of Landed Property.*

1. Land, like cotton, timber, or iron-ore, is a raw material wrought up by man. Land, like any other thing, becomes an article of property originally by occupation, and its value is enhanced by labour. There is no more reason why all land, or the rents of all land, should belong to the State, than why all house property, or all house rents, should belong to the State. If the people need land to live on, so do they need houses to live in, coals to burn, and shoes to wear. Socialism, once admitted, cannot be confined to land alone. It will exterminate "the lord manufacturer" as remorselessly as it exterminates the landlord.

2. Every man, it is contended, has a right to live on the fruits of the soil. The proposition is needlessly long. It should be put simply: Every man has a right to live. For as to living on the fruits of the soil, there is absolutely nothing else that man can live on. All human nutriment whatever is derived from what geologists call pulverized rocks, that is, soil. But if it is meant that every man has a right to live on the fruits of some soil or land of his own, where is the proof? So long as

the fruits of the earth do not fail to reach a man's mouth, what matters it whose earth it is that grows them? Some of the richest as well as the poorest members of the community are landless men. Confiscate rent to take the place of taxation, and some of the richest men in the community will go tax-free.

3. The land on which a nation is settled, we are told, belongs to that nation. Yes, it belongs to them as individuals, yet not so that a foreigner is excluded by natural law from owning any portion of it. But the government have over the land, and over all the property upon it, what is called *altum dominium*, or *eminent domain*, which is a power of commanding private proprietors to part with their property for public purposes, with compensation, whenever compensation is possible. Thus when a railway gets its Act of Parliament, the owners through whose estates the projected line is to run are compelled by an exercise of *eminent domain* to sell to the company. By the same power the government in a besieged city, when hard pressed, might seize upon all the stores of food and fuel within the walls, even without compensation. *Altum dominium*, which is not dominion properly so called, is sufficient for all national emergencies, without making the State the universal landlord.

4. It seems impossible to imagine an emergency that would justify any government in nationalizing all the land at once without compensation. None but a wealthy government could afford the compensation requisite; and the emergency would have to be severe indeed, to make it wise of them to incur

such an expense. We can imagine a government
in a newly settled country starting on the understanding that all land was State land, and that all
ground rents were to be paid into the State exchequer. This would amount to taking rents for
taxes; and instead of a landlord in every district
we should have a tax-gatherer. Probably further
taxation would be necessary: in England at any
rate the annual expenditure exceeds the rental by
some twenty millions. Government, we may suppose, would grant leases of land: when the lease
fell in, the rent would be raised for unearned increment, and lowered for decrement, but not raised
for improvements effected by the tenant himself.
In that case the tenant in two or three generations
might be a quasi-proprietor, his rent being ridicu-
lously small in comparison with the annual value of
the holding. The improvements might be the improvements of his grandfather, or even those of a
complete stranger, from whom he had bought the
tenancy. Anyhow they might be the better portion
of the value of the land, and would not be government property. Or would the government insist
on purchasing the improvements, and look out for a
new tenant paying a higher rent? Lastly, would the
government themselves make such improvements as
many an English landlord makes now, for love of
the country about him and love of his own people?

5. It would be most difficult to prevent private
property arising in land, even if it all did belong to
the State to start with. "Suppose £10 paid for a
piece of land for a year, and suppose the occupier

said, Let me have it for ten years, and I will give you £20 a year, ought not the State to accept the offer? Then suppose he said, Give it me for ever and I will pay £30 a year? Again, ought not the State to agree? He would then be that hateful creature a landowner, subject to a rent-charge. Now suppose the State wanted to do work and had to borrow money, and suppose he offered to give for the redemption of the rent-charge a sum which could not be borrowed for less than £40 a year. Again, ought not the State to accept his offer? Yet in that case he would become a hopelessly unmitigated landlord." (Lord Bramwell.)

6. When there is an alarm of fire in a theatre, any one who could convince the audience that there was time enough for them all to file out in slow succession by the door, would avert the greatest danger that threatened them, that of being crushed and trampled on by one another. Mankind in pursuit of wealth are like a crowd rushing excitedly through a narrow place of exit. Whatever man, or body of men, or institution, or doctrine, will moderate this "love of money" (φιλαργυρία), which St. Paul (1 Tim. vi. 10) declares to be " the root of all evils," the same is a benefactor to the human race, preventing that cruel oppression of the poor, which comes of ruthlessly buying land, labour, everything, in the cheapest market and selling it in the dearest. The landlord who always evicts, if he is not paid the highest competition rent,—the employer who brings in from afar the hands that will work at the lowest starvation wage,—these vultures are worse enemies to society than Socialists, for they occasion Socialism

7. Socialism, whether in land alone or in all capital, is an endeavour to accomplish by State control the results that ought to be achieved by private virtue. A landlord, or an employer, who remembers his position as being what Homer calls "a king of men," ἄναξ ἀνδρῶν,—remembers too, with Aristotle, that a prince exists for his people,—and who, besides a quasi-royal care for the body of tenantry or workmen over whom he presides, has something too of a fatherly interest in every one of them, their persons and their families, holding it to be a personal tie with himself, to be in his employment or settled upon his land,—such a man and the multitude of such men form the best bulwark a country can possess against Socialism. Such a landlord or employer is a *praesens numen* to his workpeople or tenants. In the absence of this protective, personal influence of the rich over the poor; in the disorganization of society consequent upon the misconduct of its subordinate chiefs; in the stand-off attitude of the higher classes, and the defiant independence of the lower; and in the greed of material goods that is common to them both, there lurks a danger of unknown magnitude to our modern civilization.

Reading.—Leo XIII. on the Condition of Labour, Encyclical of 15th May, 1891.[1]

[1] "The right of property attaches to things produced by labour, but cannot attach to things created by God." So Henry George, *Condition of Labour*, pp. 3, 4. How then do we read in *Progress and Poverty*, bk. 7. ch. 1: "The pen with which I am writing is justly mine," and that, in the last resort, on account of "the rights of those who dug the material from the ground and converted it into a pen"? Was not that material, iron-ore, "created by God," equally with any other portion of the earth's crust that we may please to call *land*?

CHAPTER VIII.

OF THE STATE.

SECTION I.—*Of the Monstrosities called Leviathan and Social Contract.*

1. THOMAS HOBBES, than whom never was greater genius for riding an idea, right or wrong, to the full length that it will go, was born in 1588: and notwithstanding his twelve pipes of tobacco daily, his vigorous constitution endured to his ninety-second year. The first half of his life fell in with the age of the greatest predominance of Calvinism. In religion he was scarcely a Calvinist, indeed he laboured under a suspicion of atheism : but his philosophy is accurately cast in the mould of the grim theology of Geneva. We may call it the philosophy of Calvinism. It has for its central tenet, that human nature either was from the first, or is become, bad, "desperately wicked," depraved, corrupt, and utterly abominable, so that whatever is natural to man, in so far forth as it is natural, is simply evil. The remedy for our evil nature Hobbes finds in no imputed merits of a Redeemer, no irresistible victorious grace, but in the masterful coercion of a despotic civil power. But, lest any one should suspect that there was at least this good in man, a propensity to civil society

and obedience to the rulers of cities, Hobbes insists that man is by nature wholly averse to society with his kind : that the type of the race is an Ishmael, "a wild man, his hand against all men, and all men's hands against him : " in fact that the state of nature is a state of war all round. He writes (*Leviathan,* c. xiii.) : "Men have no pleasure, but on the contrary a great deal of grief, in keeping company where there is no power able to overawe them all. For every man looketh that his companion should value him at the same rate he sets on himself; and upon all signs of contempt or undervaluing naturally endeavours, as far as he dares (which among them that have no common power to keep them quiet, is far enough to make them destroy each other), to extort a greater value from his contemners by damage, and from others by the example. . . . Hereby it is manifest, that during the time that men live without a power to keep them all in awe, they are in that condition which is called war, and such a war as is of every man against every man. . . . In such condition there is no place for industry, because the fruit thereof is uncertain, and consequently no culture of the earth : no navigation, nor use of the commodities that may be imported by sea : no commodious building : no instruments of moving and removing such things as require much force : no knowledge of the face of the earth : no account of time : no arts, no letters, no society ; and which is worst of all, continual fear and danger of violent death ; and the life of man, solitary, poor, nasty, brutish, and short. . . . To this war of every man against every man this also is consequent, that nothing can be unjust. The notions of right and wrong, justice and injustice, have there no place. Where there is no common power there is no law: where no law, no injustice. . . . It is consequent also to the same condition, that there be no pro-priety, no dominion, no *mine* and *thine* distinct, but only that to be every man's that he can get, and for so long as he can keep it."

2. Such is what Hobbes is pleased to call "the natural condition of mankind," a condition which man would have every natural reason for getting out of with all speed, were he ever so unhappy as to fall into it. It is true that, apart from civil government, violence would reign on earth. But it is not true that to live apart from civil government is the natural condition of mankind. It is not true that the only motive which draws men into civil society is the fear of violence, as though there were no such facts and exigencies of human nature as sympathy, friendship, intellectual curiosity, art, religion. It is not true that the one reason for the existence of the civil power consists in this, that without the restraining hand of the magistrate men would bite and devour one another. Lastly, it is not true that all rights, notably rights of property, are the creation of the State. A man is a man first and a citizen after-wards. As a man, he has certain rights actual and potential (c. v., s. i., p. 244): these the State exists, not to create, for they are prior to it in the order of nature, but to determine them, where indeterminate, to sanction and to safeguard them.

Natural rights go before legal rights, and are pre-supposed to them, as the law of nature before that law which is civil and positive. It is an "idol of the tribe" of lawyers to ignore all law but that upon which their own professional action takes its stand.

3. "In considering man as he must have come from the hands of nature," writes Jean Jacques Rousseau, "I behold an animal less strong than some, less active than others, but upon the whole in organism having the advantage of them all. I behold him appeasing his hunger under an oak, slaking his thirst in the first brook, finding a bed at the foot of the same tree that furnished his repast, and there you have all his cravings satisfied." (*Discours sur l'origine de l'inégalité.*) This noble savage—quite a contrast to Hobbes's ruffian primeval, "nasty, brutish," and short-lived—observes and imitates the industry, and gradually raises himself to the instinct, of the beasts among whom he lives. His constitution is robust, and almost inaccessible to malady. He attains to old age, free from gout and rheumatism. He surpasses the fiercest wild beasts in address as much as they surpass him in strength, and so arrives to dwell among them without fear. Yet withal he is distinguished from brutes by free-will and perfectibility, qualities which gradually draw him out of his primeval condition of tranquil innocence, lead him through a long course of splendours and errors, of vices and virtues, and end by making him a tyrant at once over nature and over himself.

4. Rousseau's life, 1715—1778, was a continual protest against the formalism, affectation, pedantry

and despotism of the age of the Bourbons. His
ideal of man was the unconventional, unconstrained,
solitary, but harmless and easy-going savage. Hobbes
was the growth of a sterner and more serious age.
The only reality to him in heaven and on earth was
force: his one idea in philosophy was coercion.
Human nature to him was an embodiment of brute
violence ever in need of violent restraint. Rousseau,
an optimist, saw nothing but good in man's original
nature: to the pessimist mind of Hobbes all was
evil there. Neither of them saw any natural adapta-
tion to social life in the human constitution. To
live in society was, in both their views, an artificial
arrangement, an arbitrary convention. But Hobbes
found in the intolerable evils of a state of nature an
excellent reason why men should quit it for the
unnatural condition of citizens. Rousseau found
no reason except, as he says, *quelque funeste hasard.*
The problem for Hobbes stood thus: how men,
entering society, might be "cribbed, cabined, and
confined" to the utmost in order to keep down
their native badness. Rousseau's concern was, how
one might so become a citizen as yet to retain to
the full the delightful liberty of a tropical savage.
Hobbes's solution is the *Leviathan,* Rousseau's the
Social Contract. The prize, we think, rests with the
Englishman: but the reader shall judge.

5. And first of the Social Contract. Rousseau
proposes "to find a form of association which shall
defend and protect with all the strength of the community the person and the goods of each associate,
and whereby each one, uniting himself to all, may

nevertheless obey none but himself and remain
as free as before." (*Contrat Social*, i. 6.) This
proposal is hopeless, it is a contradiction in terms.
No man can contract and remain as free as before,
but he binds himself either under a *wider* obligation
to do or abstain, where he was not bound before, or
under a *stronger* obligation where he was bound
already. Nevertheless Rousseau finds a means of
accomplishing the impossible and the self-contra-
dictory. "Each of us puts into a common stock
his person and all his power under the supreme
direction of the general will; and we receive in our
turn the offering of the rest, each member as an
inseparable part of the whole. Instantly, instead
of the private person of each contracting party,
this act of association produces a moral and collective body, composed of as many members as the
assembly has voices, which body receives by this
same act its unity, its common Ego, its life and its
will." (*ib.*) This awful signing away of all your
rights, so that your very personality is merged in
that of the community—a self-renunciation going far
beyond that of profession in any religious order—
ought certainly, as Rousseau says, to be "the most
voluntary act in the world;" and he adds the
characteristic reason: "every man being born free
and master of himself, none can, under any pretence
whatsoever, subject him without his own consent."
(*Contrat Social*, iv. 2.) Then you ask: When have
I made this large contract by the most voluntary act
in the world? Rousseau replies: "When the State
is instituted, consent is in residing." (*ib.*) But, you

reply, my residence is anything but the most voluntary act in the world: it would be awkward for me to emigrate; and if I did emigrate, it would only be to some other State: I cannot possibly camp out and be independent in the woods, nor appease my hunger under an oak. To this plea Rousseau quite gives in, remarking that "family, goods, the want of an asylum, necessity, violence, may keep an inhabitant in the country in spite of himself; and in that case his mere sojourn no longer supposes his consent to the contract." (*ib.*) Then none of us have made the contract, for we have never had the option of living anywhere except in some State.

6. Hobbes, after laying down the necessity of men combining for protection against mutual injustice, observes that a mere promise or agreement not to injure any one will not suffice: "for the agreement of men is by covenant only, which is artificial; and therefore no wonder if there be something else required besides covenant to make their agreement constant and lasting, which is a common power to keep them in awe and to direct their actions to the common benefit." He continues: "The only way to erect such a common power . . . is to confer all their power and strength upon one man or upon one assembly of men, that may reduce all their wills by plurality of voices unto one will: which is as much as to say, to appoint one man or assembly of men to bear their person; and every one to own, and to acknowledge himself to be the author of, whatsoever he that so beareth their person shall act or cause to be acted in those things which con-

cern the common peace and safety; and therein to submit their wills every one to his will, and their judgments to his judgment. This is more than consent or concord,—it is a real unity of them all in one and the same person, made by covenant of every man with every man, in such manner as if every man should say to every man: I authorise, and give up my right of governing myself to this man or to this assembly of men, on this condition, that thou give up thy right to him, and authorise all his actions in like manner. This done, the multitude so united in one person is called a *commonwealth*, in Latin *civitas*. This is the generation of that great Leviathan, or rather, to speak more reverently, of that mortal god, to whom we owe under the immortal God our peace and defence." (*Leviathan*, c. xvii.)   This idea of all the rights and personalities of the individuals who contract to live socially being fused and welded together into the one resultant personality and power of the State, has evidently been borrowed by Rousseau from Hobbes. We shall deal with the idea presently. Meanwhile several points claim our notice.

7. The hideous piece of cynicism whereby Rous seau (*Contrat Social*, iv. 2), after promising you that, if you join his commonwealth, you shall obey none but yourself, then goes on to tell you that you obey yourself in obeying the will of the majority, even when it puts you in irons or leads you to death— because as a citizen you have once for all renounced your own will, and can only wish what the majority wishes,—has its root in the position of Hobbes, that

"every subject is author of every act the sovereign doth." (*Leviathan*, c. xxi.)

8. A real and important difference between the *Leviathan* and the *Social Contract*, is that Hobbes (c. xix.) allows various distributions of sovereign power, but prefers monarchy: Rousseau (l. ii., c. i.) will have it that sovereignty is vested inalienably in the people: of which doctrine more to follow.

9. *Men are by nature equal,* say Rousseau and Hobbes and many more respectable authors. Yes, in their specific nature, that is, they are all equally men. Similarly you have it that all triangles are equal, if that is a proposition of any value. But men as individuals are not all equal. One is stronger in body, another more able in mind: one predisposed to virtue, another to vice: one born in affluence and honour, another in squalor. Not men in the abstract, but living men, start at different points of vantage, and the distance between them widens as they run the race of life. We may lay it down as an axiom, in diametric opposition to Rousseau, that inequalities are natural, equalities artificial.

10. *Man is born free:* so opens the first chapter of the *Contrat Social.* If free of all duties, then void of all rights (c. v., s. i., nn. 5, 7, pp. 246, 247): let him then be promptly knocked on the head as a sacrifice to Malthus; and with the misformed children born in Plato's *Republic,* "they will bury him in a secret and unseen spot, as is befitting."

11. Hobbes and Rousseau go upon this maxim, which has overrun the modern world, that no man can be bound to obedience to another without his

U

own consent. The maxim would be an excellent one, were men framed like the categories of Aristotle —substance, quantity, quality, relation, and the rest —each peering out of his own pigeon-hole, an independent, self-sufficient entity. But men are dependent, naturally dependent whether they will or no, every human being on certain definite others,—the child on the parent, the citizen on the State whose protection he enjoys, and all alike on God. These natural dependences carry with them natural uncovenanted obediences,—to parents, filial duty—to country, loyalty—to God, piety: all which are embraced in the Latin term *pietas*. (See St. Thomas, 2a 2æ, q. 101, art. 1, in corp.) The fatal maxim before us is the annihilation of *pietas*. In lieu of loyal submission we get a contract, a transaction of reasoned commercial selfishness between equal and equal. This perverse substitution has called forth Leo XIII.'s remark on the men of our time, "Nothing comes so amiss to them as subjection and obedience," *Nihil tam moleste ferunt quam subesse et parere.* (Encyclical on Christian Marriage.)

12. The common extravagance of the *Leviathan* and the *Social Contract* is the suppression of the individual, with his rights and his very personality, which is all blended in the State. (See Rousseau's words above quoted, n. 5, and those of Hobbes, n. 6.) The reservations in favour of the individual made by Hobbes, *Leviathan*, c. xxi., and by Rousseau, *Contrat Social*, l. ii., c. iv., are either trifles or self-contradictions. But it is not in man's power by any contract thus to change his nature, so as to

become from autocentric heterocentric (c. ii., s. i., n. 2, p. 203; c. v., s. i., n. 1, p. 244), from a person a thing, from a man a chattel, void of rights and consequently of duties, and bound to serve this Collective Monster, this Aggregated Idol, with the absolute devotedness that is due to God alone. The worship of the new Moloch goes well with the dark misanthropism of Hobbes: but in Rousseau, the believer in the perfect goodness of unrestrained humanity, it is about the most glaring of his many inconsistencies. It is of course eagerly taken up by the Socialists, as carrying all their conclusions. It is the political aspect of Socialism.

Reading.—Burke, *Warren Hastings,* Fourth Day, the passage beginning, "He have arbitrary power!"

SECTION II.—*Of the theory that civil power is an aggregate formed by subscription of the powers of individuals.*

1. The Greeks had a name ἔρανος, which meant a feast where the viands were supplied by each guest contributing in kind. If, in a party of four, one man brought a ham, another a rabbit, a third a dish of truffles, and a fourth a salmon, no one would expect that, when the cover was raised, there should appear a pigeon-pie. That would not be in the nature of an ἔρανος. Now not only Hobbes and Rousseau, but Locke and a great multitude of modern Englishmen with him, hold that the power of the State is an aggregate, the algebraic sum of the powers whereof the component members would have stood possessed, had they lived in what is called, by a misleading phrase, "the state of nature,"

that is, the condition of men not subject to civil
authority. These powers,—either, as Hobbes and
Rousseau virtually say, *all* of them, or, as Locke
and the common opinion has it, only *some* of them,
—men are supposed to resign as they enter into
the State. If therefore there appears in the City,
Nation, State, or Commonwealth, a certain new and
peculiar power, which belongs to no individual in
the "state of nature," or, as I prefer to call it, the
extra-civil state, then what we may designate as
the Aggregation Theory breaks down, and another
origin must be sought of civil principality. But
there is such a power in the State, new and peculiar,
and not found in any of the component individuals :
it is the power and authority to punish on civil
grounds. It is the right of the rods and axes, that
were borne before the Roman magistrate. It is, in
its most crucial form, the right to punish with
death.

2. We are not here concerned with proving the
existence of this right. It is generally admitted :
we assume it accordingly, and shall prove it later
on. Nor are we concerned with *domestic punishment*, inflicted by the head of a family within his
own household, for the good of that household,
stopping short of any *irreparable harm* to the sufferer.
(St. Thos., 2a 2æ, q. 65, art. 2, ad. 2.) Leaving this
aside, we say, and have proved already, that one
private individual has no right to punish another,
neither *medicinally* for the amendment of the delinquent, nor by way of *deterrent* for the good of the
community, nor in the way of *retribution* for his own

satisfaction. He has the right of self-defence, but not of punishment: the two things are quite different. He may also exact restitution, where restitution is due: but that again is not punishing. If he is in the extra-civil state, he may use force, where prudence allows it, to recover what he has lost. This *right of private war* really is surrendered by the individual, when the State is established: but war and punishment are two totally different ideas. Subjects are punished: war is levied on independent powers. (*Ethics*, c. ix., s. iii., nn. 4—6, pp. 171—174; *Natural Law*, c. ii., s. ii., n. 6, p. 212.)

3. Opposite is the opinion of Locke, who writes:

"The execution of the law of nature is in that state [of nature] put into every man's hands, whereby every one has a right to punish the transgressors of that law to such a degree as may hinder its viola- tion: for the law of nature would, as all other laws that concern men in this world, be in vain, if there were nobody that in the state of nature had a power to execute that law." We observe that the punish- ment of offenders against the law of nature, as such, belongs to the Legislator, who is God alone. Cer- tainly it is well, nay necessary, that there should be human law to bear out the law of nature: but human law is the creation of human society in its perfection, which is the State. Man is punished by man for breaking the laws of man, not—except remotely—for breaking the laws of God. Nor would it be any inconvenience, if the law of nature were in vain in a state wherein nature never intended

men to live, wherein no multitude of men ever for
any notable time have lived, a state which is neither
actual fact nor ideal perfection, but a mere property
of the philosophic stage, a broken article, an out-
worn speculation. Such is "the state of nature,"
as identified with the extra-civil state by Hobbes,
Locke, and Rousseau.

SECTION III.—*Of the true state of nature, which is the state
of civil society; and consequently of the divine origin of
power.*

1. The State is defined by Aristotle (*Politics,*
III., ix., 14): "the union of septs and villages in
a complete and self-sufficient life." The first and
most elementary community is the *family,* οἰκία.
A knot of families associating together, claiming
blood-relationship and descent, real or fictitious,
from a common ancestor, whose name they bear,
constitute a γένος, called in Ireland a *sept,* in Scotland a *clan,* nameless in England. When the sept
come to cluster their habitations, or encampments,
in one or more spots, and to admit strangers in
blood to dwell among them, these hamlets, or camps,
gradually reach the magnitude of a *village.* When
a number of these *villages,* belonging to different
septs, come to be contiguous to one another, this
mere juxtaposition does not make of them a State.
Nor does interchange of commodities, nor intermarriage, nor an offensive and defensive alliance:
these are the mutual relations of a *confederacy,* ξυμμαχία, but all these and more are needed for a State,
πόλις. To be a State, it is requisite that these septs

and villages should agree to regulate the conduct of their individual members by a *common standard of social virtue*, sufficient for their well-being as one community. This common standard is fixed by common consent, or by the decision of some power competent to act for all and to punish delinquents. The name of this common standard is *law*. (*Ethics,* c. vii., n. 1, p. 126.) The community thus formed leads a life *complete and self-sufficient*, not being a member of another, but a body by itself,—not part of any ulterior community, but complete in the fulness of social good and social authority.

2. Among the ancient Greeks and Italians, and to some extent also in mediæval Italy and Germany, the city or municipality, with the small country district attached, was the State. With us the nation is the State; and accordingly we say *my country* where the Greek said *my city*. Bearing this difference in mind, as also the fact that the *sept* is not known amongst us except to antiquarians, and likewise that the *village* with us coincides with the *parish*, and that there are town as well as country parishes,—upon these modern data we may amend Aristotle's definition thus: *The State is the union of parishes and municipalities in a perfect and self-sufficient community.*

3. The City State is well illustrated in the following narrative of Thucydides (ii., 15):

" In the time of Cecrops and the early kings as far as Theseus, Attica was always divided among several independent cities, with their own town-halls and magistrates; and when there was no alarm of an enemy, the inhabitants did not resort for common deliberation to the King, but severally managed their own affairs and took their own counsel, and some of them even went to war. But when Theseus came to the throne, he abolished the council-chambers and magistracies of the other cities, and centralised all the people in what is now the city [of Athens], where he appointed their one council-chamber and town-hall; and while they continued to occupy their own properties as before, he forced them to recognise this as their one city and State." Attica before Theseus was a *confederacy*, ξυμμαχία, not a State, πόλις.

4. A *citizen* is defined: "one who has access to a share in deliberative and judicial functions." (Ar., *Pol.* III., i., 12.) It is not necessary that he actually should share these functions, but the way to them should lie open to him: he should be a person qualified to share in them. There are various degrees of citizenship. Under a parliamentary government, we distinguish the member of parliament, the elector, and him who will be an elector as soon as he gets a house of his own; and again, the judge, and him who is liable to serve on juries. In an absolute monarchy there are no *citizens*, only *subjects*.

5. "The distribution of power in the State, and especially of the sovereign power, is called the *polity*" (πολιτεία, Ar., *Pol.*, III., vi., 1),—a word immortalised by the judicious Hooker, and happily recovered recently to the English language. The *polity* then is the distribution of the sovereignty. The person, singular or collective, in whose hands

the full sovereignty rests, is called the *ruler*. Be it
observed that what we call *the ruler* is never one
man, except in absolute monarchy. By the theory
of the British Constitution, the *ruler* is King, Lords,
and Commons, together.

6. *Nature requires that men generally live in society,
domestic and civil, so that the individual be of the family,
and families form associations, which again conspire to
form one perfect community, which is the State.* The
requirement of nature may be gathered from the
universal practice of mankind. "If it (the word
savage) means people without a settled form of
government, without laws and without a religion,
then, go where you like, you will not find such a
race." (Max Müller, in *Nineteenth Century*, Jan. 1885,
p. 114.) The same may be gathered from a consideration of what the State is, and of the ends
which it serves. The State, as we have seen (n. 2),
is a union of septs and villages, or of parishes
and municipalities. The individual is born and
nurtured in the family, and ordinarily becomes
in time the parent of a new family. Families
must combine to form septs by blood, or villages
(or parishes) by locality. Municipalities we may
leave aside, for a municipality is a potential State.
But we must consider the sept, village, or parish,
which is the community intermediate between family
and State. Among the cogent reasons which require
families to enter into this association, we may
mention friendship, intermarriage, the interchange
of services and commodities, the cultivation of the
arts, the preservation of traditions and inventions.

7. But it is further necessary that these septs, villages, or parishes, should band together and combine to form a higher community, self-sufficient and perfect,—for the determining of rights which Natural Law leaves undetermined,—for the punishing of disturbers of the peace, if need be, even with death, —for defence against a common enemy,—for a union of counsels and resources to the execution of magnificent works. This self-sufficient and perfect community, which is not part of any higher community, is the State.

8. We may observe that the whole reason for the being of the State is not mutual need, nor the repression of violence. Main reasons these are, no doubt, but not the whole main reason. Even if men had no need of one another for the supply of their animal wants, they would still desire to converse for the satisfaction of their intellectual curiosity and their social affections. And even if we had all remained as void of guile, and as full of light and love, as our first parents were at their creation, we should still have needed the erection of States. In a State there are not only criminal but civil courts, where it is not wicked men alone who come to be litigants. From sundry passages of Scripture it would appear that even angels may disagree as to what is best and proper: angelic men certainly may and do. It is a mistake to look upon civil government, with its apparatus of laws and judgments, simply as a necessary evil, and remedy of the perverseness of mankind. On the contrary, were all men virtuous, States would still be formed, towering in magni-

ficence above the States known to history, as the
cedars of Lebanon above the scanty growths of a
fell-side in our north country.

9. *There can be no State without a power to guide
and govern it.* It has indeed become the fashion to
repeat, as the latest discovery in politics, that what
a State needs is not government but administration.
This saying comes of a theory, to be examined presently, that sovereign power abides permanently
with the people at large, and that the sole function
of princes, cabinets, and parliaments, is to provide
means of giving effect to the popular will. This
however is not quite a repudiation of government,
but a peculiar view as to the seat and centre of
government. Those who hold it, vigorously maintain the right of the Many to govern, control, and
command the Few. The need of some governing
authority in a State can be denied by none but an
Anarchist, a gentleman who lives two doors beyond
Rousseau on the side of unreason.

10. *Every State is autonomous, self-governing, independent.* Either the whole people taken collectively
must rule the same whole taken distributively, or a
part must rule the rest. The ruler is either the whole
commonwealth, or more frequently a part of the
commonwealth. An autocrat is part of the State
which he governs. Sovereignty whole and entire is
intrinsic to the State. A community that is to any
extent governed from without, like British India or
London, is not a State, but part of a State, for it is
not a *perfect community*.

11. We have it therefore that *man is a social*

animal. Naturally he is a member of a family.
Nature requires that families should coalesce into
higher communities, which again naturally converge
and culminate in the State. Nature further requires
that in every State there should be an authority to
govern. But authority to govern and duty to obey
are correlatives. Nature therefore requires submission to the governing authority in the State. In
other words, Nature abhors anarchy as being the
destruction of civil society, and as cutting the ground
from under the feet of civilised man. The genuine
state of nature, that state and condition, which
nature allows and approves as proper for the evolution of the human faculties, is the state of man in
civil society. That is lost where there is no judge
in the land.

12. There are men full of a sentimental deference
to authority and professions of obedience, who yet
will not obey any of the authorities that actually are
over them. These are disobedient men. He is an
anarchist in practice, who meditates treason and rebellion against the "powers that be" actually over
him in the State wherein he lives. To obey no actual
power is to obey no power, as to wear no actual
clothes is to go naked. To keep up the comparison,
—as a man may change his clothes upon occasion,
and thus go through a brief interval of unclothedness
without injury to health or violation of decency, notwithstanding the requirement of nature to wear
clothes : so it may be or it may not be consonant
with the exigency of our nature at times to subvert
by insurrection the existing government in order to

the substitution of a new authority; that does not concern us here. We are stating the general rule under ordinary circumstances. The submission to civil authority, which nature requires of us, must be paid in the coin of obedience to the actual established "powers that be."

13. Any one who understands how morality comes from God (*Ethics*, c. vi., s. ii. nn. 6—9, 13, pp. 119—125), can have no difficulty in seeing how civil power is of God also. The one point covers the other. We need no mention of God to show that disobedience, lying, and the seven deadly sins, are bad things for human nature, things to be avoided even if they were not forbidden. All the things that God forbids are against the good of man. Their being evil is distinguishable from their being prohibited, and antecedent to it. Now as drunkenness and unchastity are evil for man, so too is anarchy. The one remedy for anarchy is civil government. Even if there were no God, it would be still imperatively necessary, as we have seen, for mankind to erect political institutions, and to abide by the laws and ordinances of constitutional power. But there would be no *formal obligation* of submission to these laws and ordinances; and resistance to this power would be no more than *philosophic sin*. (*Ethics*, c. vi., s. ii., n. 6, p. 119.) What makes anarchy truly sinful and wrong is the prohibition of it contained in the Eternal Law, that law whereby God commands every creature, and particularly every man, to act in accordance with his own proper being and nature taken as a whole, and to avoid what is repugnant to the same. (*Ethics*, c. vi., s. ii., n. 9, p. 120.)

Therefore, as man is naturally social, and anarchy is the dissolution of society, God forbids anarchy, and enjoins obedience to the civil power, under pain of sin and damnation. " They that resist, purchase to themselves damnation " (Rom. xiii. 2) : where the theological student, having the Greek text before him, will observe that the same phrase is used as in I Cor. xi. 29 of the unworthy communicant, as though it were the like sin to rend our Lord's mystical Body by civil discord as to profane His natural Body by sacrilege. But to enjoin obedience and to bestow authority are the obverse and reverse of one and the same act. God therefore gives the civil ruler power and authority to command. This is the meaning of St. Paul's teaching that there is no power but from God, and that the powers that be are ordained of God. (Rom. xiii. 1.)

14. The argument is summed up in these seven consequent propositions :

(a) Civil society is necessary to human nature.

(b) Civil power is necessary to civil society.

(c) Civil power is naught without civil obedience.

(d) Civil obedience is necessary to human nature.

(e) God commands whatever is necessary to human nature.

(f) God commands obedience to the civil power.

(g) God commissions the civil power to rule.

15. If any one asks how the State and the civil power is of God any otherwise than the railway company with its power, or even the fever with its virulence, a moment's reflection will reveal the answer in the facts, that railway communication,

however convenient, is not an essential feature of
human life, as the State is: while diseases are not
requirements in order to good, but incidental defects
and evils of nature, permitted by God. Why God
leaves man to cope with such evils, is not the question here.

Readings.—Ar., *Pol.,* I., ii.; III., i.; III., ix.,
nn. 5—15.

Section IV.—*Of the Variety of Polities.*

1. *One polity alone is against the natural law; that
is every polity which proves itself unworkable and in-
efficient: for the rest, various States exhibit various
polities workable and lawful, partly from the circumstances, partly from the choice, of the citizens: but the
sum total of civil power is a constant quantity, the same
for all States.* We proceed to establish the clauses
of this statement in succession.

2. If a watch be necessary to a railway guard, and
he is bound to have one accordingly, it is also necessary, and he is bound to procure it, that the watch
shall go and keep time. A watch that will not keep
time is an unlawful article for him to depend upon,
being tantamount to no watch, whereas he is bound
to have a watch. Otherwise, be his watch large or
small, gold, silver, or pinchbeck, all this is indifferent, so long as it be a reliable timekeeper. In
like manner, we must have a State, we must have a
government, and we must have a government that
can govern. Monarchy, aristocracy, parliaments,
wide or narrow franchise, centralisation, decentralisation, any one of these and countless other forms

—apart from the means whereby it is set up—is a lawful government, where it is a workable one; unlawful, and forbidden by God and nature, where it cannot work. A form of government that from its own intrinsic defects could nowhere work, would be everywhere and always unlawful.

3. You cannot argue from the accomplished fact the lawfulness of the means whereby it was accomplished. Nor do we say that every form of government, which succeeds in governing, was originally set up in justice; nor again that the success of its rule is necessarily due to the use of just means. The Committee of Public Safety in Paris in 1794 did manage to govern, but it was erected in blood, and it governed by an unscrupulous disregard of everybody's rights. All that we say is, that no distribution of civil power as a distribution, or no polity as a polity (s. iii., n. 5, p. 312), is unlawful, if by it the government can be carried on. And the reason is plain. For all that nature requires is that there should be an efficient civil authority, not that this man should have it, or that one man or other should have it all, or that a certain class in council assembled should engross it, or that all the inhabitants of the country should participate in it. Any one of these arrangements that will work, satisfies the exigency of nature for civil rule, and is therefore in itself a lawful polity.

4. Working, and therefore, as explained, lawful polities are as multitudinous as the species of animals. Besides those that actually are, there is a variety without end, as of animals, so of polities, that might be and are not. We can classify only the main

types. We ground our classification upon Ar., *Pol.*, III., vii., modernising it so as to take in forms of representative government, whereof Aristotle had no conception.

(1) *Monarchy*, or the rule of the Single Person, in whose hands the whole power of the State is concentrated, *e.g.*, Constantine the Great.

(2) *Aristocracy*, or the rule of the Few, which will be either *direct* or *representative*, according as either they themselves by their own votes at first hand, or representatives whom they elect, make the laws.

(3) *Democracy*, or the rule of the Many, that is, of the whole community. Democracy, again, is either *direct* (commonly called *pure*) or *representative*. The most famous approach in history to pure democracy is the government of Athens, B.C. 438—338.

(4) *Limited Monarchy*.

(a) *Monarchy with Aristocracy*, the government of England from 1688 to 1830.

(b) *Monarchy with Democracy*.

5. All civil government is for the governed, that is, for the community at large. The perversion of a polity is the losing sight of this principle, and the conducting of the polity in the interest of the governing body alone. By such perversion monarchy passes into *tyranny*, aristocracy into *oligarchy*, and democracy into *ochlocracy* or *mob-rule*. It might appear strange that, where the power rests with the whole people collectively, government should ever be carried on otherwise than in the interest of the entire community, did we not remember that the majority, with whom the power rests in a democracy,

V

may employ it to trample on and crush the minority. Thus the Many may worry and harass the Few, the mean and poor the wealthy and noble : though commonly perhaps the worrying has been the other way about. Anyhow it is important to observe that there is no polity which of itself, and apart from the spirit in which it is worked, is an adequate safeguard and rock of defence against oppression.

6. The wide range of polities that history presents is not drawn out by the caprice of nations. The very fact of a certain nation choosing a certain polity, where they are free to choose, is an indication of the bent of the national character, and character is not a caprice. No North American population are ever likely to elect an absolute monarch to govern them. That polity which thrives on the shores of the Caspian, can strike no root on the banks of the Potomac. The choice of a polity is limited by the character of the electors and by the circumstances in which the election is made. Not every generation in a nation is free to choose its polity : but the choice and institution of the fathers binds the children. Up to a certain point ancestral settlements must be respected, or instability ensues, and anarchy is not far off. Thus the spirit of freedom should always act as Burke says, "as if in the presence of canonized forefathers."

7. The smallest State in the world is the little republic of Andorra in the Pyrenees. Though it be a paradox to say it, there is as much political power in Andorra as in Russia,—one and the same measure of it in every State. In every State there is power

for civil good to the full height of the emergencies
that may arise. The same emergencies may arise
everywhere, and everywhere there is full power to
see that the commonwealth take no harm by them.
What a great empire can do for this purpose, *e.g.*,
proclaim martial law, search houses, lay an embargo
on the means of transport, impress soldiers, the
same can the tiniest commonwealth do in the like
need. And the ordinary functions of government
are the same in both.

8. This seems at variance with the theory of
some constitutions, according to which there are
certain so-called *fundamental laws*, which the legislature cannot call in question, nor deal with in any
way, but must take them in all its deliberations for
positions established and uncontrovertible. The
British Constitution recognizes no fundamental
laws. There is no reform that may not legally be
broached in Parliament and enacted there. Parliament is said to be "omnipotent," "able to do everything, except to make a man a woman." But in
many legislatures it is not so. At Athens of old
there were certain measures which no one could
introduce for discussion in the Sovereign Assembly
without rendering himself liable to a prosecution,
γραφὴ παρανόμων. And there have been many
monarchs termed absolute, who yet were bound
by their coronation-oath, or by some other agreement with their people, to preserve inviolate certain
institutions and to maintain certain laws. It may
be contended that such a government as we have in
England, which is theoretically competent to pass

any law within the limits of the natural law, has a greater range of power than a government whose operation is limited by a barrier of fundamental positive law. But this contention vanishes when we observe that there must remain in the State, which has fundamental laws, a power somewhere to reverse them. They can be reversed at least by the consent of the whole people. Thus at Athens the γραφὴ παρανόμων could be suspended by a vote of the Assembly. A people can release their monarch from his coronation-oath in such portions of it as are not binding absolutely by divine law. Where *fundamental law* obtains, a portion of the civil power becomes *latent*, and only a diminished remainder is left *free* in the hands of the person or persons who are there said to rule. Such person or persons are not the *adequate ruler* of the State, as they have not the full power, but the people, with whom rests the latent authority to cancel certain laws, are to that extent partakers in the sovereignty. Where there is agreement of the whole people, great and small, no part of the power remains *latent*, but all is set *free*. With us, it may be observed, the omnipotence of parliament has become a mere lawyer's theory. On every great issue, other than that on which the sitting parliament has been elected, it is the practice of ministers to "go to the country" by a new General Election. Thus only a certain measure of available authority is *free* at the disposal of parliament: the rest remaining *latent* in the general body of the electorate. Such is our constitution in practice.

9. If in any State the whole power were *free* in the hands of one man, there we might look to see made good the *dictum* of the judicious Hooker (*Ecclesiastical Polity*, bk. i., s. x., n. 5): "To live by one man's will became the cause of all men's misery." In a monarchy untrammelled by senate or popular assembly, it were well that some of the sovereign power should remain *latent*, and that His Majesty should rule in accordance with certain laws, not within his royal pleasure to revoke.

10. The State and the power of the State, apart from the polity, is of God. (s. iii., n. 14, p. 318.) The State under this or that polity and this or that ruler, is also of God. But, apart from the polity, the State is of God *antecedently* to any determination of any human will: because, willy nilly, man must live in civil society and God commands him so to do. But the State under *this* polity and *this* ruler is of God *consequently* to some determination of human volition. In this consequent sense we write *Victoria Dei gratia*.

11. There is little use in the enquiry, Which is the best polity? There is no polity which excels all other polities as man does the rest of animals. We judge of polities as of the various types of locomotives, according to the nature of the country where they are to run. Aristotle tells us that if we meet with a Pericles, we shall do best to make him our king, and hand over all our affairs to him. (Ar., *Pol.*, III., xiii., 25: cf. Thucydides, ii., 65.) Otherwise, "for most cities and for most men, apart from exceptional circumstances, or a condition of ideal perfection, but having regard to what is ordinarily

possible," he recommends a moderate republic under middle-class rule. (Ar., *Pol.*, VI., xi., Ed. Congreve.) This he calls *par excellence* "a polity," πολιτεία. Democracy, δημοκρατία, with Aristotle, always means that perversion of democracy, which we call *mob-rule*. (Ar., *Pol.*, III., vii., nn. 3, 5.)

12. In the English monarchy the whole majesty of the State shines forth in the Single Person who wears the Crown. The Crown is the centre of loyalty and gives dignity to the government. The Crown is above all parties in the State, knows their secrets, their purposes when in office as well as their acts, and is able to mediate, when party feeling threatens to bring government to a standstill. The British Crown has more weight of influence than of prerogative.[1]

Readings.—St. Thos., 1a 2æ, q. 105, art. 1, in corp., ad 2, 5; Ar., *Pol.*, III., xv.; *ib.*, III., xvi., nn. 5—8; *ib.*, VIII. (al. V.), xi. nn. 1—3.

SECTION V.—*Of the Divine Right of Kings and the Inalienable Sovereignty of the People.*

1. "Those old fanatics of arbitrary power dogmatized as if hereditary monarchy were the only lawful government in the world, just as our new fanatics of popular arbitrary power maintain that a popular election is the only lawful source of authority." (Burke, *Reflections on French Revolution*.)

We here stand between two idols of the tribe of politicians. We may call them Gog and Magog:

[1] Written in the month and year of Jubilee, June, 1887.

Gog, the divine right of kings; Magog, the inalienable sovereignty of the people.

2. The position known in history as "the divine
right of kings" may be best described as a *political
popedom*. It is the belief of Catholics that our
Divine Redeemer, instituting His Church by His
own personal act as a perfect society and spiritual
commonwealth, instituted in like manner the polity
under which He willed it to be governed, namely,
the Papal monarchy, begun in St. Peter and carried
to completion according to our Lord's design under
the line of Popes, Peter's successors. The monarchy
thus established is essential to the Catholic Church.
We speak not here of the temporal power which
the Pope once enjoyed in the Roman States, but
of his spiritual sovereignty over all Christendom
The Pope cannot validly resign and put out of his
own and his successors' hands, nor can the Cardinals
take away from him, nor the Episcopate, one jot
or tittle of this spiritual prerogative. He cannot, for
instance, condition his infallibility on the consent of
a General Council, or surrender the canonization of
saints to the votes of the faithful at large. Such
are the inalienable, Christ-given prerogatives of the
Papacy. Henry VIII. feloniously set himself up for
Pope within the realm of England. Blending together
temporal and spiritual jurisdiction, he made out his
rights and prerogatives as a monarch, even in the
civil order, to be inalienable as in the spiritual.
Spiritual and civil attributes together formed a
jewelled circlet, one and indivisible, immoveably
fixed on the brow of the King's Most Sacred

Majesty. Grown and swollen by their union with the spirituality, the civil attributes of the Crown were exaggerated to the utmost, and likewise declared inalienable. They were exaggerated till they came to embrace all the powers of government. The privileges of Parliament, and the limitations to the royal authority, set forth in the Petition of Right in 1628, were regarded as mere concessions tenable at the King's pleasure: from which point of view we understand the readiness of so conscientious a monarch as Charles I. to act against such privileges after he had allowed them. But to vest all the powers of government inalienably in the King, so that whoever else may seem to partake in them, shall partake only by royal sufferance, is tantamount to declaring monarchy the sole valid and lawful polity. This declaration the ministers, lay and clerical, of our Charleses and Jameses do not seem to have made in express terms. It is, however, contained by implication in their celebrated phrase of "the inalienable prerogatives of the Crown," as interpreted by the stretches of prerogative which they advised. They virtually asserted of one particular polity, or distribution of civil power (c. viii., s. iii., n. 5, p. 312), that which is true only of civil power taken nakedly, apart from the mode of its distribution— they said of *monarchy* what is true of *government*—that the sum of its power is a constant quantity (c. viii., s. iv., n. 7, p. 322), and that it is of God *antecedently* to and irrespectively of any determination of popular will. (c. viii., s. iv., n. 10, p. 325.)

3. Such a position is easily refuted, *negatively*, by

its being wholly unproven, unless the English Reformation, and the servile spirit in Church and State
that promoted and was promoted by the Reformation, can pass for a proof; and again the position
is *positively* refuted, when we come to consider how
all that nature requires and God commands, is
government under some polity, not government
everywhere under monarchy; there being many
workable polities besides monarchy. (s. iv., nn. 1—4,
p. 319.)

4. The same argument that demolishes Gog,
also overturns Magog. The two idols, opposed to
one another, stand upon the same pedestal, the
identification of government in general with one
particular polity, as though *a* polity were *the* polity.
The great assertor and worshipper of the inalienable
sovereignty of the people is Jean Jacques Rousseau.
He starts from postulates which we have already
rejected—that all men are equal (c. viii., s. i., n. 9,
p. 305)—that man is born free (*ib.*, n. 10)—that none
can be bound to obey another without his own consent (*ib.*, n. 11)—that civil society is formed by an
arbitrary convention (*ib.*, n. 4)—which convention
is the Social Contract. (*ib.*, n. 5.) From these unreasonable postulates Rousseau draws the conclusion, logically enough, that the sovereign will
in every State is the will of the majority of the
citizens: but the will of the majority, he goes on,
cannot be alienated from the majority: therefore
neither can the sovereignty be alienated, but must
abide permanently with the people ruling by a
majority of votes. The argumentation is excellent,

but the premisses are all false. The conclusion is
vastly popular, few minds considering from what
premisses it is drawn.

5. If sovereignty rests inalienably with the
people, the one valid polity is pure democracy.
This proposition, however, Rousseau was not
forward to formulate. The Stuarts had shrunk
from formulating a similar proposition about
monarchy, though they virtually held and acted upon
it. They were willing enough to allow of a parliament, whose privileges and functions should be at
His Majesty's gracious pleasure. Thus Rousseau
will allow you to have your senate, king, emperor,
if you will: only remember that he is *the prince*, not
the sovereign. (*Contrat Social*, l. iii., c. i.) The people
collectively are the sovereign, always sovereign.
The *prince*, that is, he or they to whom the administration is entrusted—since all the citizens cannot
administer jointly—is the mere official and bailiff
of the Sovereign People, bound to carry out their
mandate in all things, and removable at their
pleasure. The people must meet periodically, not
at the discretion of the prince. "These meetings
must open with two questions, never to be omitted,
and to be voted on separately. The first is:
Whether it pleases the Sovereign (People) to continue the present form of government. The second
is: Whether it pleases the People to leave the
administration to the persons at present actually
charged with it." (*Contrat Social*, l. iv., c. xviii.)

6. The claim of a pure democracy like this to
supersede all other polities cannot be established

by abstract arguments. That we have seen in examining the Social Contract. The alternative way of establishing such an exclusive claim would be to prove that the practical efficiency of pure democracy immeasurably transcends the efficiency of every other possible polity. There is indeed yet a third mode of proof resorted to. It is said that pure democracy everywhere is coming and must come ; and that what is thus on the line of human progress must be right and best for the time that it obtains. A grand invention this of Positivist genius, the theory, that whatever is is right ; and the practice, always to swim with the stream ! But supposing that pure democracy is coming, how long is it likely to last ? The answer may be gathered from a review of the working difficulties of such a polity.

7. It is made only for a small State. Railway and telegraph have indeed diminished the difficulty ; and have removed the need of all the voters meeting in one place, as was done at Athens. Newspapers echo and spread with addition the eloquence of popular orators, beyond the ears that actually listen to them. Still, think what it would be to have a general election upon every bill that passes through Parliament : for that is what pure democracy comes to. The plan would scarcely work with a total electorate of thirty thousand. You say the people would entrust a committee with the passing of ordinary measures, reserving to themselves the supervision. I am not arguing the physical impossibility, but the moral difficulties of

such an arrangement For either the people throw the reins of government on the neck of this committee, or they keep a tight hold upon the committee and guide it. In the former case the popular sovereignty becomes like that of a monarch who leans much on favourites, a sovereignty largely participated in by others than the nominal holder of the control. On the other hand, if the people do frequently interfere, and take a lively interest in the doings of the subordinate assembly, the people themselves must be a small body. An active governing body of three hundred thousand members would be as great a wonder as an active man weighing three hundred pounds. Only in a small State is that intense political life possible, which a pure democracy must live. There only, as Rousseau requires, can the public service be the principal affair of the citizens. " All things considered," he says, " I do not see how it is any longer possible for the Sovereign (People) to preserve amongst us the exercise of his rights, if the city is not very small." (*Contrat Social*, l. iii., c. xv.) And the difficulty of size in a democracy is aggravated, if, as Socialists propose, the democratic State is to be sole capitalist within its own limits. The perfect sovereignty of the people means the disruption of empires, and the pushing to extremity of what is variously described as *local government, home rule, autonomy,* and *decentralisation,* till every commune becomes an independent State. But for defence in war and for commerce in peace, these little States must federate ; and federation means centralisation, external control over the majority at home, restricted foreign relations, in fact the corruption of pure democracy.

8. Again, the perfect sovereignty of the people cannot subsist except upon the supposition that one man is as much a born ruler as another, which means a levelling down of the best talent of the community, for that is the only way in which capacities can be equalised—a very wasteful and ruinous expedient, and one that the born leaders of the people will not long endure. Then there is the proverbial fickleness of democracy, one day all aglow, and cooled down the next, never pursuing any course steadily, in foreign policy least of all, though there the dearest interests of the State are often at stake. As one who lived under such a government once put it: "Sheer democracy is of all institutions the most ill-balanced and ill put together, like a wave at sea restlessly tossing before the fitful gusts of wind : politicians come and go, and not one of them cares for the public interest, or gives it a thought." (Quoted by Demosthenes, Speech on the Embassy, p. 383 A.) What they do care for and think of sedulously, is pleasing the people and clinging to office. In that respect they are the counterparts of the favourites who cluster round the throne of a despotic monarch, and suck up his power by flattering him. Peoples have their favourites as well as kings. To these persons, the Cleon or Gracchus of the hour, they blindly commit the management of their concerns, as the *roi fainéant* of old Frankish times left everything to his Mayor of

the Palace, till the Mayor came to reign in his master's stead ; and so has the popular favourite ere now developed into the military despot. Strong-minded kings of course are not ruled by favourites, nor are highly intelligent and capable peoples : but it is as hard to find a people fit to wield the power of pure democracy as to find an individual fit for an absolute monarch, especially where the State is large.

9. From all this we conclude that the new-fashioned Magog of pure democracy, or the perfect sovereignty of the people, is not to be worshipped to the overthrow and repudiation of all other polities, any more than the old-fashioned Gog of pure monarchy, idolised by Stuart courtiers under the name of "the divine right of kings." Neither of these is *the polity :* each is *a polity,* but not one to be commonly recommended. The study of polities admirably illustrates the Aristotelian doctrine of the Golden Mean (*Ethics,* c. v., s. iv, p. 77), teaching us ordinarily to affect limited monarchy or limited democracy. But as the mean must ever be chosen in *relation to ourselves,* a Constantine or an Athenian Demos may represent the proper polity in place under extraordinary circumstances.

Reading.—The Month for July, 1886, pp. 338, seqq

SECTION VI.—*Of the Elementary and Original Polity.*

1. " All things are double, one against another." (Ecclus. xlii. 25.) The son of Sirach may have had in view the human body as divisible by a vertical median line into two symmetrical halves. But in

each of the halves thus made, the same organ or limb is never repeated twice in exact likeness, nor do any two parts render exactly the same service. This variety of organs in the bodies of the higher animals is called *differentiation*. As we descend in the animal series we find less and less of differentiation, till we reach the lowest types, which are little more than a mere bag, whence their name of Ascidians. In that State which has London for its capital city, we behold one of the highest types of political existence. Sovereignty is there divided, as usual in modern States, into three branches, Legislative, Judicial, and Executive. Each of these branches is shared among many persons in various modes and degrees, so that in practice it is not easy to enumerate and specify the holders of sovereignty, nor to characterize so complex a polity. At the other end of the scale we may represent to ourselves 250 "squatters" forming an independent State in the far West of America. They are a pure democracy, and the sovereignty belongs to them all jointly. Is a man to be tried for his life? The remaining 249 are his judges. Is a tax to be levied on ardent spirits? The 250 vote it. Is there a call to arms? The 250 marshal themselves to war. That clearly is the condition of minimum differentiation, where one citizen is in all political points the exact counterpart of all the rest. Of all polities it is the most *simple and elementary* possible. And so far forth as the natural order of evolution in polities, as in all other things, is from simple to compound, this is also the *original* polity. It is also the *residuary* polity, that, namely, which comes to be, when all other government in the State vanishes. Thus, if the Powder Plot had succeeded, and King James I., with the royal family, Lords and Commons, with the judges and chief officers of the Executive, had all perished together, the sovereign authority in England would have devolved upon the nation as a whole.

2. Certain monarchical writers shrink from the recognition of pure democracy as either the first or the last term of the series of polities. They do not recognize it as a polity at all. When there is no governing body distinct from the mass of people at large, a government must be formed, they say, by popular suffrage. Meanwhile, according to them, the sovereign power rests not with the body of electors: either it is not yet created, or it has lapsed: but as soon as the election is made, they see sovereignty breaking forth like the sun rising, in the person, single or composite, who is the object of the people's choice. This would be the correct view of the matter, if no choice were left to the electors, but they were obliged to acquiesce in some pre-arranged polity, as a Monarchy, or a Council of Ten, and could do nothing more than designate the Monarch or the Council. Under such a restriction the Cardinals elect the Pope. But our electors can institute any polity they see fit. They are a Constituent Assembly. They may fix upon a monarchy or a republic, two or one legislative chambers, a wide or a narrow franchise, home rule or centralization: or they may erect a Provisional Government for five years with another appeal to the people at

the end of that term. More than that. They could impose a protective duty upon corn, or endow the Roman Catholic religion, making such protection or endowment a fundamental law (s. iv., n. 8, p. 323), and withholding from the government, which they proceed to set up, the power of meddling with that law. They are then not only a Constituent but likewise a Legislative Assembly. But this power of making laws and moulding the future constitution of the State, what else is it but sovereign power, and indeed the very highest manifestation of sovereignty?

3. So far we follow Suarez in his controversy with James I. The *natural* order of evolution certainly is, that the State should be conceived in pure democracy, and thence develop into other polities. But in speaking as though the natural order had always been the *actual* order, Suarez seems to have been betrayed by the ardour of controversy into the use of incorrect expressions. It is true in the abstract, as he says, that "no natural reason can be alleged why sovereignty should be fixed upon one person, or one set of persons, rather than upon another, short of the whole community." This is true, inasmuch as in the abstract we view men as men, in which specific character they are all equal. But in the concrete and real life, the primeval citizens who start a commonwealth are rarely alike and equal, as the founders of the American Republic at the separation from Great Britain pretty well were, but some men, or some order of men, will so much excel the rest in ability, position, or posses-

w

sions, that the rest have really no choice but to acquiesce in those gifted hands holding the sovereignty.

Readings.—Suarez, *De Legibus*, III., iii., 6; *ib.*, III., iv., nn. 2, 3, 4; *Defensio Fidei*, III., ii., nn. 7, 8, 9; Ar., *Pol.*, III., xiv., 12; *ib.*, VIII., x., nn. 7, 8; *The Month* for July, 1886, pp. 342—345.

SECTION VII.—*Of Resistance to Civil Power.*

"When they say the King owes his crown to the choice of his people, they tell us that they mean to say no more than that some of the King's predecessors have been called to the throne by some sort of choice. Thus they hope to render their proposition safe by rendering it nugatory." (Burke, *Reflections on French Revolution.*)

1. The great question about civil power is, not whence it first came in remote antiquity, but whence it is now derived and flows continually as from its source, whether from the free consent of subjects so long as that lasts, or whether it obtains independently of their consent. Can subjects overthrow the ruler, or alter the polity itself, as often as they have a mind so to do? or has the ruler a right to his position even against the will of his people? A parallel question is, can a province annexed to an empire secede when it chooses, as South Carolina and other Confederates once attempted secession from the American Union?

2. These questions raise two totally different issues, which must be first carefully distinguished and then severally answered. The first point at

issue is whether subjects may dethrone their ruler, a people alter their polity, or a province secede from an empire, *at discretion.* The second point is, whether the same may be done *under pressure of dire injustice.* One little matter of phraseology must be rectified before an answer is returned to this first point. The question whether *subjects* may dethrone their *ruler* at discretion, from the terms in which it is drawn, can lead to none but a negative answer. From the fact that they are subjects, and this man, or this body of men, their ruler, their allegiance cannot be wholly discretionary. That sovereign is a mere man of straw, there is no soul and substance of sovereign power in him, who may be knocked down and carted away for rubbish, any moment his so-called subjects please. Rousseau is quite clear on this point. The true debateable form of the question is, whether the people, being themselves sovereign, can remove at will the official persons who actually administer the State; whether they can change the polity, and whether the inhabitants of a province can secede. The answer now is simple: all depends upon the polity of the particular country where the case comes for discussion. And if so it be that the constitution makes no provision one way or another, any dispute that may occur must be settled by amicable arrangement among the parties concerned: if they cannot amicably agree, they must fight. To save this last eventuality, it were well that any claim which the people in any country may have to remove princes and statesmen from office, to alter the polity, or to divide the empire, should be made matter of the

clearest understanding and most express and un-
ambiguous stipulation.   Even so, such a provision
must be generally viewed with disfavour by the
political philosopher, seeing how it tends to the
weakening and undermining of government; whereas
the same considerations that make out government
to be at all a boon and a necessity to human nature,
argue incapacity and instability in the governing
power to be a deplorable evil.   We must add, that
where the people keep in their hands any power to
alter the polity, or transfer the administration to
other hands, there they hold part at least of the
sovereignty; and the alteration or transference is
effected by them, not as subjects, but as partial ruler.

3. The second point we raised was, whether a
dethronement, or an alteration of polity, or a secession, may be brought about, not indeed at discretion
for any cause, but under pressure of dire injustice.
It comes to this: May the civil power be resisted
when it does grievous wrong?   Let us begin our
reply with another question: May children strike
their parents?   No.   Not even in self-defence? when
the parent is going about to do the child some
grievous bodily hurt?   That is an unpleasant question, but the answer is plain.   We can make no
exceptions to the rule of self-defence.   Self-defence
in extreme cases may raise the arm of a child
against its parent: in a similar extremity it may set
a people in conflict with their civil ruler.   Still we
regard with horror the idea of striking a parent,
and speak of it generally as a thing never to be
done: so should we regard and speak of rebellion.

We should not parade it before men's eyes as a deed to be contemplated, admired, and readily put in execution. "I confess to you, Sir," writes Burke, "I never liked this continual talk of resistance and revolution, or the practice of making the extreme medicine of the constitution its daily bread."

4. The conditions under which the civil authority may be withstood in self-defence, are fairly stated in the *Dublin Review* for April, 1865, p. 292. We must premise, that such a course of self-defence once publicly entered upon is like a rock rolled over the brow of a steep mountain: down it rolls and re-bounds from point to point, gathering momentum in the descent, till in the end the ruler, once defied, has to be dethroned, the polity subverted, the empire rent, or they who made the resistance must perish.

"Resistance is lawful :—(1) When a government has become substantially and habitually tyrannical, and that is when it has lost sight of the common good, and pursues its own selfish objects to the manifest detriment of its subjects, especially where their religious interests are concerned. (2) When all legal and pacific means have been tried in vain to recall the ruler to a sense of his duty. (3) When there is a reasonable probability that resistance will be successful, and not entail greater evils than it seeks to remove. (4) When the judgment formed as to the badness of the government, and the prudence of resistance thereto, is not the opinion only of private persons or of a mere party: but is that of the larger and better portion of the people, so that it may morally be considered as the judgment of the community as a whole."

5. Side by side with this we will set the teaching of Leo XIII., Encyclical, *Quod Apostolici*.

"If ever it happens that civil power is wielded by rulers recklessly and beyond all bounds, the doctrine of the Catholic Church does not allow of insurgents rising up against them *by independent action* (*proprio marte*), lest the tranquillity of order be more and more disturbed, or society receive greater injury thereby : and when things are come to such a pass that *there appears no other ray or hope of preservation*, the same authority teaches that a remedy must be sought in the merits of Christian patience and in earnest prayers to God."

The words we have italicized seem to point to conditions (4) and (3) respectively, as laid down by the writer in the *Dublin Review*.

For an instance of a king dethroned, not *proprio marte*, but with every appearance at least of an act of the whole nation, see the dethronement of Edward II., as related by Walsingham, *Historia Anglicana*, I., pp. 186, 187, Rolls Series.

6. "We save ourselves the more virulent and destructive diseases of revolution, sedition, and civil war, by submitting to the milder type of a change of ministry. (*Times*, April 7, 1880.)

7. It is not monarchical governments alone that can ever be resisted lawfully : but what is sauce for the king's goose is sauce also for the people's gander. There is no special sanctity attaching to democracy.

It might seem that, since resistance requires to be justified by the approval of " the larger and

better portion of the people" (n. 4, condition [4])
no just resistance can ever be offered to the will of
the democratic majority. But the said majority
may be in divers ways coerced and cajoled, a mere
packed majority, while the malcontents may be, if
not "the larger," clearly "the better" portion of
the community. (s. iv., n. 5, p. 321.)

Readings.—St. Thos., *De Regimine Principum*,
i., 6; 2a 2æ, q. 42, art. 2; 2a 2æ, q, 69, art. 4, in
corp.; Locke, *Of Civil Government*, nn. 200, 201, 203,
204, 208, 209, 223, 224, 225, 227, 229, 230, 232.

SECTION VIII.—*Of the right of the sword.*

1. By *the right of the sword* is technically meant
the right of inflicting capital punishment, according
to the Apostle's words: "But if thou do that which
is evil, fear: for he beareth not the sword in vain."
(Rom. xiii. 4.) We commonly call it *the power of
life and death.*

2. That a government may be a working government, as it should be (s. iv., n. 2, p. 319), it must not
only make laws, but bear out and enforce its legislation
by the sanction of punishment. "If talk and argumentation were sufficient to make men well-behaved,
manifold and high should be the reward of talkers.
. . . But in fact it appears that talking does very
well to incite and stimulate youths of fine mind;
and lighting upon a noble character and one of
healthy tastes, it may dispose such a person to take
up the practice of virtue: but it is wholly unable to
move the multitude to goodness; for it is not their
nature to obey conscience, but fear, nor to abstain

from evil because it is wrong, but because of punishments. The multitude live by feeling: they pursue
the pleasures that they like and the means thereto,
and shun the opposite pains, but they have no idea,
as they have had no taste, of what is right and fair
and truly sweet. . . . The man who lives by feeling
will not listen to the voice of reason, nor can he
appreciate its warning. How is it possible to divert
such a one from his course by argument? Speaking
generally, we say that passion yields not to argument but to constraint. . . . The multitude obey on
compulsion rather than on principle, and from fear
of pains and penalties rather than from a sense of
right. These are grounds for believing that legislators, while exhorting to virtue and putting certain
courses of conduct forward as right and honourable,
in the expectation that good men will obey the call,
as their habits lead them, should at the same time
inflict chastisements and punishments upon the
crossgrained and disobedient; and as for the incurably vicious, put them beyond the pale altogether. The result will be, that the decent and
conscientious citizen will listen to the voice of
reason, while the worthless votary of pleasure is
chastened by pain like a beast of burden. . . . Law
has a coercive function, appealing to force, notwithstanding that it is a reasoned conclusion of practical
wisdom and intelligence. The interference of persons
is odious, when it stands out against the tide of
passion, even where it is right and proper to interfere ; but no odium attaches to statute law enjoining
the proper course." (Aristotle, *Ethics*, X., ix.)

3. Aristotle seems hard upon the masses, likening them to brutes who must be governed by the whip. He may be supposed to speak from experience of the men of his time. If humanity has somewhat improved in two and twenty centuries, yet it cannot be contended that the whip is grown unnecessary and beyond the whip the sword. But we must observe a certain *modus operandi* of punishment which Aristotle has not noted, a more human mode than the terror of slavish fear. Just punishment, felt as such, stimulates the conscience to discern and abhor the crime. Men would think little of outraging their own nature by excess, did they not know that the laws of God and man forbid such outrage. Again, they would think little even of those laws, were not the law borne out by the sanction of punishment. A law that may be broken with impunity is taken to be the toying of a legislator not in earnest. Men here are as children. A child is cautioned against lying. He reckons little of the caution: he tells a lie, and a flogging ensues. Thereupon his mind reverts to what he was told: he sees that the warning was meant in earnest. He reflects that it must have been a wicked thing, that lie which his father, the object of his fond reverence, chastises so sternly. If the thing had been let pass, he would scarcely have regarded it as wicked. Next time he is more on his guard, not merely because he fears a beating, but because he understands better than before that lying is wrong. The awe in which grown-up people stand of "a red judge," is not simple fear, like that which keeps the wolf from the flock guarded by shepherds and their dogs : but they are alarmed into reflection upon the evil which he is God's minister to avenge, and they are moved to keep the law, "not only for wrath, but for conscience sake." From this we see that for punishment to be really salutary, its justice must be manifest to the culprit, or to the lookers on, at least in their cooler moments. A punishment the justice of which is not discernible, may quell for the moment, but it does not moralise, nor abidingly deter. There must be an apparent proportion between the offence and the punishment. A Draconian code, visiting petty offences with the severity due to high misdemeanours, is more of an irritant than a repressor of crime, because it goes beyond men's consciences.

4. There is in every human breast a strong sense of what the learned call *lex talionis*, and children *tit for tat*. "If a man has done to him what he has done to others, that is the straight course of justice ; " so says the canon of Rhadamanthus, quoted by Aristotle. (*Eth.*, V., v., 3.) We have argued the fundamental correctness of this rule. (*Ethics*, c. ix., s. iii., n. 2, p. 169.) It appears in the divine direction given to Noe : "Whoso sheddeth man's blood, his blood shall be shed." (Gen. ix. 6.) It appears in that popular sentiment, which in some parts of America displays itself in the lynching of murderers, who have unduly escaped the hands of the law; and which, under a similar paralysis of law in Corsica, broke out in blood-feuds, whereby the nearest relative of the deceased went about to slay the murderer.

Such taking of justice into private hands is morally unlawful, as we have proved. (*Ethics,* c. ix., s. iii., n. 4, p. 171; *Natural Law,* c. viii., s. ii., nn. 2, 3, pp. 308, 309.) It is a violent outburst of a natural and reasonable sentiment deprived of its legitimate vent. Unquestionably then there is an apparent and commonly recognized fairness of retribution in the infliction of capital punishment for murder. Thus the first condition of appropriate punishment is satisfied, that it be *manifestly proportioned to the crime.*

5. Capital punishment is moreover expedient, nay, necessary to the State. The right to inflict it is one of the essential prerogatives of government, one of those prerogatives the sum of which, as we have seen, is a constant quantity everywhere. (s. iv., n. 7, p. 322). No Government can renounce it. The abolition of capital punishment by law only makes the power of inflicting it *latent* in the State (s. iv., n. 8, p. 323); it does not and cannot wholly take the power away. You ask: Is there not hope, that if humanity goes on improving as it has done, capital punishment will become wholly unnecessary? I answer that— waiving the question of the prospect of improvement—in a State mainly consisting of God-fearing, conscientious men, the *infliction* of capital punishment would rarely be necessary, but the *power to inflict it* could never be dispensed with. If men ever become so ideally virtuous, the right of the State to visit gross crime with death cannot hurt them, and it will strengthen their virtue, as all human social virtue will ever need strengthening.

6. The abiding necessity of this *right of the sword*

is argued from the strength and frequency of the provocations to deeds of bloodshed and violence that must ever be encountered in human society. What these provocations are, how many and how strong, may be left to the reflection of the student who reads his newspaper, or even his novel. Not the least appalling thing about crime, atrocious crime especially, is the example that it gives and the imitators whom it begets. It is not merely that it sets the perpetrator himself on the downward path, so that, unless detected and punished, a man's first deed of blood is rarely his last : it draws others after him by a fatal fascination. Like the images which the Epicureans supposed all visible objects to slough off and shed into the air around them, such phantoms and images of guilt float about a great crime, enter into the mind of the spectator and of the hearer, and there, upon slight occasion, turn to actual repetitions of the original deed. The one preventive is to append to that deed a punishment, the image of which shall also enter into the mind, excite horror, and disenchant the recipient. This is not to be done by mere banishment of the criminal, nor by his perpetual incarceration. Exile and prison—particularly in view of the humanity of a modern penitentiary—do not sufficiently strike the imagination. One sweet hour of revenge will often appear cheap at the price of ten years' penal servitude. There is nothing goes to the heart like death. Death is the most striking of terrors; it is also the penalty that most exactly counterpoises in the scales of justice the commission of a murderous crime.

All States need this dread figure of the Sword-bearer standing at the elbow of the Sovereign.

7. But is not every capital sentence a trespass upon the dominion of God, Lord of life and death? No, for that same God it is who has endowed man with a nature that needs to grow up in civil society, which civil society again needs for its maintenance the power to make laws, to sit in judgment on transgressors, and in extreme cases, as we have proved, having tried them and found them guilty, to take away even their lives, to the common terror and horror of the crime. God, who wills human nature to be, wills it to be on the terms on which alone it can be. To that end He has handed over to the civil ruler so much of His own divine power of judgment, as shall enable His human delegate to govern with assurance and effect. That means the right of the sword.

8. It may be objected that to kill any man is to treat him as a *thing*, not a person, as an *hetero-centric*, not an *autocentric* being, which is a proceeding essentially unnatural and wrong. (c. ii., s. i., n. 2, p. 203.) St. Thomas's answer here is peculiarly valuable:

"Man by sinning withdraws from the order of reason, and thereby falls from human dignity, so far as that consists in man being naturally free and existent for his own sake [autocentric]; and falls in a manner into the state of servitude proper to beasts, according to that of the Psalm (xlviii. 15): *Man when he was in honour did not understand: he hath matched himself with senseless beasts and become like unto them;* and Proverbs xi. 29: *The fool shall serve the wise.* And therefore, though to kill a man, while he abides in his native dignity, be a thing of itself evil, yet to kill a man who is a sinner may be good, as to kill a beast. For worse is an evil man than a beast, and more noxious, as the Philosopher says." (2a 2æ, q 64, art. 2, ad 3.)

Hence observe:—(1) That a Utilitarian who denies free will, as many of that school do, stands at some loss whence to show cause why even an innocent man may not be done to death for reasons of State, *e.g.*, as a sanitary precaution.

(2) That the State must come to a conclusion about inward dispositions by presumption from overt acts, arguing serious moral guilt before proceeding to capital punishment. To this extent the State is remotely a judge of sin. But it does not punish sin *retributively* as sin, nor even *medicinally*. It punishes the violation of its own laws, to *deter* future offenders. (*Ethics*, c. ix., s. iii., nn. 4—6, pp. 171—174.)

Readings.—St.Thos., 2a 2æ, q. 64, art. 2, 3 ; 2a 2æ, q. 108, art. 3.

SECTION IX.—*Of War.*

1. War, a science by itself, has no interest for the philosopher except as an instance on a grand scale of self-defence. When the theory of self-defence has been mastered (c. ii. s. ii., p. 208), little further remains to be said about war. In a State, the self-defence of citizen against citizen is confined to the moment of immediate physical aggression. But in a region where the State is powerless and practically non-existent, self-defence assumes a far greater amplitude. (s. ii., n. 2, p. 309.) When the Highland chief

lifted the cattle of the Lowland farmer, and the King of Scotland lay unconcerned and unable to intervene, feasting at Holyrood, or fighting on the English border, then, if there were a fair hope of recovering the booty without a disproportionate effusion of blood, the farmer did right to arm his people, march after the robber, and fight him for the stolen oxen, as the gallant Baron of Bradwardine would fain have done. (*Waverley*, c. xv.) Here is the right of self-defence in its full development, including the right of private war. But in a private individual this is an undesirable, rank, and luxuriant growth; and when the individual comes to live, as it should be his aim to live, in a well-organized State, the growth is pruned and cut down: he may then defend himself for the instant when the State cannot defend him; but after the wrong is done, he must hold his hand, and quietly apply to the State to procure him restitution and redress. But there is no State of States, no King of Kings, upon earth; therefore, when of two independent States the one has wronged, or is about to wrong the other, and will not desist nor make amends, nothing is left for it; Nature has made no other provision, but they must fight. They must fall back upon the steel and the shotted gun, the *ratio ultima regum*.

2. The Lowland farmer above mentioned might be spoken of as *punishing* the Highland robber, *chastising* his insolence, and the like. This is popular phraseology, but it is not accurate. Punishment, an act of *vindictive justice*, is from superior to in-

ferior. (*Ethics*, c. v., s. ix., n. 4, p. 104.) War, like other self-defence, is between equals. War is indeed an act of authority, of the authority of each belligerent State over its own subjects, but not of one belligerent over the other. We are not here considering the case of putting down a rebellion : rebels are not properly belligerents, and have no belligerent rights.

3. The study of Civil and Canon Law flourished in the Middle Ages, while moral science, which is the study of the Natural Law, was still in its infancy. No wonder that the mediæval jurists occasionally formulated maxims, which can only be squared with the principles of Natural Law by an exceeding amount of interpretation,—which are in fact much better dropped, quoted though they sometimes be by moralists of repute. One such maxim is this, that *a wrong-doer becomes the subject of the injured party by reason of the offence*. Admit this, and you can hardly keep clear of Locke's doctrine of the origin of civil power. (s. ii., *per totum*, p. 307; cf. Suarez, *De Caritate*, d. xiii., s. iv., nn. 5, 6.)

4. We have only to repeat about war what we said of self-defence, that all the killing that takes place in it is *incidental*, or *indirect*. The cannon that you see in Woolwich Arsenal, the powder and torpedoes, have for their end what St. Thomas (*De Potentia*, q. 7, art. 2, ad 10) declares to be the end and object of the soldier, " to upset the foe," to put him *hors de combat*. This is accomplished in such rough and ready fashion, as the business admits of; by means attended with incidental results of extremest horror. But no sooner has the bayonet

thrust or the bullet laid the soldier low, and converted him into a non-combatant, than the ambulance men are forward to see that he shall not die. If indeed even in the dust he continues to be aggressive, like the wounded Arabs at Tel-el-Kebir, he must be quieted and repressed a second time. Probably he will not escape with life from a second repression: still, speaking with philosophic precision, we must say that "to quiet, not to kill him," is, or should be, the precise and formal object of the will of his slayer in war. St. Thomas indeed (2a 2æ, q. 64, art. 7, in corp.) seems to allow the soldier fighting against the enemy to mean to kill his man. But by *enemy* in this passage we should probably understand *rebel*. The soldier spoken of is the instrument of the feudal lord bringing back to duty his rebellious vassal. In the Middle Ages, till the end of the fifteenth century, the notion of independent nations scarcely found place.

In war, as all cases of self-defence, the killing is indirect. In capital punishment, on the other hand, the killing is direct: it being *chosen as a deterrent means*, that the offender be "hanged by the neck" till he is "dead, dead, dead." This disposes of the error, that capital punishment is an act of self-defence on the part of the State against evil-doers. We may observe finally that by the right of the sword, and by that alone, not in self-defence, not in war, but by the hand of public justice raised against a guilty subject, can human life ever be taken *directly*.

Reading.—St. Thos., 2a 2æ, q. 40, art. 1.

X

SECTION X.—*Of the Scope and Aim of Civil Government.*

1. I beseech the pious reader not to be shocked and scandalised by the conclusions of this section. He will find them in the end a valuable support to theology. The most religious mind can have no difficulty in allowing that cookery, as such, is a business of this world only: that you retain your cook, not to save your soul, but to prepare palatable and wholesome nourishment for your body; that honesty, sobriety, and good temper are officially requisite qualifications, simply inasmuch as the contrary vices would be the plague of your kitchen and the spoiling of your dinner. In a Catholic house the soup on a Friday is made without meat. That restriction is observed, not as a point of culinary art, but because, whereas eternal salvation is the main end of life, and cookery a subordinate end, the latter must be so prosecuted as not to interfere with the former. She who uses ingredients forbidden by the Church, is the worse Christian, but she may be the better cook. Now, to compare a great thing with a little, the State equally with the kitchen is a creation of this world,—there are no nationalities, nor kitchen-ranges either, beyond the grave. Civil government is a secular concern. The scope and aim intrinsic to it, and attainable by its own proper forces, is a certain temporal good. Suarez (*De Legibus*, III., xi., 7) sets forth that good to be,—" the natural happiness of the perfect human community, whereof the civil legislature has the care, and the happiness of individuals as they are

members of such of a community, that they may live therein peaceably and justly, and with a sufficiency of goods for the preservation and comfort of their bodily life, and with so much moral rectitude as is necessary for this external peace and happiness of the commonwealth and the continued preservation of human nature."

2. The intrinsic scope and aim of civil government is the good of the citizens as citizens. That, we have to show, is not any good of the world to come ; nor again the full measure of good requisite for individual well-being in this world. The good of the citizens as such is that which they enjoy in common in their social and political capacity : namely, security, wealth, liberty, commerce, the arts of life, arms, glory, empire, sanitation, and the like, all which goods, of their own nature, reach not beyond this world. True, a certain measure of moral rectitude also is maintained in common, but only "so much as is necessary for the external peace and happiness of the commonwealth," not that rectitude of the whole man which is required in view of the world to come. (*Ethics,* c. x., n. 4 [3], p. 182.) The intrinsic aim of the State, then, falls short of the next life. Neither does it cover the entire good of the individual even for this life. The good of the State, and of each citizen as a citizen, which it is the purpose of civil government to procure, is a mere grand outline, within which every man has to fill in for himself the little square of his own personal perfection and happiness. Happiness, as we have seen, lies essentially in inward acts. The conditions

of these acts, outward tranquillity and order, are the statesman's care : the acts themselves must be elicited by each individual from his own heart. Happiness also depends greatly on domestic life, the details of which, at least when they stop short of wife-beating, come not within the cognisance of the civil power. It remains, as we have said, that the scope and aim of the State, within its own sphere and the compass of its own powers, is the temporal prosperity of the body politic, and the prosperity of its members as they are its members and citizens, but not absolutely as they are men. We cannot repeat too often the saying of St. Thomas : " Man is not ordained to the political commonwealth to the full extent of all that he is and has." (1a 2æ, q. 21, art. 4, ad 3.)

3. From this view it appears that the end for which the State exists is indeed an important and necessary good, but it is not all in all to man, not his perfect and final happiness. To guide man to that is the office of the Christian Church in the present order of Providence. Cook and statesman must so go about the proper ends of their several offices, as not to stand in the way of the Church, compassing as she does that supreme end to which all other ends are subordinate. This limitation they are bound to observe, not as cook and statesman, but as men and Christians. A perfectly Christian State, as Christian, has a twofold duty. First, it has a *positive* duty, at the request of the Church, to follow up ecclesiastical laws with corresponding civil enactments, *e.g.*, laws against criminous clerks and

excommunicates. On this spiritual ground, being beyond its jurisdiction, the State must be careful not to forestall but to second the precept of spiritual authority. It is no business of the State, as such, to punish a purely religious offence. The second duty of a Christian State, and a more urgent duty even than the former, is the *negative* one of making no civil enactment to the prejudice of the Church : *e.g.*, not to subject clerics to the law of conscription. Useful as their arms might be for the defence of the country, the State must forego that utility for the sake of a higher end.

4. In the order of pure nature, which is the order of philosophy, there is of course no Church. Still there would be, as we have seen (c. i., s. i., n. 8, p. 197), erected on the same lines as the civil power, and working side by side with it, a religious power competent to prescribe and conduct divine worship. This power the State would be bound to abet and support, both positively and negatively; something in the same manner, but not to the same degree, as the Christian State is bound to abet the Church. The supreme direction of the natural religious power would conveniently be vested in the person of the Civil Ruler. Thus the Roman Emperor was also Chief Pontiff.

5. How in the mere natural, as distinguished from the Christian order, the provinces of marriage and education should be divided between the civil and the religious power, is perhaps not a very profitable enquiry. The only use of it is a polemic use in arguing with men of no Christianity. Among all

men of any religion, marriage has ever been regarded as one of those occasions of life that bring
man into special relation with God, and therefore
into some dependence on God's ministers. Education, again, has a religious element, to be super-
intended by the religious power. Education has a
secular element also, the general superintendence of
which cannot be denied to the State. Though
children are facts of the domestic order, and the
care and formation of them belongs primarily to
their parents, yet if the parents neglect their charge,
the State can claim the right of intervention *ab abusu.*
It certainly is within the province of the State to
prevent any parent from launching upon the world
a brood of young barbarians, ready to disturb the
peace of civil society. The practical issue is, who
are *barbarians* and what is understood by *peace.* The
Emperor Decius probably considered every Christian
child an enemy of the *Pax Romana.* But the misapplication of a maxim does not derogate from its
truth. It also belongs to the State to see that no
parent behaves *like a Cyclops* (κυκλωπικῶς, Ar., *Eth.,*
X., ix., 13) in his family, ordering his children, not
to their good, as a father is bound to do, but to his
own tyrannical caprice. For *instruction,* as distinguished from *education,* it is the parent's duty to
provide his child with so much of it as is necessary,
in the state of society wherein his lot is cast, to
enable the child to make his way in the world according to the condition of his father. In many walks of
life one might as well be short of a finger as not
know how to read and write. Where ignorance is

such a disadvantage, the parent is not allowed to let
his child grow up ignorant. There, if he neglects to
have him taught, the State may step in with compulsory schooling. Compulsory schooling for all
indiscriminately, and that up to a high standard, is
quite another matter.

Readings.—Suarez, *De Legibus*, III., xi.; *ib.*, IV.,
ii., nn. 3, 4: St. Thos., 1a 2æ, q. 93, art. 3, ad 3; *ib.*,
q. 96, art. 2; *ib.*, q. 98, art. 1, in corp.; *ib.*, q. 99,
art. 3, in corp.; *ib.*, q. 100, art. 2, in corp.

Section XI.—*Of Law and Liberty.*

1. The student of Natural Law does not share
the vulgar prejudice against civil law and lawyers.
He knows it for a precept of the Natural Law, that
there should be a State set up, and that this State
should proceed to positive legislation. This legislation partly coincides with Natural Law in urging the
practice of that limited measure of morality, which
is necessary for the State to do its office and to be
at all. (s. x., n. 2, p. 355.) This partial enforcement
of the Law of Nature is the main work of the
criminal law of the State. But State legislation goes
beyond the Natural Law, and in the nature of things
must go beyond it. Natural Law leaves a thousand
conflicting rights undetermined, which in the interest
of society, to save quarrels, must be determined
one way or another.

2. An illustration. It is an axiom of Natural Law,
that *res perit domino;* that is, the owner bears the
loss. If an article under sale perishes before delivery,
the loss falls, apart from contracts to the contrary,

upon whichever of the two parties is the owner at
the time. So far nature rules. But who is the
owner at any given time, and at what stage of the
transaction does the dominion pass? That can only
be settled by custom and the law of the land. " If
I order a pipe of port from a wine-merchant abroad ;
at what period the property passes from the merchant to me ; whether upon delivery of the wine at
the merchant's warehouse; upon its being put on
shipboard at Oporto ; upon the arrival of the ship in
England at its destined port; or not till the wine be
committed to my servants, or deposited in my cellar;
all are questions which admit of no decision but what
custom points out." (Paley, *Mor. Phil.*, bk. iii., p. 1,
c. vii.)

This leads us to remark upon the much admired
sentence of Tacitus, *in corruptissima republica plu-
rimæ leges*, that not merely the multitude of transgressions, but the very complexity of a highly developed
civilization, requires to be kept in order by a vast
body of positive law.

3. Incidentally we may also remark, that the law
of the State does not create the right of property ;
otherwise, abolishing its own creation, the State
could bring in Communism. (c. vii., s. i., p. 278.)
But finding this right of property unprotected and
undetermined, the State by its criminal law protects
property against robbers, and by its *civil* as distinguished from *criminal* law, it defines numerous
open questions between possessors as to manner of
acquirement and conditions of tenure.

4. All civil laws bind the conscience: some by

way of a categorical imperative, *Do this* : others by
way of a disjunctive, *Do this, or being caught acting
otherwise, submit to the penalty.* The latter are called
purely penal laws, an expression, by the way, which
has no reference to the days of religious persecution.
Civil law binds the conscience categorically whenever
the civil ruler so intends. In the absence of express
declaration, it must be presumed that he so intends
whenever his law is an enforcement of the Natural
Law, or a determination of the same ; as when the
observance is necessary to the preservation of the
State, or when the ruler determines what lapse of
time shall be necessary for the acquisition of property
by prescription. Very frequently, the parties to a
contract tacitly accept the dispositions of the civil
law as forming part of their agreement ; and in this
indirect fashion the civil law becomes binding on the
conscience. In this way an Englishman who accepts
a bill of exchange tacitly binds himself to pay interest
at five per cent., if the bill is not met at maturity, for
such is the disposition of the English Law. It may
be further observed that no prudent legislator would
attach a severe penalty to what was not already
wrong.

5. In Roman times it was part of the flattery of
the imperial jurists to their master, to tell him that
he was above the laws, *legibus solutus*. In the trial
of Louis XVI., the Sovereign People, or they who
called themselves such, dispensed with certain legal
formalities on that same plea. Against the law at
Athens, the generals who had fought at Arginusae
were condemned by one collective sentence, the

anger of the Sovereign People being too impatient
to vote on them separately, as the law required.
Hereupon we must observe in the first place, that
the Supreme Ruler, whether one man or a multitude,
can never be brought to trial in his own court for
any legal offence. As all justice requires two terms :
no power can do justice on itself. (*Ethics*, c. v., s. ix.,
n. 1, p. 102.) This truth is embodied in the English
maxim, that *the king can do no wrong*. Again, the
Sovereign is either expressly or virtually exempted
from the compass of many laws, *e.g.* those which
concern the flying of certain flags or ensigns, and
other petty matters. Thirdly, we have the principle,
that no being can give a law to himself. (*Ethics*, c. vi.
s. ii., n. 3, p. 117.) Lastly, we must observe that there
is no law so fundamental but what the Supreme
Power, taken in its entirety, can alter it, and by consequence dispense from it. From these considerations it follows that the Sovereign—the complete and
absolute Sovereign, be he one man or many—lies
under no legal obligation to obey any law of his own
making as such. It does not follow that he is perfectly
free to ignore the laws. He is bound in conscience
and before God to make his government effectual; and
effectual it cannot be, if the laws are despised; and
despised they will be, if the Sovereign gives scandal
by ignoring them in his own practice. Therefore
the Sovereign, be he King, Council, or Assembly, is
bound in conscience and before God, though not
legally of his own jurisdiction, so far himself to stand
to the observance of the law as not to render it
nugatory in the eyes and practice of others.

6. Law and liberty are like the strings and meshes of a net. In the one limit of minimum of mesh, the net passes into sack-cloth, where nothing could get through. In the other limit of maximum of mesh, the net vanishes, and everything would get through. We cannot praise in the abstract either a 'arge mesh or a small one: the right size is according to the purpose for which the net is to be used in each particular case. So neither can law nor liberty be praised, as Burke says, "on a simple view of the subject, as it stands stripped of every relation, in all the nakedness and solitude of metaphysical abstraction." We can only praise either as it is "clothed in circumstances." Commonly we are led to praise the one by getting too much of the other. Confounded in a tangle of fussy, vexatious, perhaps malicious restrictions, men cry loudly for liberty. When people all about us are doing things by their own sweet will, we are converted to praise of regulation and discipline and the wholesome restraint of law.

Readings.—St. Thos., 1a 2æ, q. 96, art. 5, ad 3; Suarez, *De Legibus*, III., xxxv.; *ib.*, V., iv.; Ruskin, *Seven Lamps of Architecture*, c. vii., §§ 1, 2.

Section XII.—*Of Liberty of Opinion.*

1. We are here dealing with liberty only so far as it means exemption from State control. So far as the State is concerned, a man has the fullest liberty to hold in his heart the most seditious opinions, and to think the foulest thoughts, so long as they do not appear in his public language and conduct. The heart is free from all mere humanlaw, resting in subjection to His law alone, and in responsibility to His judgment, who is the Searcher of Hearts.

2. We are dealing then not properly with opinion, but with the public expression of opinion. We are dealing with that expression as controllable by the State, not acting in deference to the invitation of any religious power, but of its own initiative and proper authority, in view of its own end, scope and aim, which is social order and public prosperity for this life. (s. x., nn. 2, 3, p. 355.)

3. That there are doctrines dangerous to social order, cannot be denied, unless we are to cease to believe in any influence of thought upon conduct. It is important to the State, that men should have the greatest possible horror of crime. (s. viii., nn. 3, 6, pp. 345, 348.) This horror is notably impaired when all idea of sin is taken away. Now the idea of sin vanishes with that of God. (*Ethics*, c, vi., s. ii., nn. 6, 7, 13, pp. 119, 123.) Therefore to pull down the idea of God among a nation of theists, whether by the wiles of a courtly Professor at a University, or by the tub-thumping blasphemy of an itinerant lecturer, is to injure the State. The

tub-thumper however is the more easily reached by the civil authority, especially when his discourses raise a tumult among the people. But where attacks upon theism have become common, and unbelief is already rampant among the masses, for the State to interfere with either "leader of thought," high or low, would be a shutting of the stable-door after the steed was stolen. Similarly we should speak of those who subvert the received notions touching the sanctity of the marriage-tie and the law of external purity generally, the obligation of civil allegiance, the rights of property and of life.

4. It will be objected: " The doctrines that you wish to express as inimical to the peace of the commonwealth, possibly may be true. Did not the first heralds of Christianity trouble the peace of the Roman world?" We reply: Let the new teachers come to us as those apostolic men came, " in weakness and in fear and in much trembling," and yet withal "in the showing of the spirit and power," with an " exhortation not of uncleanness," nor upon "an occasion of covetousness," "holily and justly and without blame " (1 Cor. ii. 3, 4; 1 Thess. ii. 3, 5, 10) ; and we will receive them as angels of God, even to the plucking out of our own eyes, if need be, and giving to them. (Gal. iv. 15.) Any hostile reception that they may meet with at first from a misapplication of our principle, will soon be made up for by welcome and veneration. There is no principle that may not be momentarily misapplied in all good faith. But the mistake in this case will readily be rectified.

5. But, writes J. S. Mill, *On Liberty*, "we can never be sure that the opinion we are endeavouring to stifle is a false opinion." If we cannot, then is there no such thing as certainty upon any point of morals, politics, or religion. Assassination of tyrants, whether in public or private life, may be wickedness, or it may be a laudable outburst of public spirit, who knows? Which of us is sure that all property is not theft? Plato's views on marriage and infanticide may be correct: the Nihilist may be your true politician; and all our religious knowledge dwindles down to the confession of Protagoras: "Concerning Gods, I find no clear evidence whether they are or are not, or what manner of beings they are." These are the sceptical tremors which this denial induces. But even scepticism has its proof, which Mill furnishes as follows: "All silencing of discussion is an assumption of infallibility." The very name *infallibility* has an effect upon the modern Englishman like that of *Popery* upon his forefathers. It shakes his nerves, obscures his judgment, and scares his seated reason to leap up from her throne. But after we have recovered from our fright, we recollect that, whereas infallibility is an all-round attribute, compassing an entire subject, certainty goes out to one particular point on the circumference; we may then be certain without being infallible. Extremely fallible as I am in geography, I am nevertheless certain that Tunis is in Africa. Silencing discussion is an assumption, not of infallibility, but of certainty. The man who never dares assume that he is certain of anything, so certain as to close his ears to all further

discussion, comes nothing short of a universal sceptic.

6. We are told, free discussion promotes discovery. Yes, free discussion in philosophical circles, free discussion among competent persons. But free discussion of a subject among the incompetent and the incapable, and the passionate and the prejudiced, is not good for the cause of truth; and if the subject be practical and momentous, it is not good for the disputants either, nor for the community. If we allow that the science and practice of morality is not advanced by free debate of ethical questions in nurseries and boarding-schools, we must also bear in mind that a vast proportion of the human family remain all their lives long, for the purpose of such discussions, as incompetent as children. The multitude cannot be philosophers. They have neither time, nor intelligence, nor love of hard thinking sufficient to arrive at the final and adequate *why* and *wherefore* of their every duty. Though capable of doing right, they are quite incapable of doing so philosophically. They do it according as they are led by custom and authority. Their inheritance is the traditionary wisdom of mankind, which they live upon as an infant on his estate, not understanding whence their support comes. It is dangerous to batter them with objections against the received moral law. You will overthrow them, not confirm them by the result of your reasonings: you will perplex their intellect, you will confound their good purpose, you will awaken their evil passions. Surely it is a more necessary point to secure that right be

done somehow, than that it be philosophically done.
The one is difficult enough, the other quite impossible
for the mass of mankind. Therefore, adapting to
our purpose the old Greek oracle : "let us not disturb
the foundations of popular morality : they are better
undisturbed "—

Μὴ κίνει Καμάριναν· ἀκίνητος γὰρ ἀμείνων.

7. But is it not immoral to interfere with conscience, and to attempt to stifle sincere convictions ?
The State, we repeat, has nothing to do with conscience as such, nor with the inward convictions of
any man. But if the State is sincerely convinced,
that the convictions openly professed and propagated
by some of its subjects are subversive of social order
and public morality, whose sincere conviction is it
that must carry the day in practice ? It is of the
essence of government that the convictions, sincere
or otherwise, of the governed shall on certain
practical issues be waived in the external observance
in favour of the convictions of the ruling power.
After all, this talk of conscience and sincere convictions is but the canting phrase of the day, according
to which conscience means mere wild humour and
headstrong self-will. Such teachings as those which
we would have the State to suppress, *e.g.*: *An oath
is a folly : There is no law of purity : There is no harm
in doing anything that does not annoy your neighbour :*
are not the teachings of men sincerely convinced :
they deserve no respect, consideration, or tenderness
on that score. We do not say, that the teachers of
these monstrosities are not convinced, but that they

are not honestly and conscientiously convinced : they have blinded themselves, and become the guilty authors of their own delusion. Not all strong convictions are honestly come by or virtuously entertained.

8. Arraigned for their utterances, men protest their sincerity, as parties indicted for murder do their innocence. We can set but small store by such protestations. It is a question of evidence to come from other sources than from the accused person's own mouth. A man indeed must be held to be sincere until he is proved to be the contrary. That is the general rule. But there are what Roman lawyers call *præsumptiones juris ;* circumstances which, it proved, will induce the court to take a certain view of a case, and give judgment accordingly, unless by further evidence that view is proved to be a false one. Now when a man proclaims some blatant and atrocious error in a matter bearing directly upon public morals—and it is for the restraint of these errors alone that we are arguing—there is a decided *præsumptio juris,* that the error in him, however doggedly he maintains it, is not a sincere, candid, and innocently formed conviction. The light of nature is not so feeble as that, among civilized men. Let the offender be admonished and given time to think : but if, for all warning to the contrary, the wilful man will have his way, and still propagate his error to the confusion of society, he must be treated like any other virtuous and well-meaning criminal : he must be restrained and coerced to the extent that the interests of society require.

Y

9. At the same time it must be confessed that when an error, however flagrant and pestilential, has ceased to shock and scandalize the general body of the commonwealth: when the people listen to the doctrine without indignation, and their worst sentence upon it pronounces it merely "queer," there is little hope of legal restraints there enduring long or effecting much. Penalties for the expression of opinion are available only so far as they tally with the common feeling of the country. When public opinion ceases to bear them out, it is better not to enforce them: for that were but to provoke resentment and make martyrs. No regulations can be maintained except in a congenial atmosphere. Allowance too must be made for the danger of driving the evil to burrow underground.

10. The censorship of opinions even in a model State would vary in method according to men and times. The censorship of the Press in particular might be either by *Imprimatur* required before printing, or by liability to prosecution after. The *Imprimatur* might be either for all books, or only for a certain class. It might be either obligatory, or merely matter of counsel, to obtain it. We are not to adopt promiscuously all the praiseworthy institutions of our forefathers.

Readings.—Cardinal Newman, *Letter to Duke of Norfolk*, § 5; *The Month* for June, 1883, pp. 200, seqq.

APPENDIX.

OF the precepts of Natural Law, some are more simple and of wider extension; others are derivative, complex, and extend to fewer cases. It is a question of more and less, and no hard and fast line of demarcation can be drawn between them. The former however are called *primary*, the latter *secondary* precepts. Again, the nature of man is the same in all men and at all periods of history for its essential elements, but admits of wide accidental variation and declension for the worse. Thirdly, it is clear that Natural Law is a law good and suitable for human nature to observe. Starting from these three axioms, we apply the reasoning of St. Thomas, 1a 2æ, q. 96, art. 2, not to human law alone, of which he is speaking, but to sundry secondary precepts of Natural Law. These are his words:

"A law is laid down as a rule or measure of human acts. Now a measure ought to be homogeneous with the thing measured. Hence laws also must be imposed upon men according to their condition. As Isidore says: 'A law ought to be possible both according to nature and according to the custom of the country.' Now the power or faculty of action proceeds from interior habit or disposition. The same thing is not possible to him who has no habit of virtue, that is possible to a virtuous man; as the same thing is not possible to a boy and to a grown man, and therefore the same rule is not laid down for children as for adults. Many things are allowed to children, that in adults are visited with legal punishment or with blame, and in like manner many things must be allowed to men not perfect in virtue, which would be intolerable in virtuous men."

This reasoning leads us up to a conclusion, which St. Thomas states thus (1a 2æ, q. 94. art. 5):

"A conceivable way in which the Natural Law might be changed is the way of subtraction, that something should cease to be of the Natural Law that was of it before. Understanding change in this sense, the Natural Law is absolutely immutable in its first principles; but as to secondary precepts, which are certain detailed conclusions closely related to the first principles, the Natural Law is not so changed as that its dictate is not right in most cases steadily to abide by; it may however be changed in some particular case, and in rare instances, through some special causes impeding the observance of these secondary precepts."

The reason for this conclusion, more pregnant, it may be, than St. Thomas himself discerned, is given briefly as follows (2a 2æ, q. 57, art. 2, ad 1):

"Human nature is changeable; and therefore what is natural to man may sometimes fail to hold good."

The precepts of Natural Law that fail to be applicable when human nature sinks below par, are only secondary precepts, and few even of them. Christianity brings human nature up to par, and *fulfils* the Natural Law (St. Matt. v. 17), enjoining the observance of it in its integrity. This is the meaning of St. John Chrysostom's saying : " Of old not such an ample measure of virtue was proposed to us ; . . . but since the coming of Christ the way has been made much narrower." (*De Virginitate*, c. 44 : cf. his 17th Homily on St. Matt. v. 37 ; indeed the doctrine is familiar in his pages.)

INDEX.

The quotations are by chapter, section, number, and page. The asterisk (*) prefixed refers to *Natural Law.*

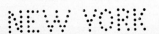

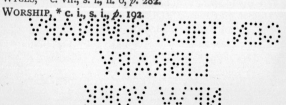

STONYHURST PHILOSOPHICAL SERIES.

EDITED BY RICHARD F. CLARKE, S.J.

Extract from a Letter of His Holiness the Pope to the Bishop of Salford, on the Philosophical Course at Stonyhurst.

"You will easily understand, Venerable Brother, the pleasure We felt in what you reported to Us about the College of Stonyhurst in your diocese, namely, that by the efforts of the Superiors of this College, an excellent course of the exact sciences has been successfully set on foot, by establishing professorships, and by publishing in the vernacular for their students text-books of Philosophy, following the principles of St. Thomas Aquinas. On this work We earnestly congratulate the Superiors and teachers of the College, and by letter We wish affectionately to express Our good-will towards them."

---

1. **Logic.** By RICHARD F. CLARKE, S.J., formerly Fellow and Tutor of St. John's College, Oxford. Second Edition. Price 5s.

2. **First Principles of Knowledge.** By JOHN RICKABY, S.J., late Professor of Logic and General Metaphysics at St. Mary's Hall, Stonyhurst. Third Edition. Price 5s.

3. **Moral Philosophy (Ethics and Natural Law).** By JOSEPH RICKABY, S.J., M.A. Lond.; late Professor of Ethics at St. Mary's Hall, Stonyhurst. Third Edition. Price 5s.

4. **Natural Theology.** By BERNARD BOEDDER, S.J., Professor of Natural Theology at St. Mary's Hall, Stonyhurst. Second Edition. Price 6s. 6d.

5. **Psychology: Empirical and Rational.** By MICHAEL MAHER, S.J., D.Lit.; M.A. Lond. Sixth Edition. Price 6s. 6d.

6. **General Metaphysics.** By JOHN RICKABY, S.J. Second Edition. Price 5s.

Supplementary Volume.

Political Economy. By C. S. DEVAS, M.A. Oxon. Sometime Examiner in Political Economy at the Royal University of Ireland. Second Edition. Rewritten and Enlarged. Fourth to Sixth Thousand. Price 7s. 6d.

LONDON: LONGMANS, GREEN, & CO.

Reviews of the First Edition.

PSYCHOLOGY.

" We regard Father Maher's book on Psychology as one of the most important contributions to philosophical literature published in this country for a long time. . . . What renders his work especially valuable is the breadth of his modern reading, and the skill with which he presses things new, no less than old, into the service of his argument. His dialectical skill is as remarkable as his wealth of learning, and not less notable is his spirit of fairness. . . . Whether the reader agrees or disagrees with the author's views, it is impossible to deny the ability, fulness, and cogency of the argument."— *St. James's Gazette*, July 8, 1892.

". . . The author has proved himself a thoroughly competent guide and teacher on the subject of his work. Almost every page of his book bears the mark of careful thought and wide reading. . . Taken for what it professes to be, this is an excellent manual. It deserves and will repay study."—*The Scotsman*, August 4, 1890.

" This book, by the Professor of Mental Philosophy at Stony-hurst College, is a sober, scholarly, and important work. . . . The author's treatment of Psychology is simple, logical, and graceful. His definitions are clear and precise, his style is crisp and nervous, and his knowledge of the literature of his subject is very considerable."—*Educational Review*, June, 1891.

" This Manual is an able and well-considered effort to reconcile mediæval and modern philosophy. The author bases his argument mainly on the works of Aquinas and the schoolmen, but he gives fair recognition to modern philosophers and to modern science. . . . We can commend the book to students of Natural Theology and Psychology."—*The Church Review*, September 26, 1890.

" Father Maher's joining of old with new in his *Psychology* is very skilful; and sometimes the highly systematized character of the scholastic doctrine gives him a certain advantage in the face of modern psychological classifications with their more tentative character. . . . The historical and controversial parts all through the volume are in general very careful and well managed."—*Mind*.

" The author is always lucid, cogent, and learned. His knowledge of the works of writers on Psychology is thorough and sound, and results in a most valuable aid to the student : particularly good examples of this are his historical sketches of the Theories of External Perception, General Cognition, and the Moral Sense, whilst the historical references and notes on almost every point should prove extremely helpful."—*The University Correspondent*, November, 1890.

"This work cannot be too highly recommended."—*The Tablet*, November 1, 1890.

". . . The book is a distinct gain to psychological science, and places its author in the front rank of the clear, deep thinkers of our time. It is a thoroughly scientific work, evincing on the part of its author great powers of analysis and discrimination, with the most profound and varied knowledge of philosophical literature."—*The Irish Ecclesiastical Record*, January, 1891.

In what does happiness
consist?
  What is moral virtue
    "   " intell
  Relation between active and
contemplative lives?
  How is friendship related to all
  Is the state absolute
  What is the best form of govt
                14

8 38,55
November 28